All's Well
that
Ends Well

New Westminster Pulpit Series

Once Saved, Always Saved

All's Well that Ends Well

Justification by Works
Sermons on James 1–3

The Way of Wisdom
Sermons on James 4–5

All's Well that Ends Well

The Life of Jacob

R.T. Kendall

Authentic
MEDIA

Authentic Media
We welcome your comments and questions.
129 Mobilization Drive, Waynesboro, GA 30830 USA authenticusa@stl.org

and 9 Holdom Avenue, Bletchley, Milton Keynes, Bucks, MK1 1QR, UK
www.authenticbooks.com

If you would like a copy of our current catalog, contact us at:
1-8MORE-BOOKS
ordersusa@stl.org

All's Well that Ends Well
ISBN: 1-932805-25-7

Cover design: Paul Lewis
Interior design: WestKey Ltd, Falmouth, Cornwall

Printed in United States of America

To Jenny and Charlie

Contents

Foreword

The natural appeal of one Bible character over another must be the experience of every Christian who reads and listens to God's word. We identify with some Bible characters more than others. Unlike Dr. Kendall, I have *always* been a Jacob man in preference to Joseph, Joshua rather than Moses, Elijah more than Elisha and so one could go on. As Bible believers we firmly accept that *all* Scripture is God-breathed and is useful for all the things that Paul describes to Timothy (2 Tim 3.16). Yet we return with greater alacrity to some passages of scripture more than to others. For me Jacob is one of the most empathetic personalities in the whole of the Bible and this is why I have come to this book with keen anticipation and have been richly rewarded in so doing.

If Dr. Kendall has become a 'Jacob' man it must be that in some particular way he identifies with the one he describes and finds echoes of himself in the scripture narrative. Why should that be? Dr. Kendall has never camouflaged himself in an effort to look like another. He is his own man. R.T. has never run away from anything. Far from it, for he has always faced everything and everyone head-on, sometimes to his personal cost. Neither did he mistakenly marry the wrong woman! So where is the connection?

Because I am the closest of friends I know something of the answer. Jacob had a deep, life-changing meeting with God. So has Dr. Kendall. Jacob was a risk taker, so is the one who writes of him here – even quoting me in one place! Jacob's was a life rooted in reality and this book has been written on the anvil of experience and has been forged from ministering to his people at Westminster Chapel for many years. The author is as real as the man of whom he writes is real.

What we have here is more than memorable Bible Readings at Keswick or a series of sermons addressed to a local Church. A man of history, a man of God is brought again to our attention in a way that is fresh, challenging, sometimes provoking but yet which breathes reality. That is the appeal of Jacob, he was a real man who met God, who could say at his darkest hour in the desert 'Surely the Lord is in this place'. What this book describes is also real and I too have met God within its pages.

For Jacob it was 'all's well that ends well'. This damaged man got there in the end. 'What is your name?' asks the wrestling God. 'Jacob' – deceiver – he answered. By grace the name was changed to Israel, the man who struggled with God. Dr. Kendall tells us about the reality of that painful struggle, his own and ours, but ever reminds us that the one with whom we often fight has the name of love. Some of us, though injured by the struggle, have like Jacob come to peace with God, our families and ourselves. Charles Wesley in perhaps his greatest hymn puts it like this

> Contented now upon my thigh
> I halt, till life's short journey end;
> All helplessness, all weakness, I
> On Thee alone for strength depend;
> Nor have I power from Thee to move:
> Thy nature and Thy name is Love.

You will find much of that love within these pages.

Robert Ames,
Senior Minister at Duke Street Baptist Church,
Richmond and Chairman of the Evangelical Alliance

Preface

When I was young, I identified more with Joseph. Now that I am getting older, I identify more with Jacob. The older we are, the longer our past – with so many memories and, in my case, so many regrets. The thought that all our past folly could actually *'work together for good'* (Rom. 8:28 AV) is almost overwhelming. That is what this book is about.

Some years ago, as I was reading Hebrews 11, this verse leapt out at me: *'By faith Jacob, when he was dying, blessed each of Joseph's sons, and worshipped as he leaned on the top of his staff '*(v. 21).

Now this doesn't happen every day, but on that occasion I *understood* Jacob. I saw him at the end of his life, leaning on his staff, worshipping and reflecting on God's utter goodness. The title of one of Shakespeare's great plays, *All's Well that Ends Well,* came to my mind. It describes Jacob's life perfectly.

When I was invited to preach at Keswick in 1991, I immediately knew I wanted to preach on the life of Jacob. I gave four Bible readings under the theme 'All's Well that Ends Well' (with apologies to Shakespeare). And I knew it was only a matter of time before I would want to preach on the life of Jacob in greater depth. This book is the result.

Having previously preached on the life of Joseph (published by Paternoster as a book entitled *God Meant It for Good*), there was some problem of overlap once Jacob's life was overtaken by Joseph's. The reader may want to consult *God Meant It for Good* for some details not dealt with here.

I would hope the reader would also take the time to read the passage from Genesis referred to at the beginning of each chapter. There are times when I assume the reader knows the background which the Bible reading gives.

There is a lovely story behind the painting on the cover. My old friend Jack Brothers, the well-known bonefishing guide in the Florida Keys (now in heaven), unbeknown to me, went to the famous artist Millard Wells and asked him to paint Westminster Chapel. Cheeky request! They even sent a photographer to London, and Millard painted what you see. He assumed it was always raining in London, hence the people with umbrellas! Millard Wells' paintings are legendary in America, and I am honoured that he and Jack presented this one to me as a Christmas present a few years ago. The original watercolour hangs in my vestry.

I am deeply indebted to Margaret Downing of Paternoster and my friend Dr Michael Eaton for their careful editing and efforts to make my sermons more readable. I am also grateful to Pieter Kwant for wanting to publish this book. My warmest thanks go to Mrs Jenny Ross for typing the original manuscript from recordings. She began this before she married Charlie and finished the task after their honeymoon. Never before has any typist worked so hard on my material. I fondly dedicate this book to them. However, the book would never have come into being without the help of my greatest friend and critic, my wife Louise.

R.T. Kendall

Westminster Chapel
London
June 1998

1

The Failure Barrier

Genesis 25:19–28

Jacob is one of the most important characters in the Old Testament. He was the grandson of Abraham, the son of Isaac and the third of the patriarchs, Abraham, Isaac and Jacob. 'The God of Abraham, Isaac and Jacob' became a cliché. As we look at Jacob, we soon recognize that the Bible does not cover up the weaknesses and frailty of its heroes. Jacob, whose name was later changed to Israel, was not a particularly attractive person. My guess is that he would be like J.R. Ewing from the TV series *Dallas*, a person you'd love to hate because there was so much about him that wasn't nice.

As I grew up, I used to identify with Joseph, one of Jacob's sons, more than with any other person in the Old Testament, but, as I got older, I have identified more with Jacob. Once, when studying the character of Jacob, I read the comment about him in Hebrews 11:21: *'By faith Jacob, when he was dying, blessed each of Joseph's sons, and worshipped as he leaned on the top of his staff.'* When I read that verse it was if a laser beam went straight to my heart, and ever since then, I have felt as if I have understood Jacob.

There is a sense in which the theme of the failure barrier will carry on right through the life of Jacob. Now there are some who would have you believe they don't know anything at all about failure, but if you are only too aware of your own failings, this book is for you.

The failure barrier separates you from personal happiness. It separates you from people. You don't want to be with people because you are haunted by a sense of failure. You distance yourself; you stay slightly away from people, lest you reach that phase in the relationship when they begin to ask you questions. There are many people who won't get close to anybody because they are afraid. They believe that if they get close to a person, it's only a matter of time before the other will feel at liberty to say, 'Well, now, tell me more about yourself. Where are you from? What do you do?'

But it can also be the failure barrier that separates you from yourself, because of a personal sense of failure. Perhaps you can't find a job, keep a job, or get the job you want. You had such great expectations, but then life began to pass you by and you felt left behind. Perhaps you know the failure of giving in to temptation, and you feel so ashamed. Perhaps you feel a failure as a parent, and the guilt is almost overwhelming. Most of all, you are convinced that you've let God down and that he is upset with you, and you can't live with yourself any longer.

If ever there was anyone who knew the guilt of failure, then Jacob is your man. The word 'Jacob' means 'heel' (or possibly 'deceiver'). Jacob was the world's greatest manipulator. He wanted to control people. He was a terrible parent and brother. He stole his twin brother Esau's blessing and, by cunning, he tricked him into selling his birthright.

The key to understanding this man is to realize that we are dealing with a person who, as he grew older, developed an ever-deepening sense of guilt which arose because of the way he deceived his own father, the way he treated his twin brother Esau, and the way he controlled his children. Let's note four things about Jacob:

1. He Failed to Keep the Family Standard

To understand Jacob, you need to see him, first, as one who was under pressure to keep up a standard because of the heritage that was passed on to him. Look at Genesis 25:19–20. It begins by saying that this is the account of Abraham's son Isaac. Then it says, *'Abraham became the father of Isaac, and Isaac was forty years old when he married Rebekah.'* And it continues in verse 21: *'Isaac prayed to the LORD on behalf of his wife, because she was barren.'* Here was a man who had a heritage of being the grandson of Abraham. How would you like to grow up being told every day, 'You had a wonderful grandfather; you had a wonderful father; now we expect great things of you!'?

In Genesis 47:9, you find these interesting words spoken when Jacob met Pharaoh. Jacob said, *'The years of my pilgrimage are a hundred and thirty. My years have been few and difficult, and they do not equal the years of the pilgrimage of my fathers.'* He was referring to Abraham and Isaac. He grew up feeling he had let the tradition down. He was no Abraham, he was no Isaac, he was just Jacob. Now in those days, your age was a measure of success and a sign of God's approval and blessing. The longer you lived, the more you sensed God's approval on you. Today, we wouldn't even think about that, but then, age was very important. Abraham lived 175 years. How did Isaac do? He lived 180 years. Our man Jacob, at the age of 130, knew it wasn't going to be much longer for him, and he was acutely aware that he didn't measure up to the standards of Abraham and his father Isaac, and he spent his life in the knowledge that he wasn't the same.

My father Wayne Kendall was regarded as the quintessence of godli - ness and respectability. He named me after his favourite preacher, R.T. Williams, and I was being groomed, not for the ministry alone, but also to fulfil the hopes of my parents that I would become General Superin - tendent in my old denomination. My father was 'Mr Nazarene', and he was well known in Ashland. I grew up hearing how wonderful he was. Yet I never felt I came up to my father's personal expectations, added to which, in my early twenties, I left the denomination in which I had been brought up. I knew then there was no chance of me ever reaching the standard my dad expected. Jacob was under pressure to keep up a standard because of the heritage that was passed on to him.

2. His Was a Special Birth

Jacob was told his very existence was an answer to prayer. His father Isaac had been an answer to prayer too. In fact, you could say Isaac was a miracle baby because Abraham was married to Sarah who couldn't bear children – she was barren for many years. Later on, it turned out that Isaac and Rebekah would have the same trouble that Abraham and Sarah had, and Rebekah would be barren. We are told that they prayed. Isaac prayed to the Lord on behalf of his wife, and God answered his prayer, and Rebekah became pregnant. This heritage was passed on to Jacob, and he was, no doubt, given the feeling that he was special. He knew God had brought him into the world, and that was a good feeling, but it also put him under pressure that he had to measure up to a particular expectation.

3. He Was Not His Father's Favoured Son

Jacob would be involved in sibling rivalry, possibly as intense as there ever was. We read further in Genesis 25:21:

> *Rebekah became pregnant. The babies jostled each other within her, and she said, 'Why is this happening to me?' So she went to enquire of the L ORD.*
> *The LORD said to her, 'Two nations are in your womb, and two peoples from within you will be separated; one people will be stronger than the other, and the older will serve the younger.'*

Rebekah had twins. Esau came out first, Jacob second, and the result was that Esau, being the elder, would receive double the inheritance, in accordance with ancient Hebrew tradition. This developed into a sibling rivalry, and Jacob grew up knowing that Esau was the firstborn and was preferred by his father. There's nothing that a boy needs more as he grows than the feeling that his father loves him and approves of him, but Jacob grew up knowing that his own dad preferred his brother.

4. He Was His Mother's Favourite

Jacob's parents were split in their parental affection for their two sons. The ideal parent would be one who loves every child equally. But what we find is this, that Isaac loved Esau, and Rebekah loved Jacob. That has to have an effect on one's development. Jacob was what we call a 'mummy's boy'. I expect John Wesley was a bit like that. He was the youngest of 18 children. His mother Susannah doted on him as the baby of the family. It shows that God can use this and God can overrule, but what it does for the other children is something else. We find that the two brothers in this sibling rivalry were actually opposites in temperament and aptitude. Esau was a 'man's man'. *'The boys grew up, and Esau became a skilful hunter, a man of the open country, while Jacob was a quiet man, staying among the tents. Isaac, who had a taste for wild game, loved Esau, but Rebekah loved Jacob'* (Gen. 25:28).

What was the result of all this? Jacob grew up to be a conniver and a conspirator. He stole his brother's birthright and blessing, and as he grew up his character was shaped in such a way that he developed an acute sense of guilt. He was ungrateful to the wife that God gave him because she wasn't his choice. He was married to Leah, whom he never really wanted, but it was Leah who gave him the sons who did more for the future of the kingdom of God than all of his other sons combined. It was through Leah that the tribes of Levi and Judah were born. But Jacob never appreciated Leah. He was so partial to his son Joseph, who was born to Rachel, whom he loved, that he caused his other sons to conspire and sell Joseph into slavery.

We are looking not only at the world's greatest manipulator but at the world's greatest complainer. Referring to Benjamin, Genesis 42:38 says: *'But Jacob said, "My son will not go down there with you; his brother is dead and he is the only one left. If harm comes to him on the journey you are taking, you will bring my grey head down to the grave in sorrow." '* Imagine the sense of guilt he was now putting on his sons. Guilty people are always experts at making others feel guilty.

Jacob may have been a complainer, a controller, but God loved him. *'Jacob I loved, but Esau I hated'* (Mal. 1:2; Rom. 9:13). Jacob, though not a very nice guy and not a very attractive person, was loved by God. When it came to the end of Jacob's life, the writer of the Epistle to the Hebrews chose one event, which says that *'Jacob . . . worshipped as he leaned on the top of his staff'* (Heb. 11:21). It shows him in his old age before he died, looking back on his life, a life riddled with guilt, but a life that, when it was all over, turned out as if it were perfect. He got his son back. He learned to appreciate Leah and the things God had done for him.

Maybe you've been controlling and manipulating. Perhaps you haven't appreciated the good things God has done for you, and the guilt is really getting to you. You've repressed it for so long, pushing it down into your subconscious, so you don't feel it. You deny it, but it may manifest itself as a physical disorder, perhaps as high blood pressure, heart trouble, an ulcer, or a migraine. The truth is, the pain is there. Once you come to terms with it, you will think, 'I don't deserve anything.'

The Jacobs of this world aren't very pleasant, but God loved Jacob. If you've been afraid to make friendships, or you are conscious of how things haven't come up to expectation, you realize life is passing you by, and you have this sense of guilt, you need to know that all this will work together for good. At the end of the day, you will just leave it all alone and say, 'God had a purpose in this.'

When Jesus came into this world, he would look out for the very kind of person that nobody else would like. In fact, the ammunition that the enemies of Jesus used against him was 'Look who his followers are!' He called Matthew, a tax collector, to be one of his disciples. He called a Zealot too. It is as though Jesus just went looking for the very person whom nobody would have chosen.

God loves failures. Do you know why? It's because he wants to take your life and turn it into a trophy of grace and bring you to the place where you see that his hand has always been on you. He wants to turn that failure into blessing.

2

The Sovereignty of God

Genesis 25:21–34

One of the most difficult aspects of the life of Jacob is the outworking of
the sovereignty of God. It is a difficult subject, and we'll begin by
remembering two facts about the Bible, where we find this fundamental
doctrine:

> *All Scripture is God-breathed and is useful for teaching, rebuking, correcting and training
> in righteousness, so that the man of God may be thoroughly equipped for every good
> work* (2 Tim. 3:16).

> *Above all, you must understand that no prophecy of Scripture came about by the
> prophet's own interpretation. For prophecy never had its origin in the will of man, but
> men spoke from God as they were carried along by the Holy Spirit* (2 Pet. 1:20–21).

These two verses from the New Testament refer to the Old Testament
so that we might know that it is equally inspired by God. Some may want
to say they accept the New Testament but not the Old Testament. Yet
remember, Jesus never apologized for the Old Testament. The God of
the New Testament upheld it to the hilt, and so should we.

The Sovereignty of God and Mystery

Why is the sovereignty of God so difficult a doctrine? Let's look at
Rebekah. She was pregnant and, feeling her babies jostling within her,
she said, *'Why is this happening to me?'* So she prayed – that's a good thing
to do when you don't understand what's happening. And God answered
her, giving Rebekah what we call a 'prophetic word' (see Gen. 25:23).
God had already decided before the two babies were born which one
would be more blessed: *'The elder one will serve the younger'*, which meant

that the younger would be the one who was blessed. The older was Esau, the younger, Jacob. When the Apostle Paul commented on that very situation, he put it like this: *'Before the twins were born or had done anything good or bad – in order that God's purpose in election might stand: not by works but by him who calls – she was told "The older will serve the younger." Just as it is written: "Jacob I loved, but Esau I hated" '* (Rom. 9:11).

Now I call that difficult. I don't understand it. But there's a lot in the Bible I don't understand. Mind you, I don't understand electricity, but I know I can go to a switch, flick it, and see a light come on. I affirm it – I just know it is so. I don't understand how. Before Jacob and Esau were born, God determined their destinies.

Jacob's grandfather was Abraham, and he didn't always understand God either. When he saw that God was going to punish Sodom and Gomorrah, he prayed, *'Will not the Judge of all the earth do right?'* (Gen. 18:25). And that should be our attitude when it comes to the sovereignty of God. We affirm it, and we trust that God knows what he is doing.

Today royalty doesn't have the power it had three or four hundred years ago, but even so the sovereign alone has the right to decide who comes to Buckingham Palace. Don't expect to go knocking on the doors. Just a few days after we arrived in Oxford in 1973, my wife and our children went into London to see Big Ben and Buckingham Palace. When we got to Buckingham Palace, my son kept looking, and said, 'I think I see her – yeah. I just saw a curtain move, and I believe she was looking out.' We stayed there for about 20 minutes but she never did come out to see us!

I don't think it would have done much good if we had asked to see her. She does the inviting; she determines who comes. A sovereign has that right. And the same is true of God. God has a right and the power to do as he pleases. I have come to the place in my Christian life where I have bowed to this teaching. God said to Moses, *'I will have mercy on whom I will have mercy, and I will have compassion on whom I will have compassion'* (Exod. 33:19). We must all bow to the sovereign God.

This subject is important for these reasons:

- We need to ensure we are acquainted with the true God. He is not bending over the banisters of heaven saying, 'Won't somebody please notice me?' God is not like a toy that you can play with.
- You and I need to be put in our rightful place. There is a feeling among many of us (until we find out better) that God owes us something. Perhaps you've had the idea that God owes you an explanation why something has happened. Maybe you have such a deep hurt, and you think, 'I don't know why God expects me to believe in him when I think of the way he has treated me. But when he explains himself, then I might just talk to him.' This is the kind of spirit you naturally feel until you understand that God owes us no explanations at all.

- We all deserve to go to hell. I don't expect you to grasp that the first time, but I can tell you it is true. If you think that becoming a Christian is doing God some kind of favour, you show that you have never been converted, you have never been broken. No. When we come to know the God of the Bible, we realize that God is gracious to save us. When we understand this, we come on bended knee and pray that he will have mercy on us.

The Sovereignty of God and Prayer

It began with Rebekah, the wife of Isaac, who had a barren womb. She had no children and it looked as though she never would have. In ancient times this was considered as a kind of curse, but it turned out that God was signalling great blessing to come. There are a number of women in the Old Testament who were barren. Eventually, many of them gave birth to people who changed the course of history. Sarah finally gave birth to Isaac. Hannah eventually gave birth to Samuel. Elizabeth gave birth to John the Baptist, also late in life. Barrenness was sometimes a symbol of promise in disguise.

Maybe you feel that you are in a similar situation and you want something to happen. Perhaps it is to have a baby, to know a particular success, or to have a prayer answered, but you have come to a dead end. You ask, 'Why?' Yet, maybe, that which looks so bleak is God's way of saying, 'Just wait a little while longer and you will see all that I have done. I do everything with a particular strategy in mind.'

Isaac prayed. One of the greatest mysteries that I know is the sovereignty of God in prayer. I know that God can do anything and doesn't have to answer to anybody, yet the same God tells us to pray. It amazes me. Perhaps you feel negative about the sovereignty of God, believing that there's no chance that he'll give you mercy. Yet that's the point: God doesn't owe us anything. If we come to understand that, it might just put us in our place and lead us to pray.

Isaac prayed to the Lord on behalf of his wife because she was barren. He need not have worried because God's oath to Abraham was at stake. God had sworn that Abraham's seed would be *'as the sand of the seashore'* (see Gen. 22:17). So Rebekah's barrenness was God's way of trying to get their attention.

Maybe the dead-end road you are on is God's way of trying to get your attention. When was the last time you prayed? How often do you pray? A thing that amazes me is that God *wants* us to pray; he *loves* it when we pray, and God wanted Isaac and Rebekah to pray. Perhaps they hadn't been praying as they should have. What is God doing to bring you to the place of prayer? Unanswered prayer is often God's way of getting our attention. You see, when we don't get what we want we are more teachable, whereas when we are blessed we can become more unteach - able. Dr Lloyd-Jones once said to me, 'The worst thing that can happen to a person is to succeed before they are ready.' God has a way of bringing you to such a place that you'll wait on him.

The Sovereignty of God and Prophecy

Prophecy is where God speaks through a person that which he wants spoken at a particular moment. It could be something to do with the present, so you could say that a preacher who expounds God's word and applies it directly to his congregation is prophesying. Sometimes we want a sensational word about the future, but what we *need* is knowing what to do now, and God speaks through the preaching of his word. Yet there *is* such a thing as predictive prophecy, when we predict and God fulfils what is said. Isaac and Rebekah prayed, then a prophetic word came to Rebekah: *'The LORD said to her, "Two nations are in your womb, and two peoples from within you will be separated; one people will be stronger than the other, and the older will serve the younger" '* (Gen. 25:23). Prophecy is God's idea. He not only determines things in advance but, sometimes, he reveals things in advance. Why? Here are six reasons to consider:

1. To show his overall plan.
2. To demonstrate that nothing ever happens to take him by surprise.
3. To show he is in complete control.
4. To prepare his people so that they too will not be surprised.
5. To let his people know that he is willing to share what he is doing.
6. To show that he knows the future.

The Sovereignty of God and People

'Two peoples from within you will be separated.' God determines our boundaries. The Apostle Paul stated that *'From one man he made every nation of men, that they should inhabit the whole earth; and he determined the times set for them and the exact places where they should live'* (Acts 17:26). It is no accident you were born when and where you were. There was a reason. You may say that your parents didn't want you, that you're an 'accident', but you'd be wrong. God wanted you to be born, and he chose the womb from which you should enter this world. I understand if you have a low view of yourself because you feel you were never wanted. You've grown up with a feeling of rejection. But consider this: God wanted you. You are here on purpose. God determines where, and when, you should be born. He alone gives life, and those who are born to us aren't ours, but his.

Equally important, God not only determines our birth but he also determines our new birth. Jesus said to a man by the name of Nicodemus, *'You must be born again'* (Jn. 3:7). The phrase *'born again'* has been abused, and people laugh at it. Nonetheless, it is a wonderful thought: 'born again' – to start all over again. Wouldn't you like to think that, just maybe, despite all you've been through, despite all your failure and frustration, you could have a second chance in life? It can happen to you, if it hasn't already. You can be born of the Spirit and come in touch with the true God. He put you here, and there is a plan for your life.

3

The Great Manipulator

Genesis 25:27–34

It will be impossible to say who will need this book more, the one who is already a Christian and is mature, or the person who has never come to Jesus Christ. Each chapter on the life of Jacob is what I call a 'double-barrelled shotgun'. It targets both the Christian and the non-Christian. Whoever you are, there is a word for you.

Esau gave up his birthright. I will define this word 'birthright' later. For now, we can note that it was the most foolish thing to do and he was so sorry. The writer of Hebrews tells us that later Esau tried to reverse what he had done. *'He could bring about no change of mind, though he sought the blessing with tears'* (Heb. 12:17). Jacob took unfair advantage of him, and this caused Jacob great grief for a long time. The result was that Jacob lived in continual fear that he would be despised, sought after and punished for what he did. Both brothers did wrong, and both knew remorse. Yet not only was Jacob responsible for being the manipulator, but he was, himself, willing to be manipulated.

Manipulation and Birthright

Let me define this word 'manipulation'. One psychologist, by the name of Everett Sholstrum, has defined a manipulator as a person who exploits, uses and/or controls people, as one would use an object, in certain self-defeating ways. So first, we are talking about one who controls others, who uses people and exploits them. Second, we are talking of a person who manipulates and treats people like things or objects, as opposed to treating them with dignity as people

We need to define the word 'birthright' at this point. We are told that Jacob manipulated Esau into surrendering his birthright. Esau was the elder and that meant he would inherit double what Jacob would receive.

In the ancient Hebrew world the birthright was very important because the firstborn had special privileges. Not only would he receive double the inheritance, but he ranked highest in the family after the father and, in his father's absence, had authority over his brothers and sisters. In short, the birthright belonging to the firstborn was a much-appreciated privilege. Only a fool would let it go.

We are all like Jacob. You say, 'Not me.' Yet, according to Sholstrum, we are all manipulators. There are two kinds: there's the 'top dog', or the silent, passive manipulator: the top politician and the high-pressured salesperson, or the passive manipulator, the person who's very quiet, who can achieve their aim by pouting or by just saying a word here and there to manipulate and get their own way. If a person manipulates you into doing something, you really only have yourself to blame, because nobody can be manipulated unless they acquiesce. So if you manipulate me, it's because I have allowed you to do it.

There is an exception to the manipulating person: Jesus Christ never manipulates us to achieve his end or purpose. He never treats us as if we are mere objects. He always treats us with dignity, as people. Perhaps people have pushed you around and have taken advantage of you over the years to such an extent that it is impossible for you to conceive what it would be like to be treated with dignity.

Mary Magdalene was possibly a prostitute. She was demon-possessed. Yet, when she met Jesus for the first time, she met a man who showed her real respect, and she adored him; she went all the way to the cross with him. When you come to see there is one who will treat you with respect and not as an object, he is worth following. The Holy Spirit, the Spirit of Jesus, is always a gentleman. He will never thrust himself upon you; he will never come and twist your arm. The Holy Spirit will never manipulate; what he does is to apply the word as it is in the Bible. When we hear his voice, the penny drops and we begin to see that God is making sense in our lives. We would be fools to reject him.

When Jesus died on the cross, he died for all the manipulators of the world. Perhaps you are reading this as one who has given in to manipu - lation, and you are so ashamed. Maybe you have manipulated someone else. Jesus took the guilt of your sins on the cross and promises a new beginning. The blood of Jesus will wash away all your sins. God promises you a home in heaven; your past is forgotten. This God will treat you with dignity. He will not manipulate you.

How Manipulation Works

Now what is manipulation? I think that perhaps the chief example is (i) emotional blackmail. If I want to blackmail you emotionally, I will make you feel so sorry for me that you'll feel awful if you don't do what

I want. I will put up a 'sob story' and make you feel guilty if you don't come to my rescue. Suppose someone says, 'I just found out this morning my mother has died. I lost my job this week, and I need to go to Liverpool, so I need £32 for the fare.' And they look at you as if you couldn't possibly deny them the money. Of course, you can refuse to be manipulated. You can go with that person to the local station to buy a ticket that can't be refunded. If they disappear from the scene, you know it was an attempt to manipulate you.

I knew a young lady who asked me what she should do about her boyfriend who had threatened to commit suicide if they split up. She thought, 'If I break up with him, he's going to kill himself. Then I'll have that on my conscience.'

Then there is (ii) the passive manipulator, the one who sulks. You ask them, 'Are you all right?'

'Yeah.'

'Are you sure?'

'Yeah, I'm fine.'

Yet, you know in your heart that they are *willing* you to ask them a few more questions. If you don't, they'll say, 'You don't care, and you know I am upset.' But if you do ask, you play right into their hands, and before you know it you are doing exactly what they want. They are brilliant at getting what they want as the 'top-dog' manipulator.

Another kind of manipulation is (iii) where people motivate others by fear. They threaten to tell what they know, or get what they want by telling others what they know. They use this kind of threat if they know they won't get their way. Then there's the manipulation of bribery, buying someone off, or promising a person material or financial gain.

Another way to manipulate is (iv) by using flattery. I can rarely resist this. If you come up to me and say, 'You know, that was the best sermon I ever heard', I know it's not true, but I love hearing it. So I'll ask, 'What can I do for you?'

They say, 'Well, I need £32 to get to Liverpool.'

You can manipulate (v) by taking advantage of someone whom you know to be lonely or weak in some way. Take a person who has a weakness when it comes to alcohol. They are trying their best not to drink but, to get what you want, you practically put it right in front of them. It is possible to take undue sexual advantage, when you know that a person has a particular weakness, yet you fail to treat that person with the respect due to a fellow human being.

Another way to manipulate is (vi) simply by blaming somebody and making them feel guilty. Or there's the person who uses illness to attract attention to get what they want. If they take advantage of somebody's good nature and know that the other person is so sweet and nice that they can just get anything they want out of them, they are manipulating.

A particularly subtle way of manipulating is (vii) to pit one person against another: 'Do you know, so and so said something about you that wasn't very pleasant? I don't agree with them, actually. But it wasn't very nice of them to say it.' When I was younger, I was in a group of four or five friends and, before I knew it, I had become suspicious of everyone in the group except one particular person. It was two or three years before I caught on. He told me little things about each of them to turn me slightly against them and to get me more dependent on him. I would say, 'I'm glad to know I've got *one* friend.' And he would assure me I could, at least, trust him, if no one else. Eventually, I realized that he was doing the same thing with the others, to get them to look only to him for friendship.

Jacob's Tricks

Jacob manipulated people by taking undue advantage of their weakened condition. Yet he knew exactly what he was doing. Probably, he had been plotting to steal his brother's birthright for years. He knew he wasn't his father's favourite and he felt cheated. Being a 'mummy's boy' wasn't fulfilling, and he knew there was only one way ahead. If somehow he could get Esau to turn over his birthright, then life would be worth living. He didn't want to go through life knowing that Esau would inherit a double portion. So he began to plot. He knew Esau had a weakness, that he had a taste for a certain kind of food. He knew that if you caught him in a weak moment, he would have to have immediate gratification and would not think clearly.

So one day Esau came in from the open country, starving, and noticed that Jacob had prepared a delicious stew. *'Quick, let me have some of that red stew!'* (Gen. 25:30). Esau was tired and worn out; the stew didn't have to be prepared; it was all ready. Jacob was ready to move in. He said, *'First sell me your birthright.'* Now we need to remember that what Esau did from this point on was done of his own free will, even though he was in a weakened state. We also know that the story of Jacob and Esau illustrates the sovereignty of God: God loved Jacob. Some say it wasn't fair, but there was another side of the coin.

You have here what I would call a double principle. On the one hand, if anybody is saved, it is by grace alone. It's just this: God is good to you. *'For it is by grace you have been saved, through faith – and this not from yourselves, it is the gift of God'* (Eph. 2:8). If you are a Christian, you cannot say you *deserve* to be a Christian. You cannot say, 'I deserve to go to heaven.' If you've been saved, you cannot say it's because of anything you have done: you can only say it's because of what God did. The word 'grace' means unmerited favour. We receive grace because of the blood of Jesus shed on the cross, because the Holy Spirit opened our hearts to believe, and we can take no credit for it.

On the other hand, it is a double principle. While some are saved because of the grace of God, some are lost because they choose to be lost. Esau could blame Jacob, up to a point, but at the end of the day, he had to live with himself. You can blame your parents, up to a point. You can blame that bad job you have, up to a point. You can blame society. You can blame politicians or the economy, up to a point. You can blame the one who took unfair advantage of you, a weakness with drink, with sex or with handling money, up to a point. Esau could blame Jacob, up to a point, but his desire for his appetite to be gratified immediately was more important to him than the high privilege of being the firstborn. Esau had such privilege yet, because he was starving, he rationalized.

Esau's Tricks

We all do this. When we are strongly tempted, we immediately start rationalizing to justify any decision we make. Here's what Esau probably said to himself: 'Well, I'm human.' When Eve partook of the forbidden fruit in the Garden of Eden, she saw that it was good for food, so she rationalized by saying, 'Eating this fruit can't be all that bad.' Perhaps you've done this and you've said, 'I've been very depressed, and this has helped me through my depression.' 'I've got a sexual problem and so and so was right there; God understands that.' In much the same way, Esau said, 'Well, I'm going to die, and what good is my birthright then?'

For some, immediate gratification is more important than the salvation of their souls. Jesus asked a question. It's one of those questions you can't answer. *'What good is it for a man to gain the whole world, yet forfeit his soul?'* (Mk. 8:36). We are talking about where we spend eternity. Am I to believe that some, in order to have sexual fulfilment or to satisfy a habit, are ready to give in to temptation and lose their souls? Some have been brought up in a Christian home and have turned their backs on the gospel. Some have heard gospel preaching and kept rationalizing, always thinking there would be another opportunity. But the Bible says, *'My spirit will not contend with man for ever'* (Gen. 6:3). The day will come when they will not hear the gospel that once stirred them.

We used to live in Ealing, beside the railway track, where trains on their way to Bristol and South Wales went past us at one hundred miles an hour. The first time we ever heard one it sounded like an earthquake. Two or three weeks later, we would hear one only now and then. Six months later, visitors would say, 'How do you put up with that sound?' Yet we didn't even notice it.

If the Holy Spirit is dealing with you, while there's a little tug in your heart, respond to him!

You see, *this* is the way the devil works. Jacob had the stew *ready*. He didn't have to say, 'Now that you've sworn the birthright is mine, I'll go and prepare it for you.' It was ready. The devil will already have someone there to drink with you, to have sex with, or to give you easy money.

Judas Iscariot was the great manipulator. He went to the chief priests and asked, *'What are you willing to give me if I hand him* [Jesus] *over to you?'* (Mt. 26:15). So they made a deal for 30 pieces of silver. After Judas realized what he had done, he offered to return the money. But they said, 'That's your problem.' Those who are manipulators, in a matter of time, live to be sorry.

While God uses his word to persuade you to do what you will wish you did, the devil will manipulate you to do what you will wish you hadn't done. Esau realized later what he had done. He wanted to turn the clock back. He wanted to do something to change everything, but he had passed the point of no return. The Bible tells us that he couldn't reverse it, though he tried with tears (see Gen. 27:38).

Now is the time to weep. Weep for your sins. Be sorry, and thank God that he is coming to you again. Look to his Son and trust him. If you hear his voice, are you willing to do that today? Jesus says, *'Come to me'* (Mt. 11:28).

4

Does One Have a Free Will?

Genesis 27:1–29

Does one have a free will? Now I don't know if that's the most exciting question you've ever had put to you – it will appeal to some more than others. Those who have gone into theology, philosophy or psychology have faced it. There are those who aren't the slightest bit bothered, yet there comes a time when we all have to ask this kind of question.

Free Will

You may say, 'It is obvious people are free.' But others disagree. B.F. Skinner, the Harvard psychologist, is a behaviourist. He believes that we are not free, that we all react the same way to given impulses, and that everybody would act the same way under the same circum - stances. Sigmund Freud said that we have unconscious repressed desires because of influences from our parents when we were children that lead to feelings we can't control.

There is an aspect of the life of Jacob that is hard to understand. Jacob was probably in his twenties. Following his mother's devices, he deceived his father in order to get the patriarchal blessing. This blessing was passed through deception and trickery. Jacob received the blessing that Isaac thought he was giving to Esau. We know that God said in advance that Jacob would be chosen and that Esau would have to bow to Jacob. It was a prophetic word to Isaac's wife, Rebekah. Does that mean that Jacob had to deceive his brother to fulfil that prophetic word to his mother? The prophetic word was that when the twins were in Rebekah's womb, the Lord said to her, *'The older will serve the younger'* (Gen. 25:23). Without this verse we wouldn't have a problem, but in the New Testament the Apostle Paul uses this very moment for the teaching of election or predestination: *'Before the twins were born or had done good or bad – in order*

*that God's purpose in election might stand . . . Just as it is written: Jacob I loved,
but Esau I hated'* (Rom. 9:11). So God made the decision before they were
born, yet we find out what Rebekah and Jacob apparently had to do to
make that word become true.

You can see the problem. Rebekah knew what no one else knew, that
Jacob was God's choice. The whole thing was God's idea. I don't
understand this at all. But there's a verse that I always turn to whenever
I don't understand what's going on in my life. I remember these words
of Abraham, *'Will not the Judge of all the earth do right?'* (Gen. 18:25). You
are not reading this by accident. There is a reason that you are supposed
to read this and God will use it. I am so often amazed how God will use
a message that you wouldn't have dreamed would make a difference in
another person's life. Nevertheless, God does that.

When Rebekah heard that Isaac, who was now blind, was going to
give his blessing to Esau, she said to herself, 'This is the moment.' So she
turned to Jacob saying, 'I want you to get that blessing. Here's what to
do.' Instead of the wild game that Isaac hoped for, they found a couple
of young goats, and Rebekah prepared the food to her husband's taste.
To deceive Isaac she had Jacob wear the goatskin on his hands, so that
when the old man touched him he would say, 'This is Esau.' And it
worked. Jacob got the blessing!

What if she had not told Jacob to do this? What if Jacob had not done
it? What would have happened? We'll never know. We only know what
happened. Maybe as you read you are asking, 'What if I had not done
that?' The truth is you did and you cannot change the past. However,
you can come to see that God has shaped your past, and no matter what
has happened in your life, whether good or bad, God will cause it to look
beautiful and wonderful, no matter how odd it may appear.

According to the Epistle to the Hebrews 12:16, it was all Esau's fault
in the first place, because Esau gave his birthright to Jacob. This meant
that the blessing would not come to Esau. But I still want to ask: Is that
the way it's supposed to be? Is this the way God works?

There are other ways, but here is the way I would define free will:
Free will is man's own ability to determine his destiny. Free will is what
appeared to be in operation when Rebekah acted as she did and Jacob
deceived his father. Free will, then, determines events: in this instance,
God's prophecy was fulfilled and Jacob received the patriarchal blessing,
which was more precious than gold.

The patriarchal blessing was an anointing, a built-in gift of God that the
patriarchs had. Abraham, Isaac and Jacob had it within their bodies, their hands,
and in their minds, in order to pronounce a blessing upon their children.
The form of the blessing would be exactly as the words they uttered in
bestowing it. The blessing was to be coveted above all else. There was still
a chance, although Esau had sold his birthright, that he would get that
blessing and it would overrule what he had done.

When Rebekah heard that the blessing was imminent, she started planning. God invested the patriarch with authority to bless or to curse. Nobody believed in God's promise more than Rebekah, and nobody worked so hard to make it happen.

Predestination

Consider people like Martin Luther or John Calvin back in the sixteenth century who shared a belief in predestination. The common way to look at predestination is to say, 'If it's true, there's nothing for us to do – it's all going to happen anyway.' As the hard-shelled old Baptist in the hills of Kentucky says, 'What is to be, will be, whether it happens or not!' Those who don't believe in predestination say, 'I don't believe that, because if I did I wouldn't do anything.' It's their way of opting out or criticizing those who do believe in it. For those on the outside looking in that's the way it always appears, but to the one who actually believes it the opposite is true. Instead of predestination making you passive or a fatalist, it makes you highly motivated. That's what made Luther and Calvin turn the world upside down. Some would abuse this teaching, and I have had to fight this over the years. That said, it's wonderful when you can find the balance. You believe in the total sovereignty of God and that he can do anything by his own will, but equally you believe you have to do something or God isn't going to bring it to pass. When I teach evangelists, I talk about strong doctrine. I teach predes - tination because I want a group of men and women who will go out on the streets, believing in the sovereignty of God, and yet try to convert people as though it were up to them. God honours that kind of thinking and action.

This does not mean that the way Jacob and Rebekah went about it was the right way. The point is that nobody believed in God's promise more than Rebekah, yet she worked so hard to bring it about. What she did brought Jacob great grief. Yet, at the end of the day, God owned it all, and Romans 8:28 was vindicated again: *'In all things God works for the good of those who love him, who have been called according to his purpose.'* Jacob would have the greatest sense of guilt – we'll see that in the next chapter – but the guilt that Jacob felt was part of the problem he experienced throughout the whole of his life. In the end, God just sanctioned his life and he became a great trophy of grace.

You may be a great sinner and know that you don't deserve God's mercy. You are aware of how you've 'blown it' and of how you've let things slip through your fingers; you've been a failure and you're ashamed. You are the very kind of person whom God loves to save, because the more complicated your problem, the greater the glory God will receive. The greater your sin, the greater the forgiveness. This is not to justify what you've done. This does not justify what Jacob did, but it shows that God will take that which was wicked, which was wrong, and cause it to work together with other things for good.

Let me put it another way. We have those who say, 'God knows whether I will be saved, so it doesn't matter what I do.' It is true that God knows. I don't know where you will be one hundred years from now, but God knows. We observe that there are two reactions to the fact that God knows whether you will be saved. You can say, 'There's nothing I can do about it', and just blame God. I find it interesting that in non-revival times that's the reaction of most people. They say, 'I'm not going to worry about it; it's not my problem. God knows. It's OK.' When there is no sense of God, there's no awakening, so that's the reaction. If that is your reaction, you are mirroring the atmosphere that is in the world and in the church today, where there isn't much God-consciousness.

How God's Sovereignty Works

Through weakness

The first thing to realize is that God works through weakness to achieve his end.

Genesis 27:1 says: *'When Isaac was old and his eyes were so weak that he could no longer see, he called for Esau his older son.'* God used Isaac's weakness to achieve his end and has been doing that ever since. God uses our weaknesses to achieve his purpose. The Apostle Paul said that he prayed for God to remove the *'thorn in the flesh'* three times (a phrase he uses in 2 Cor. 12:7). Have you prayed for something, but God has not answered your prayer? Some suggest that if you were more spiritual your prayer would be answered, but Paul was a very spiritual man. The answer he received from the Lord was, *'My grace is sufficient for you, for my power is made perfect in weakness'* (2 Cor. 12:9). This shows how God works through weakness to achieve his aim. Perhaps you have thought that in order for God to use you, you had to be strong. Wrong.

Are you weak? Are you so weak you feel ashamed? God says in reply, 'Wonderful, you're the one I want.' Maybe you are conscious of your failure. Perhaps as you grew up and you went to school, you didn't make good grades and you didn't study. Perhaps you are older, you're a parent and you say you're a failure as a parent. Maybe you took an exam and it didn't go the way you wanted it to, and you feel there's no hope for you. Perhaps you are a failure in that you haven't taken care of your body as you should and you are in ill health as a result. God works through weakness to achieve his end. Jesus was crucified in weakness. He let them do what they wanted, and they crucified him. They treated him like the scum of the earth, and he became vulnerable. Why did he do that? He did it so that you could see that. Jesus was crucified in weakness that we might know we are the very kind of people for whom he died. If, by contrast, you are the type of person who always gets things done and you think your good works are going to save you, you are not really a Christian. God looks for the weak, not the strong.

Through wickedness

We must also realize that God works through wickedness to achieve his end. Romans 5:20 says, *'Where sin increased, grace increased all the more.'* What Rebekah did was wicked; what Jacob did was also wicked. Genesis 27:16, 17 refers to their trickery:

> *She also covered his hands and the smooth part of his neck with the goatskins. Then she handed to her son Jacob the tasty food and the bread she had made. He went to his father and said, 'My father.'*
> *'Yes, my son,' he answered. 'Who is it?'*
> *Jacob said to his father, 'I am Esau, your firstborn'* (Gen. 27:16–19).

That was a lie. Not only trickery, but deceit. Perhaps you are aware of your wickedness and wilful wrongdoing. God doesn't have to explain himself. One of my favourite verses is Isaiah 55:9: *'My ways are higher than your ways and my thoughts than your thoughts.'* We think in a certain way: God thinks in a different way. He doesn't have to explain himself.

Three times in the early chapters of the book of Acts we have this principle. *'This man [Jesus] was handed over to you by God's set purpose and foreknowledge; and you, with the help of wicked men, put him to death by nailing him to the cross'* (Acts 2:23). So wickedness is what crucified Jesus. So in Acts 3:13 we read:

> *The God of Abraham, Isaac and Jacob, the God of our fathers, has glorified his servant Jesus. You handed him over to be killed, and you disowned him before Pilate, though he decided to let him go. You disowned the Holy and Righteous One and asked that a murderer be released to you. You killed the author of life, but God raised him from the dead.*

So the wickedness that lay behind the crucifixion of Jesus turned out to be God's way of saving the world. When Jesus was hanging upon the cross, he could take upon himself all our wickedness, all our deceit and trickery. The skeletons in our cupboards were charged to Jesus as though he were guilty, and all our sins were put on him. God worked through wickedness to achieve his end.

Finally, in Acts 4:27 we read these words: *'Herod and Pontius Pilate met together with the Gentiles and the people of Israel in this city to conspire against your holy servant Jesus, whom you anointed. They did what your power and will had decided beforehand should happen.'* Would you want any other God than that – a God who has control over everything, whom nothing catches by surprise?

Through wilfulness

The final point is that God works through wilfulness to achieve his end. What Rebekah did was an act of the will, her free will. What she did determined what happened. What Jacob did determined what happened. He could have rejected his mother's advice, but he did what she said and the result was that he received the blessing. And when Isaac realized what had happened, he said, *'I blessed him – and indeed he will be blessed'* (Gen. 27:33).

So it is with us, when we accept the gospel. Rejected, the gospel means that we stay as we are. In fact, things get worse and eventually we become eternally lost. In a sense, whether we go to heaven or to hell is up to us because God works through wilfulness. The Bible promises that whoso - ever is willing may come (see Rev. 22:17). If you hear his voice and open the door, he will come in (see Rev. 3:20). The same God who works through weakness, wickedness and wilfulness will also work through your will.

5

The Anointing

Genesis 27:25–40

Isaac, the father of Jacob, had a particular anointing. I would define the anointing here as God's gift to us by which we bless others. When you become a Christian, God gives you an anointing. Many Christians feel they don't have an anointing at all, but that's not the case. There are anointings that are more spectacular than others, yet every Christian has an anointing.

God's Anointing

1. Every Christian has an anointing

The anointing stems partly from the natural – the way we were made. Our parents, our environment and our background are all ingredients of no small consequence that figure in our anointing. These are the natural gifts that we operate as a result of the way we've been brought up, for the gifts we had before we became Christians don't disappear once we are saved.

But the anointing is also that which comes from above – the super - natural. The Holy Spirit comes on top of natural gifting; he is superim - posed, and that is why we call the gifts *supernatural*. In fact, the word 'anointing' is used in 1 John 2:20 when John says, *'You have an anointing from the Holy One, and all of you know the truth.'* Again, in 1 John 2:27, we read: *'As for you, the anointing you received from him remains in you, and you do not need anyone to teach you. But as his anointing teaches you about all things and as that anointing is real, not counterfeit – just as it has taught you, remain in him.'*

This anointing will do something for you and will do something for others. If that anointing flows as it should, it will be almost impossible to tell who is blessed more, you – or others. There is no such thing as an anointing which is just for you, so that you can soak it in like a sponge. No. The anointing will bless you and it will bless others. You may ask, why use that particular word, why not call it a 'gift' or a 'calling' or a 'vocation'? But, when it comes to the way the Holy Spirit blesses us, it is the best word one can use to describe what happens. 'Anointing' comes from a word that literally means to 'smear with an ointment', and that's what the anointing is. It is something that the Holy Spirit does.

2. Anointings are varied

Not everybody's anointing is the same, and no one person has every anointing that is possible. Only one person who ever lived had every conceivable anointing, and that person was Jesus. The Bible says that Jesus had the Holy Spirit without measure, that is, without limit (Jn. 3:34). When you become a Christian, you receive the Holy Spirit. Don't you dare let anyone tell you that you can have the Holy Spirit and not be a Christian or you can be a Christian and not have the Holy Spirit. If you have the Holy Spirit, you are a Christian. If you are a Christian, you have the Holy Spirit. That does not mean that further down the line there can't be a greater anointing, a 'baptism of the Spirit' and a filling, but once you become a Christian you receive the Holy Spirit and you receive an anointing. That anointing can increase. It is my most fervent prayer for an increase of the anointing that I already have, but the point is, I only have the Spirit in a limited measure, I don't have all there is. Only Jesus had all there is. That means we need each other. Not everybody's anointing is the same and no one can do everything.

Jesus said in Luke 4:18, *'The Spirit of the Lord is on me, because he has anointed me to preach good news to the poor.'* He was quoting from Isaiah 61:1. Some have an anointing to preach, and others have an anointing to heal. I don't know why it is, but those who have an anointing to heal don't see healing every time they pray for somebody. They do, however, see more healings than anyone else.

There's an anointing given to some to help others, and this is no inferior gift. It is one of the most precious anointings – it is called the gift of helping others, and is listed among the gifts in 1 Corinthians 12. There are some who, if you spend a few minutes with them, make you feel so much better. They have an anointing. They have an ability to calm you down, to encourage you, or to listen to you and give the word. It is supernatural, and also a natural gifting. That person probably had a particularly suitable temperament or disposition. So we are talking about two ingredients, the natural and the supernatural. There are those who have an anointing to make money, although not many Christians have it because most of us could not be trusted with it.

3. Anointing seems natural

This passage talks about Isaac's anointing. The anointing came easily; it was as natural as breathing. Notice how it's put in verse 27: *'So he went to him and kissed him. When Isaac caught the smell of his clothes, he blessed him.'* Now what he smelt was Esau's clothes. Jacob put on Esau's clothes and goatskin and Isaac smelt them, so that even though he was blind, he felt he knew it was his firstborn son. So we are talking about something natural. He blessed him and said, *'Ah, the smell of my son is like the smell of a field the Lord had blessed.'* The smell triggered off these words, and we can see how there's a natural explanation for the way it began.

The point is this: any anointing seems natural. To the person who is truly spiritual, the supernatural seems natural, and to the person who has a real anointing, it is as easy for him as breathing, because when you are operating within the level of the anointing God has given you, you will never be tired. There will never be fatigue.

You may have heard of the 'Peter Principle' – an ingenious idea and quite true: everybody is promoted to the level of their incompetence. The reason things break down, and the reason why you have to have that spare part so soon is because the person on the assembly line shouldn't have had that job – or the manager shouldn't have had their job – they should be on the assembly line. It seems that through death, ambition or lack of good personnel, people are given a job that they can't do. Often, due to pride or selfish ambition, a person is determined to gain promotion; they get it and celebrate. But eighteen months later, they have a nervous breakdown because they can't cope. But, you see, when you operate within the sphere of your own anointing, it's easy.

Dr Paul Cain has one of the most unusual anointings. I've never seen anything like it. When the anointing is on him, he can go straight to the fifth row in a meeting, call a person's name and say what's wrong with them. He can tell prophetically what is going to happen in the future. (I have not personally seen him do it but I have talked to those who have.) They say he can go on for half an hour, while 30 or 40 people are called out, one after the other, and he hits the nail on the head every time – and you wonder, 'How does he do it?' That's as natural for Paul to do as it is for a gifted organist to play the organ; he's not dead after an hour or more of playing, nor is a worship leader tired after he's been singing. You could define the anointing as doing what is easy for you, where you're never at the level of your incompetence.

The whole time Isaac was praying for Jacob, he thought it was Esau. Esau eventually came in from hunting and said, 'I've come for my blessing.' Isaac trembled violently and cried, *'Who was it, then, that hunted game and brought it to me? I ate it just before you came and I blessed him'* (Gen. 27:33). Isaac knew that his anointing was used in a different direction from the way he intended it. Once he realized what God allowed to happen, he was tested to the full because he wanted to bless his firstborn. But when he saw that he had blessed Jacob, he stood by it.

4. Anointing is permanent

Any anointing you are given, you will always have once God has given it because *'God's gifts and his call are irrevocable'* (Rom. 11:29). Once God has given you an anointing, you've got it. Take some of the TV evangelists from America: how was it they could preach and seem to have such power and such ability? You may see some video replays of those men and say, 'Oh, what power!' only to find out later their private lives were altogether different, inconsistent with the way they were preaching. The point is, if you have an anointing, God doesn't take it back. That is consistent with the gospel of Jesus Christ, because once you become a Christian you will always be a Christian.

Do you know what makes a person a Christian? A person is a Christian who realizes that he cannot earn his way to heaven. For those who see it, nothing is clearer. But until the penny drops and the light comes through, you can't see it. Sometimes when I preach, I spend the whole sermon explaining that you are only saved by Jesus Christ dying for you on the cross. People then come back to see me. I put to them the most elementary question: 'If you stood before God and he said to you, "Why should I let you into my heaven?" what would you say?' I think to myself, 'This is easy – I've been preaching on it for the last 35 minutes.'

But they reply: 'Well I've tried to do my best, I've tried to do the right thing.'

I can't believe it! So I'll ask, 'Were you in the service?'

'Yes, I loved your sermon.'

'And you are saying that you can get to heaven by trying to do the right thing or by earning your way?'

'Well, I'm really trying.'

This shows that even though I preached it, the Holy Spirit hasn't made the message clear. I spent 15 minutes one morning with a very intelligent man. We met out on the street. We sat down, we had some coffee and talked. He was very polite, very middle-class and sophisticated. He said he was confirmed in the Church of England and he had three children; one of them had been confirmed, and the other two hadn't. I asked, 'Do you think you are going to heaven?'

He replied, 'There's a 50/50 chance.'

So I explained that we can't earn our way to heaven – we are saved by grace. I showed him that the Bible says: *'For it is by grace you have been saved, through faith – and this not from yourselves, it is the gift of God – not by works, so that no-one can boast'* (Eph. 2:8). I was getting so excited as I talked to him, and he just watched me as I thought I was getting ready to lead him to the Lord.

Towards the end, I said, 'What do you think?'

He said, 'I still think you have to earn your way.'

He didn't hear a word I said. The point is, there is an anointing of the Spirit that will enable you to see what others see so clearly, but until the Spirit reveals it you won't see it. I will never forget talking to a lady who was 80 years old and went to church all her life. I presented the gospel to her, and this time the penny dropped. You should have seen her face! She said, 'Nobody's ever told me that.' They probably had, but the Spirit hadn't applied it.

The fact that you remain always a Christian is due to this principle of the anointing. When you are saved, you are saved because you confess your sins to God. Ask God to save you for Jesus' sake; receive the Holy Spirit and you never lose him. Jesus said, *'I will ask the Father, and he will give you another Counsellor to be with you for ever – the Spirit of truth'* (Jn. 14:16). At the very moment you are saved, God puts to your credit the righteousness of Jesus. So that one second after you are converted, you are as righteous as Jesus in the sight of God. Twenty years later, thirty years later, you're no more righteous – because you have the righteousness of Jesus. God never takes back what he gives. It's the principle of grace.

5. Anointing will be tested

The anointing that will be given to you – whatever it is – will put your faith to the test. Just as when Isaac realized what had happened when he had blessed Jacob and said to his beloved Esau, *'I blessed him – and indeed he will be blessed!'* (Gen. 27:33). Isaac affirmed what God did. That's what we have to do: we have to affirm it God's way. So if you think you get to heaven by your own efforts, you may not realize it, but you are showing contempt for God's way. God's way is sending his Son to die on a cross.

The anointing may bring difficulties for you. It may lead you where you don't want to go. You may have to go against personal desire. It may lead you to bless those whom you personally may not have chosen to bless.

A few years ago, I talked with a man in Oxford who was from Harvard University, a historian and an expert on the life of David Brainerd. This Harvard professor said that what people don't know about David Brainerd is that he didn't really like the Indians in New York to whom he ministered, yet people talk about this man who had such a burden for the Indians there. The truth is that he didn't really like them, but that's where God led him.

God's Anointing upon Isaac

1. It was effective in the direction God wanted

It was effective in the direction God wanted, but it was not effective in the way Isaac himself wanted. Isaac's anointing was the patriarchal anointing of Abraham, Isaac and Jacob, who were given special powers to anoint those on whom God put his hand. And so the content was predetermined, and the words were God's very words: '*May nations serve you and peoples bow down to you. Be lord over your brothers, and may the sons of your mother bow down to you. May those who curse you be cursed and those who bless you be blessed*' (Gen. 27:29). That was the content of the anointing that was on Isaac to give. So it was effective and it went to Jacob, and it is true to this day. Jacob was physically present and Jacob received it and, in the providence of God, that was the way it was supposed to be. As my old friend Henry Mahan used to say, 'When the gospel is preached to people as they are, it will save some and condemn others, but it will accomplish God's purpose.'

2. It passed by Esau

The anointing went to Jacob simply because Esau had stolen his birthright. According to Hebrews 12:15, this is the reason things went as they did:

> *See to it that no-one misses the grace of God and that no bitter root grows up to cause trouble and defile many. See that no-one is sexually immoral, or is godless like Esau, who for a single meal sold his inheritance rights as the oldest son. Afterwards, as you know, when he wanted to inherit this blessing, he was rejected. He could bring about no change of mind, though he sought the blessing with tears.*

The reason the anointing bypassed Esau is because Esau himself forfeited it by what he did – by giving in to immediate pleasure, by not allowing for gratification to be delayed. He had to have satisfaction right now – and in that moment, he blew his whole life away. And the reason the blessing went the way it did was because of Esau's decision; yet it could equally be said that Jacob received the blessing because he wanted it more than anything else in the world.

I want more anointing than anything else in the world. I don't pray for more money, I don't pray for fame, for prestige, or for security. I pray for the anointing, because that's the blessing of God. If you know you have the anointing, even though you don't have other little things, know that blessing from him is worth more than all the money in the world. '*If God is for us, who can be against us?*' (Rom. 8:31). Jesus said, '*The kingdom of heaven is like a merchant looking for fine pearls. When he found one of great value, he went away and sold everything he had and bought it'* (Mt. 13:45). What that means is, when you want the anointing more than anything in the world, you'll do anything to get it because you want God's blessing. It's like Elisha, who saw that, just maybe, he would receive Elijah's mantle, and so he would not let Elijah out of his sight (see 2 Kgs. 2:2).

3. It was lost beyond recovery

Once the door of opportunity is shut, nothing can reverse what has happened. This is what we learn of Isaac's anointing. It was passed to Jacob and Esau *'burst out with a loud and bitter cry and said to his father, "Bless me – me too, my father!"'* (Gen. 27:34). We can be sure that Isaac wanted so much to bless his own firstborn son. And the best he could muster up was a little blessing in verses 39 and 40 – there's not much there. It just shows, incidentally, how limited a parent is with a child. We pray for our children, but they must be converted for themselves. Isaac wanted his firstborn to have the blessing, but once the door of opportunity has been shut, nothing can reverse what has happened.

Esau missed it. And then you have these pitiful words when he wanted to criticize his brother. *' "Isn't he rightly named Jacob? He has deceived me these two times: he took my birthright, and now he's taken my blessing!"'* (Gen. 27:36). Esau wanted to blame someone else, not himself.

There's a lesson here for all of us: if we want the blessing more than anything in the world, we can have it because our very desire will be testimony to God's work in our hearts.

6

Unable to Forgive?

Genesis 27:34–46

Although I will be referring mainly to Esau in this chapter, you will see how relevant it is to the life of Jacob. Esau was Jacob's twin brother and Esau had a problem: he could not forgive Jacob. For 20 years Jacob was in hiding, in fear of his life, avoiding Esau. Esau, we are told, was determined to kill his own brother: 'Esau held a grudge against Jacob *because of the blessing his father had given him. He said to himself, "The days of mourning for my father are near; then I will kill my brother Jacob" ' (Gen. 27:41).

A Problem of Forgiving?

Do you have a problem forgiving people? Perhaps you cannot forgive an unfaithful spouse. You cannot forgive your father because he wasn't a good parent, and when you think of praying to God and calling him Father, something inside just switches off. You can talk to Jesus, you can talk to God, but you can't call him Father. Perhaps you are angry with your mother because you were not her favourite. Maybe you are angry with a relative who took advantage of you at some stage. Perhaps that boss of yours wouldn't give you that recommendation. Perhaps you know what it is to have an old friend betray you, or there was one who took advantage of you and spread an untrue rumour. Maybe someone was unkind or unfair to your child and you can't forgive them. Perhaps you have a son-in-law who has mistreated your daughter. We could go on and on. You live with the feeling of being let down. Someone gave you a promise; you believed it, but they didn't keep it.

Esau held a grudge against Jacob, and the result was that he lived for one thing: vengeance. Can you identify with that? Do you know what it is to want to see another person hurt, smashed, humiliated, put down? You'd like them to get the sack, or you would love to hear of somebody falling into sin, all because they did something to you that wasn't very nice. Did you hear that so and so is now in a lot of trouble and think, 'Good, it's about time they got their comeuppance'?

What a way to live! We can never come to terms in ourselves with being unable to forgive others. When I can't forgive, I am the one who is hurting; I am the loser. And yet, because I have such a wicked, sinful heart, even though I know in my head I'm hurting myself, I still want to hurt someone else.

I knew of a minister who had a story to tell about how he was mistreated. I wish I could say that at first this particular minister handled it well. He didn't. Whenever I saw him, I would look at him and I would say to a friend of mine, 'You know, he's a different man.' He was a shadow of himself. You knew it *was* him, but you had to do a double-take because his bitterness went so deep that it affected the look on his face, his posture and his whole outlook.

Now, whenever I hear of a story of mistreatment, I am always sympathetic. And I doubt not for a second that there are hundreds of people who could tell a story that would break your heart, and you would get riled inside and want to fight for them. And yet, even though we are sympathetic, the truth is that the degree to which we hold a grudge will be the degree to which we damage our own health, and not just mentally. A person who holds a grudge and doesn't deal with it eventually develops not only a neurosis but a psychosis, where they become paranoid, suspicious, and out of touch with reality. Not only mental health can be damaged, however. Holding a grudge will lead to high blood pressure, heart disease, or arthritis. It doesn't follow that every person who has heart disease or arthritis is holding a grudge, but unforgiveness is undoubtedly one of the causes in many cases.

Yet to be fair, forgiving another person when they have been really awful to you is not easy. I for one find this the most difficult thing I've ever come across. Of all the areas of temptation that a person can have, to forgive someone who has done us an injustice is the hardest thing. It's partly our pride; it's partly seeing the injustice which makes us angry. We think of our reputation, and what really gets our goat is that people think so highly of the person who hurt us! Then, as if that isn't enough, the person who has hurt us most seems to be blessed by God! And we might wish that it's because we've been praying that they would be blessed, but of course it isn't that at all – they just seem to get away with it.

Praying for Your Enemies

Jesus said, *'Love your enemies and pray for those who persecute you'* (Mt. 5:44). I've come to see that when Jesus said, 'pray for them', he didn't mean a perfunctory prayer where you say, 'Bless so and so, Lord.' Of course, we don't always want to say this too often, in case the Lord interrupts us and says, 'Just a minute – did I hear you say you want me to bless them?' Imagine the conversation:

'Well, I'm supposed to ask you to bless them, Lord.'

'OK,' the Lord says, 'though I'm not sure you really want me to.'

'Well . . . yes, bless them.'

'Are you sure?'

'Yeah . . . bless them.'

'OK, I'm going to.'

'You are, eh?'

I have a prayer list of people that I don't particularly like. Seriously. No one knows who is on it, but on this list there is someone I pray for whom I don't like at all. He hasn't been nice to me. I once saw an article he had written in a magazine. My immediate feeling was, 'I'm not going to read that.' And then I thought, 'Wait a minute – I prayed for that man this morning. If I really meant what I prayed, I'm going to read that article.' I did. It was a good article and I got a lot out of it. So I said to God as best I knew how, 'Lord, bless him.' I want to come to the place where, if I see an article or book he has written, or hear something about him, and people are bragging about him, I can feel the same way as others do. You may say it's not possible, but I believe it is. I think this is why Jesus told us to pray for our enemies. I have found that the more I do it and mean it, the freer I get in my spirit, and I feel good.

Jacob's Treatment of Esau

Now there were two things that Jacob had done. First, he took advantage of Esau in a weak moment. Second, he deceived his ageing, blind father and stole the patriarchal blessing that should have gone to Esau. Once it had been done, it was too late to change anything, even though Isaac was upset about it. Isaac wanted to give his blessing to Esau, but said it was too late. They all had to live with what Jacob had done. So Esau was deeply hurt and cried out in anger: *'Bless me – me too, my father!'* (Gen. 27:34). How do you suppose that made Isaac feel? The proof that Isaac had a fear of God is that he said that the blessing would remain with Jacob. He could not give a blessing to his son the way in which he wanted.

What does this say to us? We have to love God more than our children, more than any relative, any person. Listen to Jesus:

I did not come to bring peace, but a sword. For I have come to turn a man against his father, a daughter against her mother, a daughter-in-law against her mother-in-law – a man's enemies will be the members of his own household. Anyone who loves his father or mother more than me is not worthy of me; anyone who loves his son or daughter

more than me is not worthy of me; and anyone who does not take his cross and follow
me is not worthy of me. Whoever finds his life will lose it, and whoever loses his life
for my sake will find it (Mt. 10:34–37).

So there are several reasons why Esau could not forgive his brother:

- Self-pity. We are told in verse 42, *'Your brother Esau is consoling himself*
  with the thought of killing you.' Why do we console ourselves? Self-pity
  always seems right at the time, but it is self-defeating and only adds to
  the problem. Self-pity springs from a self-love. But it is always
  counter-productive. We do not begin to live productive lives until we
  stop feeling sorry for ourselves. It is essentially self-righteousness, our
  way of saying, 'I don't deserve this.' It is, therefore, aimed at God, who
  is not pleased when we give into this sulking spirit.
- The hurt went deep. There are hurts and there are hurts. Some may
  be two or three inches deep; this one was a mile deep.
- Jealousy combined with the injustice. We know Esau was jealous; we
  can't blame him. After all, he wanted the blessing, but the blessing
  went to the one who didn't deserve it. And so Esau held a grudge
  against Jacob.
- Esau's life would never be the same again. It is one thing to have
  something hurt a little and feel there's a little scar there, but life goes
  on. Esau's life would never be the same again. What Isaac had done
  resulted in Esau living for only one thing – taking vengeance on his
  brother.
- Why couldn't Esau forgive? There's no doubt he was angry with God
  for letting it happen. Perhaps if you were honest with yourself, you
  could trace your bitterness towards someone in particular. And, if you
  have any faith in God at all, you have to come to terms with the fact
  that God let it happen. This is why the Psalmist said:

Do not fret because of evil men or be envious of those who do wrong; for like the grass
they will soon wither, like green plants they will soon die away. Trust in the L ORD
and do good; dwell in the land and enjoy safe pasture. Delight yourself in the L ORD
and he will give you the desires of your heart . Commit your way to the L ORD; trust
in him . . . He will make your righteousness shine like the dawn, the justice of your
cause like the noonday sun (Ps. 37:1–6).

That's a promise. There's no doubt that Esau was angry with God, but
that is not the end of the story, as we know from the remarkable events
in Genesis 33.

Jacob had been on the run for 20 years. It is one thing not to be able to
forgive, but how would you feel if somebody wouldn't forgive you? Jacob
was now away from everybody, and nobody could find him. I expect that
for 20 years he lived in fear every time he saw a caravan – 'Could that be

Esau coming to get me?' Every time he went very far he would wonder
who people were. How would you like to live in perpetual fear of
somebody catching up with you?

A Time for Overcoming Bitterness

The time came when it was zero hour, when Jacob had to meet Esau.
He knew that his brother wanted to kill him, so he devised various ways
to protect himself for as long as possible, and he did this partly by the gifts
he had ready. We read in Genesis 33:5–10:

> *Then Esau looked up and saw the women and children. 'Who are these with you?'*
> *he asked.*
>
> *Jacob answered, 'They are the children God has graciously given your servant.'*
>
> *Then the maidservants and their children approached and bowed down. Next, Leah*
> *and her children came and bowed down. Last of all came Joseph and Rachel, and they*
> *too bowed down.*
>
> *Esau asked, 'What do you mean by all these droves I met?'*
>
> *'To find favour in your eyes, my lord,' he said.*
>
> *But Esau said, 'I already have plenty, my brother. Keep what you have for yourself.'*
>
> *'No, please!' said Jacob. 'If I have found favour in your eyes, accept this gift from*
> *me. For to see your face is like seeing the face of God, now that you have received me*
> *favourably.'*

Who would have thought it, the very thing that he had dreaded was now
reversed. What does this tell you? Something had happened to Esau. What
changed him? It may have been time. As they say, time heals all wounds.
And it could be that with time a person mellows, but if that's the way it
happens it is not a real victory. Do you know why the Bible says, *'Do not
let not the sun go while you are still angry'* (Eph. 4:26)? It's because if on the
day you are really angry, you deal with your rage, then it's a spiritual victory,
and you feel better the next day. Yet perhaps it was Esau's temperament
that was responsible for the change in his attitude to his brother. It may
have been that he was the type that wounds easily and heals quickly. There
are those who have a quick temper, but they get over it and everything's
fine. Perhaps it was because of a change of taste. Our tastes change after a
while, and it could be that after a while Esau said that being the firstborn
didn't mean that much to him, having the patriarchal blessing didn't mean
that much to him any longer. If that is the way he overcame his bitterness,
then it was a natural victory. That is to say, people who are not converted
can get over things through time, or through their temperament, or by a
change of taste. We don't know for sure how Esau did it, but there is some
reason to believe that God dealt with him, which is possibly why Martin
Luther said that he expected to see Esau in heaven.

There are those who think, because of Romans 9:13: *'Jacob I loved, but Esau I hated'*, that Esau would be eternally lost. That is not what this verse means. It is just showing God's privilege of choosing or rejecting, and it had to do with the inheritance in any case. The point is, something did happen to Esau, and we too must learn how to come to terms with our grudge. When we see ourselves with real objectivity and stand back and ask ourselves why we are as we are, we become objective.

It is so easy for us to be judgemental, but we don't know what process the mind of another is going through, or what has happened to them. Paul says in 1 Corinthians 4:7: *'For who makes you different from anyone else? What do you have that you did not receive? And if you did receive it, why do you boast as though you did not?'* The truth is that we all do things that are not right.

God totally forgives because he sent his Son to die for our sins. And the reason Jacob could say, *'To see your face is like seeing the face of God'* (Gen. 33:10) was because the God that we can turn to is a God whose justice has been satisfied by the blood of his Son. God can even take that unforgiving spirit, forgive you for your inability to forgive, give you a new heart and bring you to the place where you can sincerely pray for those who have treated you unfairly. You can come to the place that you *want* them to be blessed, and eventually it even becomes a selfish prayer because when you pray that way you get blessed more than anybody. And that's the truth.

Recently, I saw the minister I referred to earlier who had been greatly hurt. His face was like it used to be before he changed. He talked in the most loving way about the person who had hurt him so deeply, and I couldn't believe it. He wasn't trying to impress me. I don't think he even remembered that I knew. God had worked in him and he was completely free of his bitterness.

7

Our Heavenly Home

Genesis 27:41–28:9

May he [God] give you and your descendants the blessing of Abraham, so that you may take possession of the land where you now live as an alien, the land God gave to Abraham (Gen. 28:4).

By faith, he [Abraham] made his home in the promised land like a stranger in a foreign country; he lived in tents as did Isaac and Jacob, who were heirs with him of the same promise. For he was looking forward to the city with foundations, whose architect and builder is God (Heb. 11:9, 10).

Advantages and Disadvantages

There are advantages and, I would have to say, some disadvantages of being brought up in a Christian home. I think there are two advantages. One is that you've got a head start. The person brought up as a Christian hears the gospel, hears what we call the 'language of Zion'. This is language that after you have been saved for a while, you feel at home with – 'theological language', you could call it. The second advantage is that there's a greater likelihood of becoming a Christian if you've been brought up in a Christian home – statistically, this would appear to be the case. However, there's also a disadvantage. Those brought up in a Christian home often feel cheated. They feel they are left out, and they grow up wishing they had a different set of parents so that they could do things that other kids get to do. They say, 'It's not fair that we have to go to church.'

In Hebrews, it says that Abraham, Isaac and Jacob lived in tents. I wonder how Jacob felt about living in a tent. It was the only world he knew. I suppose that as he grew up, Jacob grew a little tired of living in such a home and would look at his father and say, 'Is this the best there is?' What did Jacob have to look forward to? How would you like to live this way? Perhaps Isaac wished he could do something different for his son.

I think parents often wish they could do more for their children. I myself grew up in a Christian home and I can remember how I would say to my father, 'Why can't I have this for Christmas? Micky, across the street, look what he had for Christmas.'

Dad would answer, 'Son, I'm sorry, but I work for wages. It's the best I can do.'

But that wasn't what really hurt. What really hurt was when we had Wednesday night prayer meetings on summer evenings and I would be out in the back garden playing basketball where my dad had set up a basketball court. All the other kids would use it and come and play, and at about ten past seven I would have to leave them playing basketball in my own back garden while I went to church. And I used to resent it.

It's like Abraham and Isaac providing tents for their sons to live in. It was their heritage. I had to go to church every Sunday morning, every Sunday night (every time the door was opened it seemed like we were in church), but the service didn't end until nine o'clock. At the Nazarene Church we were called 'Noisyrenes' because the people sang so loudly and shouted and did all kinds of things. So much went on that we often didn't get home by ten o'clock. I didn't always like it, I can tell you. So I can understand how anybody brought up in a Christian home feels cheated.

I have since found out where those kids who used to play in my back garden are now. When I went back to Ashland, I asked after them. One of them, I was told, couldn't even come back to the town because so many people are after him. As for the star basketball player of the Ashland Tomcats, I was told he was out on the edge of town, sipping vodka all day long. I found out more recently that he had died at an early age – an alcoholic.

A few years ago, Louise and I had the privilege of meeting Jackie Pullinger in Hong Kong. She had been living there for over 20 years. I asked her, 'Where is home?' Tears filled her eyes. Pointing upward, she said, 'There's my home, and I really mean that.' Maybe you are in difficulty at the moment and wonder why. It's God's way of making you look beyond.

God's Plans for His People

A Christian is an alien, a stranger here on earth. The main reason Jesus died is that you may go to heaven, not to heal your marriage, or to heal your body, or to make you a lot of money. It is true there are fringe benefits of being a Christian. God gives us a lot of good things along the way; he supplies our every need. He has a plan for our lives and his way will bring us to happiness more quickly than our way of doing things.

What did Isaac pass on to Jacob? The knowledge that Jacob was different, under a special covenant, a promise made binding by an oath.

Jacob was part of it. He would go to heaven, even when the people around him wouldn't. So on this earth he was a stranger.

Being born into a Christian home has its advantages, but it is no guarantee that a person will become a Christian. One of the saddest things I know is to be born into a Christian home where you have heard it all, and you let those precious years pass by without responding in your heart.

What can you be sure of once you're a Christian? The first thing is this: God has a plan. Genesis 28:1 says: *'So Isaac called for Jacob and blessed him and commanded him: "Do not marry a Canaanite woman. Go at once to Paddam Aram, to the house of your mother's father Bethuel. Take a wife for yourself there, from among the daughters of Laban." '* Generally speaking, it is God's will that you are married. The Bible says, *'It is not good for the man to be alone'* (Gen. 2:18). It was certainly God's will that Jacob should be married. Lonely people often come and ask me if they will ever find a husband or a wife. And I say that if they would be happier getting married, then they will get married. It will be God's will. Psalm 84:11 says, *'The LORD God is a sun and shield; the LORD bestows favour and honour; no good thing does he withhold from those whose walk is blameless.'* If you remain unmarried, it is a hint from God that you will be happier that way. There is something worse than being unmarried and that is being unhappily married.

God has a plan for your life, and he knows what is good and what is right for you. It's easy for us to get impatient. All of us have something we want and we don't get, whether it's the person who is lonely, or the person who wants to make money or something else. Now what God may lead one person to do, he may not lead another to do. God has a providence. The worldly definition would be 'luck', but for the Christian, it just means God sorts things out.

So Rebekah, the manipulating wife and mother, did it again. She wanted to make sure that her Jacob wasn't going to be killed by Esau, so she told him to leave. But she knew there had to be the patriarchal blessing and somehow Isaac had to give it or Jacob wouldn't go. So she went to her husband and said, *'I'm disgusted with living because of these Hittite women. If Jacob takes a wife from among the women of this land, from Hittite women like these, my life will not be worth living'* (Gen. 27:46). Persuaded by this, Isaac called for Jacob and told him to leave.

It's interesting how so often the strange things that happen to us cause us to make decisions which, when we look back later, we see were the best things that ever happened to us. In 1964, Louise and I left Ohio and went back to Florida. These were some of the loneliest days of our lives. We had no church to back us (we had left the church of the Nazarene and I had given up a church in Ohio). I started selling vacuum cleaners, and then I started a little magazine called *Redeemer's Witness*. I had a few invitations to preach here and there but those were hard days. Then, eventually, I got a church and gave up *Redeemer's Witness*. Several years later, we moved to

Kentucky to go back to the seminary. Out of the blue came a phone call from a man whom I had never met and who introduced himself as Bob Parker. He said, 'I hear you are coming to the Southern Baptist Seminary at Louiseville. Would you like to pastor a church while you are there?'

'Would I ever!' I replied. (We didn't know how we were going to make it financially: we'd given up the church in Fort Lauderdale to go back to Kentucky.)

He continued, 'I'm leaving my church the very week you're arriving. All I need do is to recommend you, and my deacons will take you on my recommendation.'

'This is wonderful,' I said. 'However did you know about me?'

'Oh, I used to read a little magazine named *Redeemer's Witness*,' he said.

And so it happened that Esau's grudge and a manipulating mother sent Jacob away. It was the last time Rebekah would ever see her son.

An Explanation for Everything

God has a purpose. He has a plan for you; he has a providence for you. That means things will happen in your life where, unknown to you, God will be at work. There is an explanation for everything that happens. Listen to me. If you are a Christian nothing happens to you without a purpose. You may not know the reason by tomorrow afternoon. You may begin scratching your head and asking, 'Why did God allow this to happen?' Don't become bitter about anything, for one day you will see God had everything under total control.

Isaac told Jacob that he was living as an alien in that land. But his family would do such good for that country, and one day the land would be named Israel. Jacob's own name was to be changed to Israel. Sometimes it is said that Christians have no influence. Someone once said that some Christians are so heavenly minded they are no earthly use. I don't believe that is often the case, because those who are willing to be the most detached from this world will do it the most good.

You may be an alien on this earth and you may wonder what good you are doing. Away with those ideas of people who say Christianity is behind the times. I want you to know Christianity is *ahead* of the times because, according to the Apostle Paul, *'God exalted him* [Jesus] *to the highest place and gave him the name that is above every name, that at the name of Jesus every knee should bow, in heaven and on earth and under the earth, and every tongue confess that Jesus Christ is Lord to the glory of God the Father'* (Phil. 2:9). Christianity is the wave of the future because the Christian bows to Jesus as Lord now – everybody will do it then. It's only a question of *when*, not *whether*, you are going to say 'Jesus is Lord'. Do it later against your will or do it now and be saved.

8

Discovering God for Yourself

Genesis 28:10−17

Discovering God for himself. That was what Jacob did. This event made such an impact on him that he referred to it on his deathbed. In Genesis 48 we read that Jacob called for Joseph who gathered round the bed with his two sons to hear Jacob say: *'God Almighty appeared to me at Luz in the land of Canaan, and there he blessed me and said to me, "I am going to make you fruitful and will increase your numbers. I will make you a community of peoples, and I will give this land as an everlasting possession to your descendants after you"'* (vv. 3–4). What happened to Jacob was the experience of all experiences. He would never forget it.

Do you remember the time when you discovered God for yourself? I don't necessarily mean remembering the time and place where you were converted, but remembering the intense power of that experience. There's nothing like discovering God so powerfully for yourself that if every other person in the world renounces their faith, and you were the only believer left, you would still trust him.

We are looking at this point in the life of Jacob and begin by reading, *'He reached a certain place.'* It was not exactly in the heart of Luz but in that general area. Little did Jacob know that the next morning that *'certain place'* would have become so special to him and so important that he would pour oil on his pillow (which was a stone, and couldn't have been comfortable), and make a little memorial and say, 'From now on, this place is called Bethel.'

We should note a number of things about Jacob throughout this experience:

1. Jacob's Dependency

Jacob had been so dependent on his parents, especially upon his mother; he had never wandered far from home. He was not like Esau, who was a man of the fields, a man of the woods, a man of the wild. Esau might have been happy wandering so far from home, but Jacob had never done anything like this before, so he must have been afraid.

We can see from a story Jesus told in Luke's gospel what it was like to travel in those days. Jesus said: *'A man was going down from Jerusalem to Jericho, when he fell into the hands of robbers. They stripped him of his clothes, beat him and went away, leaving him half-dead'* (Lk. 10:30). That was not an uncommon event in Bible times. Jesus was speaking of a short journey from Jerusalem to Jericho. How must it have been for Jacob to go from Beersheba to a totally strange land which, the scholars say, was five hundred miles away? In those days there were no roads, no public transport. Here was a man scared to death, having to leave home because his brother wanted to kill him.

Perhaps you are away from home. You've been thrust out and are wondering what life is all about and what is happening to you. Yet, perhaps God has set this up so you may learn to know him and to discover him for yourself for the first time.

At this time in Jacob's life, if he had any relationship with God at all, it was second-hand. Are you like him? Is your religion second-hand? Maybe you were spoon-fed something from your parents or from your grandparents and have a long Christian background. I have a background not unlike Jacob's. You will recall I spoke of having a Christian father and that we went to church every time the doors were open. His mother and father were Christians. So I grew up hearing it all, knowing i t all. But there came a time when I needed to find out for myself the answer to questions such as: Is there a God? Does he care? What is he like?

So we come to Jacob. He had a famous grandfather, Abraham. He had a father who figured in Abraham's greatest spiritual experience. Jacob had heard the story of how Abraham was told to sacrifice Isaac and what happened as a result a thousand times. Then there were the times when he heard how God had met with Isaac:

> *'I am the God of your father Abraham. Do not be afraid, for I am with you; I will bless you and will increase the number of your descendants for the sake of my servant Abraham.'*
>
> *Isaac built an altar there and called on the name of the L ORD. There he pitched his tent, and there his servants dug a well (Gen. 26:24–25).*

If you were to interview Jacob at this stage he would have to say, 'Nothing like that has ever happened to me.' He had never come to know God for himself.

2. Jacob's Distress

That was Jacob's own word. In Genesis 35:3 we read that he said: *'Then come, let us go up to Bethel, where I will build an altar to God, who answered me in the day of my distress and who has been with me wherever I have gone.'*

What was the nature of Jacob's distress? On this particular night, he had set out for Haram and having reached *'a certain place'* he had stopped for the night as the sun had set. Taking a stone for his pillow, he put it under his head and lay down to sleep. But he was afraid, for at any moment his brother Esau might turn up to kill him. Jacob could hardly defend himself against a 'man's man'. He was a 'mummy's boy', used to staying at home. He was no match for Esau and so he had good reason to fear. But this experience was God's way of setting Jacob free from his parents, especially from his mother, so God could have Jacob all to himself. That could be true of you too. God wants you all to himself.

There was not only the dread of Esau to worry Jacob but also the danger of the wild. Wild animals might attack him; he could fall victim to robbers and, on top of all this, he didn't know the way. Rebekah had travelled this route coming in the other direction. But that was a long time ago, and her memory of the journey had been hazy and, in any case, she had had servants to show her the way. Jacob must have been very scared and he was lonely. No parents. No friends. Everybody was a complete stranger. And there was one other thing (we know it from later accounts), the distress of his conscience. It had begun to dawn on him that what he had done to Esau wasn't very nice. His manipulation had succeeded. He had stolen the birthright; he had received the patriarchal blessing. What he had done to his brother was weighing heavily upon him. Whatever would God think of him now – if there was a God? Jacob was in trouble. There was no way he could justify his behaviour.

Could it be that you are wrestling with the question: does God exist? 'If he does,' you may think, 'he certainly wouldn't like me because of all the wicked things I have done.' One way of consoling yourself is to say, 'But there is no God.' But then you come back and say, 'If there is, what does he think of me? I am in awful shape.'

To Jacob, God must have seemed a million miles away. But you know the saying 'the darkest hour comes just before dawn', and sometimes when God seems the most remote and you are feeling the most guilty, maybe it's then you are ripe to hear God speak to you.

3. Jacob's Dream

Taking one of the stones there, he put it under his head and lay down to sleep. He had a dream in which he saw a stairway resting on the earth, with its top reaching to heaven, and the angels of God were ascending and descending on it. There above it stood the LORD (Gen. 28:11–13).

The first thing we see about his dream is that Jacob, the world's greatest manipulator, was passive. There was nothing he could have done to bring this about. Yet Jacob had always been the active one, the one who rolled up his sleeves and made things happen. He got what he wanted through manipulation. He was a genius at it.

Perhaps you are one who likes to live in the fast lane and you have been able to manipulate your way. You're the type who gets things done and you know how to make things happen. You'll never discover God like that. The only way a person can discover God is where they don't think, they *know* they had nothing to do with God speaking to them – God just did it.

So God began to speak to Jacob through a dream when he was asleep. Everything that was happening now was out of his hands.

Have I described you? You have always had your finger on the button, and now you have lost control and you wonder what on earth is happening? Yet, when someone cannot do anything in his own power, this is how God prepares him.

> 'Twas grace that taught my heart to fear
> And grace those fears relieved . . .

John Newton, who wrote these words, came to see that God had saved him by sheer grace alone. Jesus died for those who cannot save themselves. Jesus died for those who have a guilty conscience, who know they don't deserve anything good. The only way you can come to know God is to recognize you are a sinner and repent and ask God for mercy. Perhaps you were never willing to hear the gospel before, but God has got you in such a state you are hemmed in and willing to listen now. You're like Jacob in a dream; he was passive; matters were out of his hands. God may have brought events to such a situation where all you can do is just to see his mercy.

4. Jacob's Discovery

Jacob had a dream in which he saw a stairway resting on the earth with its top reaching to heaven, with the angels of God ascending and descending on it. Many theologians ask what Jacob's ladder means. The best explanation I can come up with is this. Notice it says that the angels of God were both ascending and descending on it. You may have thought the angels should just have been coming down but the Bible says they were also going up. It means the whole time Jacob was on this journey, scared to death, he had angels around him and they were going up from where he was – they had been with him the whole time. So Jacob learned what the Psalmist talked about in Psalm 91:11–12: *'He will command his angels concerning you to guard you in all your ways; they will lift you up in their hands, so that you will not strike your foot against a stone.'*

Jacob now saw he had been protected, and through all that had happened angels had been around him. Hebrews 1:14 says, *'Are not all angels ministering spirits sent to serve those who will inherit salvation?'*

But we need to consider the whole of this verse in Genesis which says, *'The angels of God were ascending and descending on it. There above it stood the LORD.'* Here was the one about whom Jacob had wondered fearfully, 'If he exists whatever does he think of me?'

Some people are afraid to meet God because they know he is a God of holiness, a God of truth.

No wonder Jacob felt so awful. But do you know what he found? God spoke and said:

> *I am the LORD, the God of your father Abraham and the God of Isaac. I will give you and your descendants the land on which you are lying. Your descendants will be like the dust of the earth, and you will spread out to the west and to the east, to the north and to the south. All peoples on earth will be blessed through you and your offspring. I am with you and will watch over you wherever you go, and I will bring you back to this land. I will not leave you until I have done what I have promised you* (Gen. 28:13–15).

It turned out to be a word of pure grace. The word 'grace' means unmerited favour, God blessing us when we don't deserve it. That's what Jacob discovered: God was with him and God was so good.

Many view God in such way they feel they have no hope. But I can tell you if you call on God in the name of Jesus, pleading with the blood Jesus shed on the cross, God will show you he has been with you all the time; there have been angels around you. And he has come to forgive you, to promise you that he will be with you wherever you go. It all happened at Bethel, Jacob's *'certain place'*.

9

How to Recognize God

Genesis 28:10–22

When Jacob awoke from his sleep, he thought, 'Surely the L ORD is in this place, and I was not aware of it' (Gen. 28:16).

The most wonderful thing that can happen to anybody is for God to turn up. The problem is we don't always recognize him at the time and we only see later that it was God. We don't recognize him for a number of reasons. It could be we don't know him. Another reason is that we may have a fixed, biased idea as to what he would be like if he came.

How God Reveals Himself: Four Examples:

1. The Welsh Revival

Every time I go to Wales I cannot help but think about the Welsh Revival. I sometimes get the impression that the people who live in Wales think that if revival ever comes to Britain it will be just like it was in 1904/1905. It is possible to have a biased idea like this because of the way we know God has turned up in history. Take a person who has known God powerfully in their life. You could say to that person, 'Do you think you would know if God turned up?' They would say, 'Yes, definitely, because I've met God.' The trouble is we think God can only come in one particular way, and that's the way we've met him. The question is, if he turned up in an unexpected way, would we affirm him?

The sooner we learn to recognize the Lord the better. For some, it may take years to see that God has been in a situation with them; for others, it may take only a few seconds. But the narrower the time gap the better, for it shows our hearts are in tune with what God is doing. I can think of nothing worse in the world than for something that God is in to be happening and I not to recognize it.

If you're not a Christian, then it's also true for you that the sooner you realize when God is there the better because the Bible says, *'My Spirit will not contend with man for ever'* (Gen. 6:3). If the Lord turns up and he is at work, then you ought to move at once. Let me put it like this. It may be that whenever you hear preaching you sense that the Holy Spirit is dealing with you, that God is on your case. You know that the preacher wouldn't know much about you, if anything at all, and the only way he could speak in this manner was if God had led him to do so. Listen to me. You know the old saying, 'Strike while the iron is hot.' If God is speaking to you, don't dare assume that he will be speaking to you next time you go to church. Don't you dare think you may have another opportunity. God has said, *'My Spirit will not contend with man for ever.'*

2. Rock group's manager

A few years ago, the manager of a very famous rock group came into one of our services, and when I had finished speaking, the person who had brought him said he had been shaken rigid and had trembled, saying, 2'I've never heard anything like that.' But he wouldn't make a move beyond that. A few weeks later, he took his own life.

If you are a Christian and the Lord turns up and you don't recognize him, you are impoverished since you miss seeing God for who he is, then. I guarantee you will wish later you had seen it was the Lord sooner.

3. A Presbyterian church

Many years ago, Louise and I lived in Fort Lauderdale, Florida, on a street where just around the corner was a vacant lot with a sign saying, 'Coral Ridge Presbyterian Church – Future Home'. Two years later that sign was still there and the lot was still vacant. We began to laugh, saying, 'Whatever is happening? Where is the Coral Ridge Presbyterian Church?' Then we moved to Ohio. Eighteen months later we returned, and in place of that vacant lot stood a church of some size – the Coral Ridge Presbyterian Church. I heard they had started something called 'Evangelism Explosion' and I said, 'God's not in that.' Yet I began to hear of ever more people who were converted through Evangelism Explosion, but I continued to criticize it until I saw changed lives. A few years passed. I became pastor of my own church and then I knew I had to climb down. I went to the pastor of that church, D. James Kennedy, on bended knee and asked if I might go out with him and watch him witness. It had taken me years to recognize that God was in that situation. God can turn up and because of our biases, we may not see the work he is doing.

4. A potential convert

It is possible to miss what God is doing in another person. The first night Arthur Blessitt preached in Westminster Chapel, London, a young man in the top gallery stood to receive Christ. But his girlfriend turned on him saying, 'Oh no! Don't!' Unlike him, she hadn't been convicted by the Holy Spirit at all. You may feel that what you are receiving others are receiving too, but this may not be the case. Or perhaps, you may be bored to tears, but God is talking to someone else near you.

How You Might Miss God

Let me give you three examples of how this can happen.

1. Missing what God is doing in someone else

In 1 Samuel 1, Eli the priest (a very religious person), saw Hannah praying in her heart and her lips moving silently. Thinking she was drunk, Eli said to her, ' *"How long will you keep on getting drunk? Get rid of your wine."*

"'Not so, my lord," Hannah replied, "I am a woman who is deeply troubled. I have not been drinking wine or beer; I was pouring out my soul to the L ORD" ' (vv. 14–15).

Eli began to see then that it was God. Yet initially, the person who was the religious authority did not see God was at work.

Just as it was then, today it is possible to be in the Lord's work, to be a minister, and yet miss what God is doing.

Do you know the greatest outpouring of God's Spirit the world has yet seen? I think we would all agree it was on the day of Pentecost (see Acts 2). Do you know who criticized it? It was the religious people of the day.

These are two interesting biblical examples of when those who opposed what was happening and thought others were drunk, failed to recognize God at work in others.

2. Being unprepared for answered prayer

Another way God may turn up unrecognized is that he may answer prayer and you may stare that answered prayer right in the face and not believe it. For example, in Acts 12 the church had prayed for Peter who had been put in prison, and in answer to their prayer an angel had delivered Peter miraculously from the jail. We read these words:

> Peter knocked at the outer entrance, and a servant girl named Rhoda came to answer the door. When she recognised Peter's voice, she was so overjoyed she ran back without opening it and exclaimed, 'Peter is at the door!'

*'You're out of your mind,' they told her. When she kept insisting that it was so,
they said, 'It must be his angel.'*

*But Peter kept on knocking, and when they opened the door and saw him, they were
astonished* (Acts 12:13–16).

Their prayer was answered, but they did not accept it. Are you like that?
Perhaps your life is in difficulties and you have been praying because you
don't know how to get out of the mess you are in. The answer to your
prayer is right under your nose. I can tell you, *'Today, if you hear his voice,
do not harden your hearts'* (Ps. 95:7). As surely as you recognize the authentic
voice of God in these words, you ought to pray right now and just say,
'Thank you Lord. You are talking to me at this very moment.'

3. Being disappointed at God's word

There's one other way I want to show you how God can turn up
unrecognized and that is when you are disappointed by the word you
receive. We read in 2 Kings 5:1–14 that Naaman was commander of
the army of the King of Aram, and he had been told about a prophet
by the name of Elisha who would be able to heal him of his leprosy.
He finally made arrangements to visit him, and he was sure that Elisha,
like everybody else, would be impressed as he was a man of considerable
stature and a high-ranking officer. He went to Elisha's house. However,
Elisha sent a servant to answer the door and didn't even see Naaman,
merely sending him a message: 'Go to the river Jordan and dip in it
seven times.' Naaman was incensed by this treatment. But somebody
got him to cool down a little, saying, 'Look, if a man of God gives you
a word, even if you don't understand it, maybe you ought to do what
he says.' So Naaman went to the river Jordan (he must have felt like a
fool) and dipped himself in once and came up. There was no change.
But when he did it for the seventh time and he came out, he had skin
like that of a baby. He couldn't believe it. He had almost missed this
miracle altogether.

Today, God's message may sound as ridiculous to you as Elisha's
message did to Naaman all those years ago. Yet Jesus Christ will take your
case because he died on the cross for you, and the only way you can be
saved (it sounds ridiculous, I admit that) is to ask God for mercy. That
means you can't snap your fingers and say, 'You've got to do it, Lord,
because I'm here.' Do you feel (like Naaman with Elisha) you are so
important that God should bow to you? No. When you ask for mercy,
know that you don't deserve it; recognize that God sent his Son into the
world to die on a cross for your sins. That may sound as ridiculous as
Elisha's word to Naaman: 'Dip in the Jordan seven times.' But he ended
up doing it and he got what he wanted.

How to Recognize God

1. Be open

Be open to the unexpected time. Jacob said, *'The LORD is in this place, and I was not aware of it'* (Gen. 28:16). Be open to the unexpected manner in which God might turn up. He came to Jacob in a dream. God can do that.

2. Recognize God's 'low profile'

What God does powerfully, he usually does in a low-profile way at first. In Isaiah 53:2 we read, *'He grew up before him like a tender shoot, and like a root out of dry ground.'* If you came upon a root sticking up, what would you think? Probably, you would take little notice of it. Yet it was Jesus who was described as *'a root out of dry ground'*. So, when Israel's prayers were answered, and the Son of God actually came and healed the sick and raised people from the dead, they didn't recognize him. The initial work of the Holy Spirit is always unconscious. At first, you feel nothing. God was at work in Jacob in *'a certain place'*, but he didn't feel anything.

3. Know that fear is often one of the first ways we begin consciously to feel God

Notice how it was put: *'When Jacob awoke from his sleep, he thought, "Surely the LORD is in this place, and I was not aware of it." '* He was afraid and exclaimed, *'How awesome is this place!'* (Gen. 28:17). Fear is often the way God begins to make you conscious of him. I've known people get up in the middle of a service and leave, unable to cope with this feeling. But if you recognize that God is not happy with the way you are living, then you *ought* to be afraid.

Jacob affirmed God. Fortunately for him, it didn't take him long. The question is, how long will it take you?

10

Our Response to God's Sovereign Mercy

Genesis 28:10–22

What is sovereign mercy? Why couldn't I just say, our response to God's mercy? It's because we need to see that when God gives mercy, he gives it to a particular individual whom he has chosen. Mercy may be offered indiscriminately, but the one who is enabled to receive it is the one whom God has sovereignly touched.

What is the difference between mercy and grace? Mercy is not getting what we deserve. What we deserve is justice. Grace is getting what we don't deserve, namely, favour.

We could ask what is the difference between mercy and justice? I heard Billy Graham give a good illustration of this. Several years ago, he was driving in North Carolina and was exceeding the speed limit. A policeman pulled him over and took him before the Justice of the Peace. Billy was pretty nervous about it but, when he saw the magistrate, he recognized him as a man he knew. 'Well,' he thought, 'this is a bit of luck – I won't have to pay the fine.' He pleaded guilty and was sentenced to pay a fine of $50.00. His heart sank, but he thought, 'Well, that's right. I'm getting justice.' However, as soon as the judge gave the sentence, he got up from his bench, walked over to the cashier, got out his wallet and paid Billy's fine himself. And so, as Billy put it, 'When the judge sentenced me to pay a fine of $50.00 I was given justice, but then, when he turned around and paid my debt, I was given mercy.' Justice is getting what you deserve. Mercy is not getting what you deserve.

When we talk about sovereign mercy, it is mercy not given to all, but to some. We are dealing here with a very great mystery. We talk about the sovereignty of God, which is God's right to do as he pleases with whom he pleases. Now, to any Briton this should come as no surprise. As we have already seen (Chapter 2), Her Majesty the Queen is sovereign, and the Sovereign alone has the right to determine who comes into her presence. Nobody ever visits the Queen unless a prior invitation has been given. The only way we could ever get to see her is if she invited us. That is exactly the way it is with the God of the Bible.

Sovereign mercy is only given to those who are pretty awful. This is why, when Jesus came, he would be seen with sinners, the biggest crooks in town. He would accept people like Zacchaeus, who would swindle people out of money, and he even chose Matthew, a tax collector, who was probably dishonest, to be one of the twelve. And it was just the very thing that the Pharisees, the religious people of the day, used against Jesus saying, 'He sits with sinners.' And Jesus replied, 'You've got it!' *'It is not the healthy who need a doctor, but the sick . . . I have not come to call the righteous, but sinners'* (Lk. 5:32).

If anyone reading this thinks they are righteous, I have bad news for them! They've been moral, they've been clean, they haven't hurt anyone, and have the sort of reputation people envy. The chances of them getting to heaven are nil. Jesus came to save sinners. God loves to find the most difficult case. He loves to find the person whose conversion would leave everyone feeling indignant. What would you think if God had saved Saddam Hussein a week after the Gulf War had ended? What would you think if he saved someone who had been unfaithful to their spouse or had abused a child? You would think, 'That person doesn't deserve to be saved.' Yet that is exactly the person God wants.

Jacob was a scoundrel. He was what we would call a 'heel', a cheat, a manipulator. He had stolen his brother's birthright; he cheated Esau out of the patriarchal blessing and now he was running for his life. Jacob was afraid. He was lonely and depressed. He had let his family down and had never come to discover God for himself. He was like those who have been brought up in a Christian home yet have never been saved. He was like those who could give you all the right answers but who had never experienced salvation in their own hearts.

I want us to see three things: the vision, the voice and the vow:

1. The Vision

When he reached a certain place, he stopped for the night because the sun had set. Taking one of the stones there, he put it under his head and lay down to sleep. He had a dream in which he saw a stairway resting on the earth, with its top reaching to heaven, and the angels of God were ascending and descending on it (Gen. 28:11–12).

The vision is known as Jacob's ladder. Jesus himself implicitly referred to this when he said to Nathaniel, *'You believe because I told you I saw you under the fig-tree. You shall see greater things than that . . . I tell you the truth, you shall see heaven open, and the angels of God ascending and descending on the Son of Man'* (Jn. 1:50).

What did this ladder (or stairway) resting on the earth, whose top reached to heaven, mean? It meant three things:

- It meant access to God. We were talking about trying to see the Queen. Who do you know who could give you access to the Queen? Yet the most wonderful thing that could happen to you is to have access to the true God, the God of heaven and earth, the God who made you, the God who holds your destiny in his hands.
- It meant dialogue with God. We saw there was a stairway reaching to heaven and that the angels of God were ascending and descending on it. Going up from earth meant they had already been with Jacob. But also, as Jacob could say a little later, this was none other than the gate of heaven, so it shows Jacob could actually talk to God and have God talk to him. I have news for you: it is not only possible for you to talk to God, but you can hear God speak to you. God will speak in a manner that you would never expect. You know the word 'gob-smacked': when we are stunned by the way God deals with us, God will speak to you just like that.
- It meant the approval of God. Suddenly, Jacob was so overwhelmed that God would literally unveil the heavens and talk to him that he said he would give God a tenth of everything in the light of God manifesting himself to him. It could be the same for you. The most overwhelming thought in the world is that God could love you and single you out.

2. The Voice

It was one thing to have had the vision of the ladder going to heaven and seeing the angels, but quite another, and a more important thing, when God spoke and said, *'I am the LORD, the God of your father Abraham and the God of Isaac'* (Gen. 28:13). Little did Jacob know that one day when God would speak, he would add his name, and that one day every Jew in Israel would never utter that language without saying, 'I am the God of Abraham, Isaac and Jacob.' But now, Jacob was discovering God for himself and little did he know he would ever be in that category.

You may feel the most insignificant and unworthy person that ever lived. God loves to pick somebody like that. He loves to find a sinner, or a person with an inferiority complex or an outcast from society.

Hearing is more important than seeing. The Psalmist said, *'Thou hast magnified thy word above all thy name'* (Ps. 138:2 AV). And we read in Romans 10:17, *'Faith comes from hearing the message, and the message is heard through the word of Christ.'* What that means is this: You have two sets of ears: with one set of ears you hear the physical voice; the other set of ears is in your heart when you know God is using someone to talk to you.

Here was Jacob, feeling scared, feeling unworthy, he had let his father down, he had let his grandfather down, he had let his brother down and, if there was a God, he had let him down too.

The greatest hymn John Newton ever wrote in my opinion is not 'Amazing Grace' but this one:

> In evil long I took delight,
> Unawed by shame or fear,
> Till a new object struck my sight,
> And stopped my wild career.
>
> I saw One hanging on a tree
> In agonies and blood,
> Who fixed His languid eyes on me
> As near His cross I stood.
>
> Sure never to my latest breath
> Can I forget that look;
> It seems to charge me with his death,
> Though not a word He spoke.
>
> My conscience felt and owned the guilt,
> And plunged me in despair.
> I saw my sins His blood had spilt
> And helped to nail Him there.
>
> Alas, I know not what I did,
> And now my tears are vain,
> Where shall my trembling soul be hid?
> For I the Lord have slain.
>
> A second look He gave which said:
> 'I freely all forgive:
> This blood is for thy ransom paid;
> I died thou mayest live.'

God said three things to him when Jacob was preparing for the worst and saw the ladder: (i) I am with you. (ii) I will bring you back home. (iii) I will never leave you.

When Jacob woke up he couldn't believe that God could talk to him like that. He thought he would get justice. He thought he would get punishment. Perhaps you know what you have been like, and certainly God knows. Could it be that the same God who rescued Jacob is singling you out above all others, not because you deserve it but because God loves a difficult case? Do you know what God is saying?

- He offers you total forgiveness for the past. Forgiveness will be given when you come to the place where you say, 'God, I am sorry. Save me for the sake of the blood of Jesus.'
- He offers you a new beginning. Isn't it wonderful to think you can start all over again! Perhaps you are a backslider. Come back, and he will say, 'The past is forgiven.'
- He promises never to leave you. God said to Jacob, 'I'll bring you back. I will never leave you.' The same God says it to you.
- One of the most wicked men who ever lived was a man by the name of Saul of Tarsus. Now he would not have accepted he was wicked had you told him. He sat at the feet of Gamaliel; he was studying to be a rabbi; he had a pedigree a mile long and he said he was blameless in his outward way of living. He was, in fact, wicked. He was giving assent to killing Christians and doing everything he could to wipe Christianity off the map entirely. Yet, one day, he was stopped dead in his tracks and saw what he was doing was wrong. The Apostle Paul never got over it. He put it like this: *'I thank Christ Jesus our Lord, who has given me strength, that he considered me faithful, appointing me to his service. Even though once I was once a blasphemer and a persecutor and a violent man, I was shown mercy'* (1 Tim. 1:12–13). God could have struck Saul of Tarsus dead, but he didn't. And God could have finished you off long ago, but you're still here.

3. The Vow

So what did Jacob do? First, the Bible simply says, *'Taking one of the stones there, he put it under his head and lay down to sleep'* (Gen. 28:11). The stone symbolized the discomfort he was feeling. We saw how the stone became so special to him that the next day he poured oil on it and called that place Bethel (see Chapter 8). What had been the moment of his deepest distress was now treasured. Second, he affirmed God as being behind everything. It says in verse 17: 'This is none other than the house of God; this is the gate of heaven.' Jacob affirmed God was at work and this is the first thing you must do. I want you to realize in your heart that God is on your case. All that has been happening is God's doing.

Can you recall your worst hour? I can recall mine. Listen to this verse of an old hymn:

> When through the deep waters I call thee to go,
> The rivers of woe shall not over flow.
> For I will be with thee thy trials to bless
> And sanctify to thee thy deepest distress.
>
> Anon.

Jacob said, 'In my hour of distress, God met me.' He was so over-whelmed he made a vow. What is that? It is a pledge. In those days it was a very solemn thing to make. If you made a vow, you kept it. Jacob pledged that Abraham's God would be his God. His father's God would be his God, and to him he would give a tenth of everything. Jacob's heart was so broken, so touched, this is what he wanted to do. How about you?

11

Love at First Sight

Genesis 29:1–30

'Love at First Sight'. This is the story of Jacob having obeyed the patriarchal blessing. He has at long last reached his destination five hundred miles away from home, and lo and behold all things coalesced: there before him was the woman who was God's choice for him. He was so overcome with a sense of gratitude to God that he wept openly. Here was a man hoping to get married who had found what he was seeking. Jacob discovered that God had done everything he was supposed to do after he obeyed. To put it another way, obedience comes before confir - mation. By 'confirmation', I'm not talking about a particular ritual in church, I'm talking about when God has come alongside and made it obvious that you've done the right thing by letting powerful things happen.

God's Confirmation: Finding a Wife

I want us to see what it is like before, and after, you become a Christian. Do you realize that becoming a Christian is obedience? Do you realize that until you become a Christian you are in disobedience to God? That's a fact. So if you think you are not a sinner, if you are not a Christian you *are* a sinner because it is sin to disobey. You may say, 'Well, I never thought I had to be a Christian because God said I had to be.' I'm telling you it is what God commands. The Bible says, *'In the past, God overlooked such ignorance, but now he commands all people everywhere to repent'* (Acts 17:30). So if you are not Christian, you are in disobedience.

Perhaps you ask, 'Why should I become a Christian? I want first of all to see there is evidence that it's going to turn out all right for me.' Do you know if you wait for something to happen, for a sign, you will wait for ever? Becoming a Christian is obedience, however curious you might be. 'Will I get married if I become a Christian? Will I prosper? How do I know I can live the Christian life? After all, I'm not sure I am ready.' Nobody is ever ready. We are all by nature against the idea of becoming Christians. What makes us become Christians is that the Holy Spirit creates such an unrest in the way we've been. St Augustine said it a long time ago, 'Thou hast made us for thyself. Our hearts are restless until they find their rest in thee.' If you're not a Christian, I'm going to tell you something I know about you: in your heart you are miserable. You can pretend and protest, but I know there's misery there. And it will not do to wait until you see things happen and then say, 'Ah, now I'll get in on it.' No. That's to put the cart before the horse. Obedience comes before confirmation.

Now I'm not hinting for a second that you are going to get married if you become a Christian, assuming you are looking to be married. However, as I said in Chapter 7, it is God's will for you to marry, probably, if you're not married. The Bible says, *'It is not good for the man to be alone'* (Gen. 2:18). What has long gripped me is that if man in his pre-fallen state in the Garden of Eden, before sin entered the world, could be lonely, how much more is it true today! In 1 Corinthians 7:9 Paul says, *'It is better to marry than to burn with passion.'* Note carefully, the Bible says that it is better to *marry* than to burn. The modern idea is that it is better to sleep with a person than to burn. Not so. The assumption in the Bible is that we do not engage in sex until we marry. Marriage is what sanctifies sexual union. You may say, 'The problem is I am faced with so many tempta - tions; I have a weakness in this respect.' Let me quote a most important verse: *'No temptation has seized you except what is common to man. And God is faithful; he will not let you be tempted beyond what you can bear'* (1 Cor. 10:13).

There was never any doubt that Jacob would get married. God had sworn an oath to his grandfather Abraham and then to his father Isaac that their seed would be as the sand of the sea, and the only link between that promise and the sand of the sea was Jacob, so he didn't need to worry (see Gen. 22:17). God had a wife for him, and so for you. If you're lonely, whether you are male or female, God has the right person for you, if it is right for you to marry. If for any reason that blessing is withheld then God will give you grace to cope.

Jacob and Rachel Meet

It was an inconspicuous beginning for Jacob. He came to the land of his eastern peoples and there he saw a well in a field. What's so significant about that? There were three flocks of sheep lying near it, and so Jacob walked over to them. Nothing romantic was happening at this stage. He saw some shepherds and asked, 'Where are you from?'

'We are from Haran.'

'Do you know Laban, Nahor's grandson?'

'Yes, we know him,' they replied. 'As a matter of fact, here comes his daughter Rachel, with the sheep.'

So no sooner than he had asked about Laban's health, Jacob heard the name 'Rachel'. Now whether that name rang bells, I cannot say, but when he knew she was coming, Jacob the manipulator got to work. I wonder if you have ever noticed this: as soon as he knew Rachel was coming with the sheep, here was Jacob talking to total strangers. 'Look,' Jacob said, 'the sun is still high. It is not time for the flocks to be gathered. Water the sheep and take them back to the pasture.' Imagine a stranger coming up and telling the shepherds how to run their business! Do you know why he was doing that? He wanted to get them out of the way so that when Rachel came he could have her all to himself. They were still talking with him when Rachel turned up with her father's sheep because she was a shepherdess.

When Jacob saw Rachel, he saw how beautiful she was. He rolled up his sleeves and he went up to that well and rolled the stone cover away. He was out to impress her already. Then he went up to her and Genesis 29:11 says, *'Then Jacob kissed Rachel and began to weep aloud. He had told Rachel that he was a relative of her father and a son of Rebekah.'* And so it was an emotional, romantic moment. It was love at first sight. After a long journey, this unexpected meeting with this beautiful young lady released his pent-up tensions in oriental fashion, and he wept openly without any sense of embarrassment.

Now, how do we know it was love and not a passing infatuation? The answer is that Jacob was willing to wait. True love can be tested with time. Nowadays, a man and a woman won't wait seven *days* before sleeping together, and their excuse is 'Ah, but we're in love!' They don't have a clue what love is. This is a love story. Jacob was willing to wait seven *years*.

Before you become a Christian, you need to see you have to obey. But then, after you become a Christian, things start to happen, and things fall into place. Jacob knew God was with him, and we have seen how he was so overcome with emotion that he wept openly. Maybe you'll do that too, or perhaps you will weep in private. There is such a sense of God's faithfulness in everyone who puts him first that they are almost overwhelmed. Jacob could see all that was promised to him was exactly right.

The Manipulator Meets His Match

I want to say one more thing: your commitment to Jesus Christ will be tested. I'm not promising you that if you become a Christian it's going to be downhill all the way. I want you to see Jacob's love was put to the extreme test. Mind you, those seven years working for his Uncle Laban seemed like days. Verse 20 says: *'So Jacob served seven years to get Rachel, but they seemed only like a few days to him because of his love for her.'* When we have something to live for time passes quickly.

Now for the extreme test. Jacob, the manipulator, had met his match. Let me introduce Laban. Jacob got his comeuppance (deserved fate or punishment). Little did Jacob know that God was doing two things at the same time, and he will do them for every believer. (i) He gives you something to live for. (ii) He will be in the process of breaking you.

Jacob needed to be broken. We all need to be broken. What does that mean? It means God has to break us of having a hard heart and walking over everybody. Jacob did not realize it then, but for the next 20 years, after falling head over heels in love, he would see what it was like to be on the other end of manipulation, because Laban proved to be one of the rudest, most ruthless manipulators the Bible describes.

So this was a parallel period where, on the one hand, while Jacob had something to live for, he also had Laban. You could say Laban was made for Jacob and Rachel was made for Jacob. As Christians, we will all have what the Apostle Paul calls a *'thorn in the flesh'* to keep us humble (see 2 Cor. 12:7). And I have to tell you, speaking of a *'thorn in the flesh'*, all the manipulation we've seen in Jacob was a drop in the ocean compared to what Laban could do. The way Laban treated Jacob was so unfair.

Do you know when we are broken? It is when we are treated unfairly and learn to keep quiet about it. Peter said, 'If you suffer for doing evil, well, that's one thing. But when you suffer for doing good and are quiet about it, that's pleasing to God' (see 1 Pet. 3:13, 14). God wants to bring us to the place where we can take pain and injustice without complaining because that is what Jesus did. On the cross, he who knew no sin was made sin. Jesus did not deserve to be crucified and could only say, *'Father, forgive them, for they do not know what they are doing'* (Lk. 23:34). And even when they shouted up to him and said, 'Hey, Son of God, come down from the cross and then we'll believe!' Jesus never made reply. He knew what it was like to take injustice, unfairness and hate. *'As a sheep before her shearers is silent, so he did not open his mouth'* (Isa. 53:7).

You see, it's one thing when you suffer because you deserve it – quite another thing when it's unfair. Perhaps you are wondering why you have been treated unfairly. It's so that you can accept what is unfair and keep quiet about it. That is the goal and that is brokenness. If you are in a situation where what you are having to endure is very unfair indeed, then have I got news for you! That means that God has great plans for you, because the greater the injustice, and the quieter you are, the greater blessing you are going to be to others.

So what Jacob was going to have to endure for the next 20 years was being manipulated and mistreated. What happened? At the end of seven years Jacob went to Uncle Laban and said, 'Look, my time is completed. I'm ready to get married.'

'All right,' replied Laban. 'Let's have a great feast together.' So they prepared the food and took out their tambourines. It was a great oriental moment. Behind the scenes Uncle Laban took the elder daughter Leah, and slipped her into a dark, unlit tent. (The scholars think that Laban probably tried to get Leah married off years ago but that nobody wanted her; they all wanted Rachel.) So Laban put Leah into the tent on the night for which Jacob had waited so long. They slept together, and the next morning Jacob discovered Leah! What would you have done? Jacob went to Laban and asked, 'What on earth is going on? You've deceived me.'

Laban answered, 'Oh, by the way, I meant to tell you that it's not our custom to give the younger daughter in marriage before the older one!'

Facing Disappointment

Most relationships, according to Gerald Coates, go through three stages:

- Stage One: It is lyrical: you are just over the moon. Do you remember the first thing Laban said to Jacob? *'You're my own flesh and blood.'* Jacob thought then Laban was the most wonderful person that ever lived.
- Stage Two: This is when disillusionment comes. Most friendships go through that – you go to the other extreme.
- Stage Three: Reality dawns. What we know is that Jacob is now disillusioned and do you know what he found out? He discovered what you will discover. Once you become a member of the Christian family, most of your trouble is going to be (I hate to say this and I wish it wasn't so) with other Christians.

> To live with the saints above,
> Oh, that will be glory.
> To live with the saints below,
> Well, that's another story.
>
> Anon

There may be someone at the office, there may be some worldly friend who will laugh at you if you become a Christian, and you will face a little persecution – just a little. But once you are in the family, you are going to find we're not perfect. No Christian is perfect. Your faith will be tested. You'll be tested to the hilt when somebody you thought so wonderful lets you down and disappoints you.

12

The Unloved Woman

Genesis 29:31–35

Leah, Jacob's first wife, not his choice and not part of his plans, can be seen in the Bible as the unloved woman. Can you identify with that? Leah's father, Laban, took advantage of her and insisted that Jacob take her as his wife. Jacob was in love with Rachel, her younger sister. Leah was plain; Rachel was beautiful. Every man wanted Rachel. She turned heads wherever she went, but not Leah. Jacob agreed to serve seven years for Rachel. At long last time was up and on his wedding night Jacob went into a dark, unlit tent and we read in Genesis 29:25, *'When morning came, there was Leah!'* Most people ask, 'How did this make Jacob feel?' I want to ask the question, 'How did this make Leah feel?'

Here was an unloved woman. Perhaps she was unloved by everybody. Jacob didn't love her. She was plain and Jacob never pretended to notice Leah. Her father Laban told Jacob, *'It is not our custom here to give the younger daughter in marriage before the older one. Finish out this daughter's bridal week; then we will give you the younger one also, in return for another seven years of work'* (Gen. 29:27). This tells us Laban had been wanting to marry off his daughter Leah for years. No one would take her so he got rid of her this way. He showed such insensitivity to her feelings. So we see Leah was also unloved by her father because no father would have treated his daughter like that if he cared about the way she felt. Leah was manipulated and controlled by an uncaring father.

Why is this story relevant? It is especially relevant to any woman who feels unloved. It could be because of an unhappy relationship with her father. Many young people grow up unable to call God Father because, in their minds, they immediately picture a father who didn't care. Perhaps you are like that. You have felt unloved as long as you can remember because you haven't known a father's love. Perhaps you feel unloved because of an unhappy relationship with a brother or a sister. It could be you feel unloved because of a husband or because of another man who has hurt and rejected you. My word to you is this: God cares about that. Furthermore, this story is relevant not only to women, but to any man, any husband, any father. If you have been insensitive to a woman's feelings and have underestimated the hurt she feels by her rejection, you may come to appreciate the depth of her pain.

God cares about women who have known rejection. In the same book of Genesis there is a woman named Hagar. She was the maidservant of Sarah, Abraham's wife. Sarah was barren and unwisely told Abraham to lie with Hagar, and he did. Yet as soon as Hagar became pregnant, Sarah turned against her and Hagar fled into the desert. But the angel of the Lord appeared to her and Hagar gave this word to the Lord: *'You are the God who sees me . . . I have now seen the One who sees me'* (Gen. 16:13). God turned up in Hagar's worst moment, when she felt rejected by another woman. Perhaps you know what it is to be rejected by a woman. It may not be a man who has treated you unkindly.

We are all different and, because we do not share the same problems and weaknesses, we may feel it is hard to find someone else who will understand how we feel. The point is that God sees and understands and, to prove it, he sent his Son into the world, who lived on this earth, tempted at every point just like we are, yet he was without sin. And even if no one else does, Jesus will understand completely. Do you know we can talk to him and tell him just what we're feeling? No one ever cared for us like Jesus.

Perhaps you think Jesus never knew what it was like to be unloved. Listen to me. He was hanging on a cross two thousand years ago, and he knew physical pain beyond anything you or I could conceive. The pain of crucifixion was the worst kind of pain known to mankind and Jesus endured that. He went through physiological pain and the test to his spirit, but he was not prepared for the moment when, without notice, his unbroken, intimate fellowship with his Father suddenly came to an end. His Father didn't say, 'Oh, by the way, you will notice that between twelve o'clock and three o'clock, I am going to desert you, my Son.' There wasn't a hint this would happen, but Jesus suddenly cried out, *'My God, my God, why have you forsaken me?'* (Mk. 15:34). He knew what it is to be deserted, to be rejected. That was the hardest moment for Jesus to bear.

There are a number of things about Leah, the unloved woman, I want us to see:

1. Leah's Calamity

This is described in verse 25: *'When morning came, there was Leah! So Jacob said to Laban, "What is this you have done to me? I served you for Rachel, didn't I? Why have you deceived me?"'* The worst scenario that could have been imagined happened. Maybe Laban was hoping that Jacob would love Leah. Maybe Leah was hoping against hope that Jacob would love her, but instead Jacob was angry and resented both Leah and her father. How do you think that made Leah feel?

Some bad relationships that women have with men can be traced to events earlier in their lives. Perhaps you can identify with this. Maybe you don't trust men; you're afraid of men, and these feelings can be traced to your past. You may have been abused as a child by someone you trusted, but you felt cheap and blamed yourself. You thought you must have done *something* to bring it about. Now you feel unloved and you don't want to feel the way you do.

Leah's calamity did not begin at an early age, but it was obvious her father didn't respect her. The day came, and she was told what to do. She had to go into that tent and prepare for the worst when Jacob would find out the next morning. What an ordeal it must have been for her! She knew he didn't want her. Perhaps you would say that she shouldn't have co-operated with her father. This sort of thing wouldn't happen in our culture today, but in those days she had to do what her father ordered, and it was obvious she wanted to make the most of the situation. She just hoped, maybe . . . Jacob would love her.

2. Leah's Complaint

Let's read from Genesis 29:31–34: *'When the LORD saw that Leah was not loved, he opened her womb, but Rachel was barren. Leah became pregnant and gave birth to a son. She named him Reuben, for she said, "It is because the L ORD has seen my misery. Surely my husband will love me now." '* That is a 'dead give-away'. She had hoped that despite what her father made her do, Jacob would love her, even though she knew there was no mutual physical attraction and that she was plain; she was hoping that Jacob would start to love her, and the way to make it happen was by giving him a son. Her complaint was that her husband didn't love her and, for all I know, it was also that she was not beautiful. Perhaps she was angry with God about this.

There are many women who are angry with God because they feel he did not give them good looks, and so men find them unattractive. Perhaps you feel this way. Let me ask you a question: Do you wish you looked different, that you were better-looking than you are? I suppose we all wish that. But maybe, one day, when we get to heaven, we'll see it was a particular kindness which we couldn't see at the time that God made us just like we are. Do you know what God wants to achieve in you and me? He wants us to come to terms with our looks, with our gifts, with our limitations, with our place in society, with our parents, with the way we've been treated, and to learn to like ourselves like that. One of the greatest evidences of grace is that we like ourselves just as we are.

3. Leah's Conversion

I'm going to show you something you may not know about Leah: she became a disciple of the Lord. I will prove it. Laban was an idol-worshipper and he didn't know anything of the God of Abraham, Isaac and Jacob. Leah knew nothing of Yahweh, the God of the Old Testament, who became her personal Redeemer and Saviour. But to his everlasting credit, Jacob must have witnessed to the true God and, at some point, it must have changed Leah. This is extraordinary considering how rejected she felt. Yet she believed despite the fact her husband didn't love her, and she gave all the credit to God for what he did. We read in verses 32 and 33: *'Leah became pregnant and gave birth to a son. She named him Reuben, for she said, "It is because the LORD* [Yahweh] *has seen my misery." . . . She conceived again, and when she gave birth to a son she said, "Because the LORD* [Yahweh] *heard that I am not loved, he gave me this one too." '* So here was a woman talking about the true God. Something had happened to her.

The proof of conversion is that you see through to the true God and don't let circumstances divert you. I have often been amazed how black people in the Deep South ever became saved when I consider how badly their masters treated them. Yet they heard talk of heaven and knew one day they were going there, where they would be out of their misery. They could identify with that. That's why they were converted. God has a way of getting us past our circumstances. No matter how dreadful our experiences might have been, God has a way of reaching us, and the most unlikely person can be the most glorious convert. The experience which may have caused us to feel the deepest bitterness can turn out to be our salvation. God has designed all things to get us to look to him. And lo and behold, Leah was now giving glory to God. She had sons.

4. Leah's Compensation

It says in verse 31, *'When the LORD saw Leah was not loved, he opened her womb, but Rachel was barren.'* I will tell you something about God the Father. In Isaiah we read, *'I, the LORD, love justice'* (Isa. 61:8). The God of the Bible loves justice, and if you are being treated unfairly, God knows it. It is only a matter of time and he is going to compensate. That's a promise. Let me tell you something about Jesus, God the Son: Jesus is full of compassion. Luke 7:12 says this: *'As he approached the town gate, a dead person was being carried out – the only son of his mother, and she was a widow. And a large crowd from the town was with her. When the Lord saw her, his heart went out to her and he said, "Don't cry." '* Jesus sees your tears. He knows you're hurt. *'Then he went up and touched the coffin, and those carrying it stood still. He said, "Young man, I say to you, get up!" The dead man sat up and began to talk, and Jesus gave him back to his mother.'*

Did the Lord notice how Leah was feeling? The Bible says, *'When the LORD saw Leah was not loved, he opened her womb.'* Standing somewhere in the shadows, you'll find Jesus. He's the only one who cares and understands. You'll know him by the nail prints in his hands. What was Leah's compensation? Rachel, whom Jacob loved, was barren. Leah, the unloved woman, came through where it ultimately mattered. Nothing could stop Jacob being the father of many sons because God had foreordained it. Therefore, God's word was at stake (see Gen. 22:17). You could call it his sense of humour, you could call it his sense of justice, but when God saw that Leah was not loved, he opened her womb. Rachel, the one who was loved, was contributing nothing to this oath that God swore to Abraham, Isaac and Jacob.

Are you an unloved woman? God knows that. He's going to do things for you, and if you start counting your blessings, he's going to make it up to you – it's only a matter of time. All Christians have their 'thorn in the flesh'. I can think of one great composer whose voice is mediocre, he'd like a better voice. The Lord says, 'I've given you an anointing: you can write hymns.' We all want what we don't have. And we all feel some sense of rejection. I can remember when I was a little boy my dad built me a basketball court in my backyard and I was hoping to become really good at the game. In fact, I did become pretty good, but I never made the first team. And whether it was basketball, football or baseball, I was never asked to be captain, and I would be the last person to be picked for a team.

5. Leah's Crown

Her crown was twofold. First, Leah came to terms with her affliction, with her hurt. This is the remarkable thing about Leah: she came to terms with her complaint. Until a particular moment, she kept saying, 'If I have one more son my husband will love me.' She was so excited when she had her first baby and he was a boy. She named him Reuben which means 'see a son', saying, *'Surely my husband will love me now.'* So far it hadn't worked. She conceived again and gave birth to her second son Simeon, but still Jacob did not love her. *'Again she conceived, and when she gave birth to a son she said, "Now at last my husband will become attached to me, because I have born him three sons." '* She got it wrong every time, but then something happened to her. In verse 35 we read, *'She conceived again, and when she gave birth to a son she said, "This time I will praise the LORD." '* Until then, she was hoping her husband would love her, but the Lord said, 'I love you – will I do?' Leah came to terms with that.

But there was second part to Leah's crown. Not only did she come to terms with things here below, but the legacy of Jacob that mattered in years to come came through Leah. The tribe of Levi came through that third son. Who would have known that one day a book would be named after Levi, the book of Leviticus, and through him would come the tribe of Levi, the priesthood? She also gave birth to Judah, the one through whom the Messiah, God's Son, came. Her crown was that she graced the church with glory as no other wife of Jacob could have done. Leah's desire was to have a husband who loved her, but her crown was what she did for the future of Israel. Jacob never appreciated Leah, but God did. And so do we.

13

The Woman Who Had Everything?

Genesis 29:1–30:2

If Leah could be called 'the unloved woman', Rachel, on the other hand, was the woman who, apparently, had everything. There are many of us, men and women, who feel deprived, and when we look at others we look at those who have everything (so it seems) and we feel rather cheated, rather deprived and sorry for ourselves. The question is, should we feel like that?

When I was a student in High School, back in 1953, there was a fellow who had absolutely everything. You know the type. He was top of his class. He made A's in everything. I had a class with him in Algebra: he made an A, I made a D. I had a class with him in Latin: he made an A, I made a C. He excelled in everything. He was the first stringer on the Ashland Tomcat basketball team; he had the perfect body, the perfect physique. He could hit a goal from 30 feet away. To top it all, he always had a girlfriend and she would be pretty!

A Woman Who Had Almost Everything

But, of course, the person who has it all is only an illusion. They only *appear* to have everything. You would say Rachel had everything. First, she had a beautiful body. Genesis 29:17 says she was *'lovely in form'*, and the Bible can be very descriptive; you don't have to use your imagina-tion. The same verse tells us she also had beauty. Moreover, Rachel was brave. She was the only woman in the Bible called a shepherdess. That work took a lot of courage and meant she had a lot of self-confidence. There's more: she had brains. I will prove this to you. Later in our story, when Jacob, Leah and Rachel fled from Laban and he caught up with them, her father angrily demanded, *'Why did you steal my gods?'* Then he began to search everybody, but when he came to Rachel, Genesis

31:35 tells us, *'Rachel said to her father, "Don't be angry, my lord, that I cannot stand up in your presence; I'm having my period." So he searched but could not find the household gods.'* It shows she must have been very clever to have come up with that excuse at the last moment. Not only did Rachel have all these attributes, but she had a sense of belonging. She was loved. Jacob loved her. And there's nothing that gives a person a feeling of security, of confidence and being at ease, than when they know someone loves them.

Perhaps you feel unloved. Maybe you were rejected as a child and you never felt your mother or your father loved you. Perhaps, now you are married, you don't feel your husband or your wife loves you. It may be that you are single and you have always wanted someone to love you. Rachel didn't have that problem: she was loved by Jacob. Feeling rejected has its effect on your personality. But Rachel seemed to have everything.

However, there was one thing she lacked. Rachel was barren. She had *almost* everything. We have seen that by comparison Leah (to use a modern expression) was a 'loser'. She was plain; she was rejected.

A rivalry developed, but not as far as Rachel was concerned. If you were to ask Rachel, 'Is there a rivalry between you and your sister Leah?' she would have replied, 'Oh, goodness, no!' You see, the person who has everything isn't usually aware how other people feel. You couldn't have told Rachel there was a problem, but here's what we know. God looked down from heaven and he saw that Leah was not loved, and he opened Leah's womb.

Being Loved by God

Isaiah 61:8 says, *'I, the LORD, love justice.'* You may think that God is not fair in what he allows to happen, but he knows what you are thinking. He knows every thought you have ever had. Remember, he loves justice and he is the one who is determined to compensate and make up for that deprivation. Leah was unloved by her husband but was loved by the Lord, whereas Rachel was loved by her husband but she was barren. The Lord did not honour Rachel in the thing that began to matter more than her beauty, her brains, and everything else she had going for her. What is the difference between having love from someone here below and receiving love from the Lord? The love that is here below is only for the here and now, but the love that is from above has the future in mind. I want to ask you this: Do you feel deprived because you are not a Rachel, because you haven't had a great education, you don't have a brilliant brain, a great body or good looks, you don't have a good job and you feel you aren't really appreciated? But there's more to life than beauty, than having a good body, than having brains that make people excel.

I have this question: Are you loved by the Lord? That's what matters. You ask, 'How can I know?' Well, to begin with, Hebrews 12:6 says, *'The Lord disciplines those whom he loves.'* What does this mean? It means God begins to deal with you; he forces you to learn something in a way that is pretty rough. He gets the whip out, as it were, and gives you one or two lashes. It may be the Lord who has kept you from getting that job, or from getting married. It may be the Lord who has brought you to a place where everything happening around you is bad, and you wonder where God is. Are all the bad things that happen God's doing? Yes. God brings you so low that there's nowhere to look but up, and then, when you start looking at him, he says, 'Oh, good, you're coming to me. This is what I wanted.' And you begin to realize that the Lord loved you that much, he beckoned you in his direction. You see, those whom the Lord loves, he deals with, and those that are dealt with are truly his, and they will go to heaven and no one else.

When you die you'll go either to heaven or to hell. The Bible is true, and what will matter eventually is where you will spend eternity. It may be that the Rachels of this world get the attention here below: they make the front cover of the magazines; they turn heads when they walk down Oxford Street, and nobody notices you. But one day you will find out that God loved you so much that, to get your attention, he brought you to the place where you just looked to him. And you come to see what the Rachels of this world can't see because they are blind, what they can't see because they are preoccupied with what people think about them. You will know that God brought you to the place where you had to come to terms with the fact that you're a sinner on the road to hell and the only way to be saved is by the blood of Jesus Christ.

Loved by a Man – but Dissatisfied

Another thing to think about is this. Rachel had her husband's love, but soon that wasn't enough. She had now come to the place where she wanted a baby more than beauty; she wanted to be a mother more than she desired her husband's affection. And if you knew the person who appears to have everything very well, the chances are you wouldn't want to change places with them for anything.

Some years ago, when I had to sell vacuum cleaners for a living, I met some of the wealthiest and most famous people in America. When they got to know me, they would confide in me and ask me to sit and talk to them. I could tell you one pathetic story after another. I wouldn't want what they've got for anything. Believe me, I would leave them thinking, 'Thank God, I'm not in that situation.' You would go up to their beautiful, wealthy houses feeling envious, and leave thinking, 'It's true; all that glitters is not gold.'

Changing Priorities

There is another thing to learn if you feel deprived because you are not
a Rachel. Our priorities and values change in time. You couldn't have
told Rachel that one day bearing children would be more important to
her than her beauty. Not only was Leah's deprivation compensated, but
now look how things have changed. Rachel was jealous of Leah. Who
would ever have thought that would happen? But that is exactly what it
says in Genesis 30:1: *'When Rachel saw that she was not bearing Jacob any
children, she became jealous of her sister.'* No matter who you are, I promise
you the day will come when that which is so special and so important
now won't compare to the set of values you will have then.

The Last Becomes First

The last point I want to make is summed up in the words of Jesus: *'Many
who are first will be last, and many who are last will be first'* (Mt. 19:30). Leah
was the one who had the babies, not the beauty. But what Leah had going
for her meant more to the future of the kingdom of God than what Rachel
had going for her, because Leah bore four babies and later would have
two more. As we saw in the previous chapter, Leah's son Levi gave the
people of Israel the tribe of Levi, and her son Judah gave the world a
Saviour.

I want to ask this question: What are you doing that will survive? It
is better to be last now and in the future to be first. It is only a matter of
time before the person you have envied will be jealous of you! You say,
'Me?' Yes, you! Who would have thought Rachel would become jealous
of Leah?

It turned out that even Rachel and her husband began to have their
quarrels, for Rachel went to Jacob and said, ' *"Give me children, or I'll die!"
Jacob became angry with her and said, "Am I in the place of God, who has kept
you from having children?"'* (Gen. 30:1–2). And you thought the grass was
greener on the other side of the fence! Rachel had love: Leah had life.
Rachel had the looks: Leah had the legacy.

God was dealing with Rachel. Rachel appeared to have everything,
but what she didn't have brought her to brokenness. Perhaps you are like
Rachel; you have the brains, the beauty, you're self-confident, you've
been on top and people have envied you. But really you are lost and,
maybe, God is trying to bring you to the place where you see your need
of him.

14

Coping with a Rival

Genesis 30:1–24

A rival is a competitor, someone who is a threat, a person who could upstage you. Sooner or later most of us know what it is to have a rival. It may be a close friend. Perhaps you don't mention the rivalry between you, you rarely think about it, and yet it's just beneath the surface. Sometimes that rival is an enemy, and it would seem in this case it almost came to that. Leah and Rachel were so jealous of each other because, although Rachel had the looks, Leah could produce children and that was her claim to fame. Leah was obviously a very plain woman and Rachel was very beautiful. We don't know whether this caused rivalry between Leah and Rachel as they grew up, but it's possible. This would be sibling rivalry.

Many have speculated as to what Paul's *'thorn in the flesh'* was (see 2 Cor. 12:7). Some have thought he was referring to somebody who was always needling him, somebody who got under his skin. Perhaps you have a rival who is a *'thorn in the flesh'*, not a particularly pleasant thing. But the truth is, a rival can be good for us. A rival will keep us on our toes, and the day will come when that rival ceases to be a threat, and then you will say, 'I'm glad now I had that experience.'

Let's learn more of the story of Rachel and Leah. Rachel was so desperate that she even offered her maidservant to her own husband and said, *'Here is Bilhah, my maidservant. Sleep with her so that she can bear children for me and that through her I too can build a family'* (Gen. 30:3). So Jacob did, and Rachel said, *'God has vindicated me; he has listened to my plea and given me a son.'* And there was a second son. Rachel said, *'I have had a great struggle with my sister, and I have won'* (Gen. 30:8).

Do You Have a Rival?

Do you have a rival? Is there someone who is in competition with you?
Is there someone who gets under your skin? They may want to upstage
you or damn you with faint praise which, instead of making you feel
good, makes you feel worse. A rival spirit.

A famous quote of Martin Luther is, 'God uses sex to drive a man to
marriage, ambition to drive a man to service, fear to drive a man to faith.'
Lets talk of the ambition that drives a man to service. Some time ago, I
was reading Ecclesiastes 4:4. I was so gripped with this verse, so shattered
by it, that the letters jumped out at me as if they had been written in gold.
It says: '*I saw that all labour and all achievement spring from man's envy of his
neighbour.*' It is saying ambition will get things done, but achieving that
ambition will make another person jealous. You know the feeling when
you've achieved something and someone says, 'I'm very happy for you,'
and somehow you don't really think they are. It's a lot easier to weep
with those who weep than to rejoice with those who rejoice. Sometimes,
it's the loneliest thing to have accomplished something and you don't
have anyone you can tell who will be glad for you.

So we are motivated at a natural level so people will admire us.
Accordingly, we discover Leah was motivated by something more than
just wanting to win her husband over. It's true that was a part of it, but
she had reached the place where she wanted to please God.

Ambition at the natural level is something God uses to get us started;
it drives us to want to do things and to do them. In the same way, God
uses sex to make a person want to get married. But sexual love will not
keep a marriage going for ever. Eventually, unselfish love must come in.
And so it is with ambition. Ambition that makes you want to do things
won't be sufficient to last on and on. Eventually, you must have an
ambition to please God.

One of the most moving things about this story is that when Leah first
had a baby she said, '*Surely my husband will love me now.*' When she had
another baby, she said, '*Because the LORD heard that I am not loved, he gave
me this one too.*' And then she had a third baby and she said, '*Now at last
my husband will become attached to me, because I have born him three sons.*' She
conceived again, and then she said, '*This time I will praise the LORD.!*'
Something had happened to Leah (see Gen. 29:32–35).

You see, an ambitious person may start out wanting people to admire
them, but that won't be enough, ultimately, to bring glory to God. God
wants to bring you to the place where you just want to please him. Leah
had reached that place, and it is what drove her to God. Having a rival
will help do that. I want you to understand that God will use a person
who competes with you, a person who is a '*thorn in your flesh*'.

However, an unhappy event occurred that must have been a real trial
to Leah. True, she had begun to learn something of the praise of God,

but that didn't mean everything would be happy for her thereafter. Not only did having four babies *not* win her husband's love, but now Jacob stopped sleeping with her altogether. We know this because we read: *'During wheat harvest, Reuben went out into the fields and found some mandrake plants, which he brought to his mother Leah. Rachel said to Leah, "Please give me some of your son's mandrakes."*

'But she said to her, "Wasn't it enough that you took away my husband? Will you take my son's mandrakes too?" ' (Gen. 30:14–15).

We don't know what these mandrakes were, but the common view is that they had something to do with fertility. So Rachel was hoping these would work for her. She answered Leah by saying, *'Very well . . . he can sleep with you tonight in return for your son's mandrakes.'* Can you see the rivalry between them and the humiliation Leah felt then?

Perhaps a rival spirit has brought you to a place where you have lost all sense of pride, you've been put down, you have lost all sense of self-esteem. Often a rival lives for one thing, and that is to make you look bad. It is very painful. What can you do if you have a rival? You can let a rival spirit throw you, or destroy you, or you can let them be the best thing that has ever happened to you. The day will come when you are so thankful for that *'thorn in the flesh'*.

Kinds of Rivalry

There are various kinds of rivalry. There is social rivalry. Leah was affected socially. She said, *'Women will call me happy'* (Gen. 30:13). She wasn't only thinking of Jacob, she was thinking of her reputation generally. Leah had the edge here because she was the one having babies. Do you know what it is like to have a social rival? Perhaps you know someone who uses their education, their background and the important people whom they appear to know, to make you feel inferior.

Another kind of rivalry – a sexual rivalry – had developed here. In a different sense, Rachel had the edge because she had the appeal, she was more attractive and Leah was no match for her. Perhaps you know the feeling of being upstaged when it comes to sexuality or sex appeal, and you feel such a lack of self-esteem. Yet I want you to know that God has a purpose in that, and the day will come when what was once an area of deep concern, and almost something you didn't want to think or talk about, becomes what you treasure most. One day you will thank God that he made you just as you are.

There is also a special rivalry, and that is when God sovereignly raises up somebody to keep you on your toes. John Cotton and Thomas Hooker were two Puritans who left England for America. Cotton founded Boston and Hooker the state of Connecticut. But the rivalry between them was so great that one of them had to leave. Often, you will find two very towering people just cannot stay in the same area very long. When you get to heaven, you will get to see a video replay and understand how Simon Peter (Number One among the 12 disciples you might say) felt when out of the blue came Saul of Tarsus – a 'Johnny-come-lately'. That was hard for Peter. I can tell you that was not easy at all. We are all easily threatened; every one of us has a fragile ego. Yet it is to Peter's everlasting credit that at the very end of 2 Peter he says:

> *Bear in mind that our Lord's patience means salvation, just as our dear brother Paul also wrote to you with the wisdom that God gave him. He writes the same way in all his letters, speaking in them of these matters. His letters contain some things that are hard to understand, which ignorant and unstable people distort, as they do the other Scriptures* (2 Pet. 3:15–16).

Peter affirmed Paul.

There is one other kind of rivalry implied in this passage – a salvation rivalry. In verse 2 we read: *'Jacob became angry with her and said, "Am I in the place of God who has kept you from having children?" '* What does that tell us? It tells us that, at the end of the day, the very thing that meant most to Leah and also to Rachel eventually was that they could have children. This is something only God can bring about. Of all the rivalries we could talk about, sibling rivalry, a special rivalry, a sexual rivalry, a social rivalry, the one rivalry you must understand is that there is no rival to the way you can be saved. The rivalry to your salvation could be your church membership, your baptism, having been born into a Christian home, your good works. They rival the only way to be saved. Only God can save. The only way to be saved is to see that Jesus died on the cross. Faith in Christ alone will save you.

There was a time when Rachel said, *'I have had a great struggle with my sister and I have won.'* Are you wanting to win? Who did win? Was it Rachel or was it Leah? Neither won. God won. The future of Israel was secured, and we all won because Judah was born, and Jesus is the Lion of the Tribe of Judah. God gave us a Saviour. Through the rivalry of those two sisters the kingdom of God was advanced. God did it, and God is still adding to the church.

15

Vindication at Last

Genesis 30:22–24

Then God remembered Rachel; he listened to her and opened her womb. She became pregnant and gave birth to a son and said, 'God has taken away my disgrace.' She named him Joseph, and said, 'May the LORD add to me another son.'

We are all introduced to a particular subject in an individual way. I will never forget how, in the summer of 1956, the subject of vindication came to me. The word 'vindication' means to be cleared of any blame or suspicion. In the summer of the previous year, when I was a student in Tennessee, I had had what I can only call a 'Damascus Road experience'. It was almost as extraordinary as that of the conversion of Saul of Tarsus. God became so real to me that if the whole world became atheistic, nothing would cause me to renounce my conviction that Jesus Christ has been raised from the dead and is now at the right hand of God.

The experience opened me to certain teachings that, at that time, were new to me. I came to see the doctrine of election, that God, in his sovereign purpose, for reasons I do not understand, chooses some and not others. I had never been taught that and thought I had discovered something new, but it came to me from the Lord. That was not all, I came to see that those who were saved could never be lost. I had heard of that teaching but had always been told it was not true. I knew then it was and that I would never change my opinion and I still haven't. I also became aware of sin in my life in a way I had never known before. There was a change in my attitude towards God. I felt that God had shown me he was going to use me one day.

When I went home to Ashland, Kentucky, I thought that my family would welcome it and clap their hands saying, 'That's thrilling!' However, that wasn't their reaction at all.

My father was broken-hearted over my discovery and the things I was saying to him. It seemed that, instead of being used by the Lord, I had

no future at all and no church that believed in me. I didn't know where
to find anyone who shared my theology. My father, who loved me (and
whom I loved), said, 'Prove to me God is going to use you.' But I couldn't
do this. What I longed for was to be vindicated, to be cleared of any
suspicion.

I had received a new set of teaching that had been revealed to me by
the Holy Spirit and by my experience. I saw the need to be vindicated,
and I also saw that vindication was a biblical teaching. Furthermore, I
came to understand the teaching of the Lord's chastening. The Bible says.
'The Lord disciplines those he loves, and he punishes everyone he accepts as a son'
(Heb. 12:6). This teaching has been special to me.

Rachel's Disgrace

Have you ever known what Rachel called 'disgrace'? Here are her words:
'God has taken away my disgrace.' (The Authorized Version uses the word
'reproach'.) What is disgrace or reproach? It is sheer embarrassment. It
has mostly to do with our pride. It was the very thing the disciples
overcame. Sometimes God takes away the feeling of shame or embarrass -
ment. There are also times when God gives you such an internal victory
that there is no disgrace or feeling of shame at all. In Acts 5:41 we read,
*'The apostles left the Sanhedrin, rejoicing because they had been counted worthy
of suffering disgrace for the Name.'* They had been embarrassed over what
had happened to Jesus. He had let them down. He had left them high
and dry. They couldn't understand how one who could walk on water,
who could raise a man from the dead, could now let himself be crucified.
They felt disgrace; they felt reproach, but they had reached the place
where they rejoiced to suffer the shame and disgrace for the name of Jesus.
There is the kind of disgrace which is not removed from you but which
you can surmount. This is what the disciples overcame.

Many say Rachel shouldn't have worried about not having children.
After all, she had the love of her husband. Rachel was loved and she was
beautiful. You could say she had everything. But all of us want something
we can't have. It lies within God's power to do something about it. Who
would have thought the day would come when Rachel would want
vindication? Her disgrace was that she was barren. She was loved but was
unfulfilled. She wanted to be part of a very rich tradition, to be a sovereign
vessel.

Chosen vessels wait a long time before God uses them in the way
for which they were destined. There is a long tradition that those who
were used the most, waited the longest. Remember how Sarah, the
wife of Abraham, said, *'The LORD has kept me from having children'* (Gen.
16:2). Perhaps there is something you want. Are you prepared to admit
that the Lord has kept you from having that, and not to be angry with

God? Are you willing to come to terms with what the Lord has done? Rebecca, the wife of Isaac, was barren. Hannah was barren. Elizabeth, the mother of John the Baptist, had gone to the age of the menopause, and when it looked certain she could never conceive, God gave her a son. But God often lets those whom he is going to use be without what matters so much to them. *'Sing, O barren woman, you who never bore a child; burst into song, shout for joy, you who were never in labour'* (Isa. 54:1). Isaiah could say that about one who longed for a special touch, a breakthrough or vindication even, and that is God's word for you. Do not be afraid. You will not suffer shame. Do not fear disgrace. You will not be humiliated.

In ancient times barrenness was regarded as a sign of God's disapproval. Rachel believed her inability to conceive and the withholding of vindi - cation meant that God did not approve of her. Perhaps you are blaming yourself for what you don't have. You keep thinking, 'What have I done wrong? What can I do?' The truth is that God is sovereign. He can do what he pleases, with whom he pleases, when he pleases. That is his word for you. The day came when God remembered Rachel. He listened to her and opened her womb. She became pregnant and gave birth to a son and said, *'God has taken away my disgrace.'*

Rachel's Vindication

Rachel's vindication, while seeming to come all at once, came in stages. Rachel had what I can only call premature vindication. We read *'Rachel said, "God has vindicated me; he has listened to my plea and given me a son"'* (Gen. 30:6). But Rachel did not bear that baby: it was Bilhah, her servant, who slept with Jacob with Rachel's permission. Bilhah conceived and Rachel got the credit. Rachel said, *'I have had a great struggle with my sister, and I have won'* (v. 9). Someone can want something so badly that they grab any shadow of what they want and say, 'Look what God has done.' But Rachel had sold herself short. She had said, 'This is it. God has vindicated me.' The truth was that God hadn't even begun to do what he was going to do with her.

I think many people find something they hang on to before they discover the real thing. Perhaps you are like this. You think you are saved and are not. 'Don't judge me,' you say. 'I don't even know you.' But I'll tell you why I say this. You think you have a fairly good chance of going to heaven, and are basing your belief that you are a Christian on the fact that you have done good things. You're like Rachel who claimed to have won, as if it were something she did. (God would one day do something beyond her power.) What you call salvation is as hollow and as shallow as Rachel claiming she had been vindicated when nothing of the sort had happened. It was a counterfeit victory.

The Christianity you are clinging to is called a 'gospel of works'. You think that good works count for something and will get you to heaven. You have done your best to live a good life and assumed that meant you were a Christian. Perhaps you were baptized, have given money to the church or have become a church member. It is a false victory that is based on what *you* have done. A gospel of works is no comfort at all. It is a 'do-it-yourself' religion. There are thousands of different religions, and you may not have realized that whether it is Islam, Buddhism, Hinduism or Shintoism, to name but a few, they are all alike: DIY religions. What separates the Christian faith from all other religions of the world, what separates the true God from the false, is who initiates your actions. Have you sold yourself short and have never come to see that God's salvation is what *he* does for you in his time?

The day would come when Rachel had a real vindication, and what she would experience then made her servant girl having a child seem like nothing. The day would come when she would have her own son, and this would bear no comparison with what she had once called 'vindication'.

There is a possibility that God wants to do something for you in the future that will make it seem that what you have now is nothing in comparison. One day you will look back and say, 'I can't believe I thought I was saved.' You are not saved until you see the only way to heaven is through Jesus Christ alone, who shed his blood on the cross, until the day when you stand back and say, 'He did it all.'

What do we know of Rachel's vindication?

1. It was a scheduled vindication. God had it in mind all along. He knew one day she would have a baby. God has your vindication scheduled too. He has a plan for you, and it's far greater than the thing you thought would give you satisfaction. The Bible says, *'Humble yourselves, therefore, under God's mighty hand, that he will lift you up in due time'* (1 Pet. 5:6).

2. We should note that God is sovereign and takes his time. I'll never forget one man in Fort Lauderdale who was gloriously converted many years ago. One night, after church, I saw George looking up at the stars and tears running down his cheeks. I said, 'OK, George, what's wrong?'

'Oh, nothing's wrong,' he answered. 'It's wonderful! I'm just standing here, wondering why I waited so long.'

I said, 'George, be thankful that God came when he did. Some never see it.'

God takes his time. You wonder why he waits, and then the penny drops and your immediate reaction is 'Why didn't I see it sooner?' Verse 24 puts it this way: *'Then God remembered Rachel.'* The timing was in his hands.

3. It was a sudden vindication. It came slowly but God has a way of turning things around in the shortest span of time. You wouldn't think it was possible. He can take a long time, and then, when he works, everything changes in no time at all.

4. It was a sensational vindication. It came openly, visibly, obviously. When Rachel spoke of her premature vindication, she was like many who speak of signs and wonders; she was fooling herself. When God really does work and people are healed, it will be open and obvious. When God worked to vindicate Rachel, it was a sweet vindication.

5. It was satisfying. You will find it satisfies you when you trust Jesus alone and not yourself. Romans 10:11 says, *'Everyone who trusts in him will never be put to shame.'* Her vindication was secure. She would never lose it. What God finally did would be hers and it would never go away. When you come to Christ because your salvation is not based on your own works, but on the righteousness of another, you will be saved for ever.

6. It was strategic. Rachel's first son was the future Prime Minister of Egypt, although she wouldn't live to see it. She named him Joseph because she wanted another baby. Indeed, God did give her another son, Benjamin. She couldn't have known how strategic he would be. Paul said, *'If anyone else thinks he has reasons to put confidence in the flesh, I have more: circumcised on the eighth day, of the tribe of Benjamin'* (Phil. 3:4). What Rachel finally received was worth waiting for. To this very hour we all benefit from it, for it was Paul who took the gospel to the Gentiles.

We should see that her vindication was the result of prayer. The Bible says that God remembered Rachel. He listened to her. This means she had been praying. She needed and wanted something only God could do.

Have you settled for a premature, shallow vindication? Have you said, 'Ah, I've got it!' What God would do is to make that look like nothing. Remember, *'No eye has seen, no ear has heard, no mind has conceived what God has prepared for those who love him'* (1 Cor. 2:9). What you may have called salvation, you now see is nothing. You have to climb down and affirm what God alone can do and your life will change.

16

How to Cope with Mistreatment

Genesis 30:25–43

How do you cope with mistreatment? The story about Laban and the way he treated Jacob may have much to teach us.

Jacob had been living in Paddam Aram now for 20 years. For 14 years he worked for Laban, keeping his agreement in exchange for Laban's two daughters. Then another six years elapsed before Jacob finally made the break, and it was after Joseph was born when Jacob turned his thoughts towards going home. During all those years Jacob had received scant, if any, remuneration from Laban beyond board and lodging. If Jacob received any more than that, then there's no hint of it. Even when Rachel and Leah became his wives, Jacob wasn't allowed to set up his own establishment. He was obliged to live under his Uncle Laban's jurisdic - tion, until one day Jacob said, 'Enough is enough.' So Jacob said to his uncle, *'Give me my wives and children, for whom I have served you, and I will be on my way. You know how much work I've done for you'* (Gen. 30:26).

For someone living under a controlling spirit, in an area that was not home, and knowing everything was against him, speaking up like that probably took a lot of courage. Maybe you can identify with the kind of mistreatment Jacob endured for so many years. I have known many people who have put up with so much from others, a controlling parent, or a spouse, for instance, who make life so unpleasant. It may be the boss one has to work for. I dare say many reading this dread returning to work on Monday mornings.

There are three things to note about this passage:

1. Delayed Appreciation

Most of us like a compliment. Jacob never received a compliment from Laban until the day he said, 'I'm going home. Send me on my way!'

He had waited 14, if not 15 years, to be appreciated. Now Laban wanted to admit that not only did he appreciate Jacob, but he had good reason to do so, as he believed that all the prosperity he had been enjoying was because of him. So we read in verse 27: '*Laban said to him, "If I have found favour in your eyes, please stay. I have learned by divination that the* LORD *has blessed me because of you." He added, "Name your wages, and I will pay them." '*

What is divination? It's possible that Laban, who was not a worshipper of the true God Yahweh, discerned things by some occultic means. Yet it is also possible that Laban needed an excuse to say why he hadn't appreciated Jacob before now. Jacob had been a blessing to Laban. Is it possible that the prosperity and wealth coming to Laban were *really* because of Jacob? The answer is 'Yes'. But why is this the case?

One reason is that Jacob was accommodating despite Laban's unfair - ness. Second, it was because of Jacob's ability. There's no doubt about it, Jacob had a gift, an ability, when it came to working with sheep and cattle. He knew how to make them multiply. The third reason for Jacob being such a blessing was his accountability to God. Jacob was a man under orders. God was with Jacob.

Later in Genesis we find a similar thing when Joseph, Jacob's son, worked for Potiphar, for we are told that because the Lord was with Joseph, the household of Potiphar profited and prospered. So, when God is with you, wherever you go you are going to be a blessing. This should not surprise us. But in every case it all comes down to this: an anointing (see Chapter 5).

His anointing didn't mean Jacob was perfect – far from it. The fact that God blesses someone because of you, is not because of how good you are. But it is true, if there is an anointing upon you, you will be a blessing wherever you go. We are told that in the days of the Soviet Union, when a person was converted, the government wasn't always as unhappy as you might have thought. Even though they claimed to be atheistic and they hated Christianity, they knew one thing about Chris - tians: they made good workers. They were honest; they didn't steal and they worked hard, which made them stand out. There is a way of testifying just by being such a good worker. I am going to ask you a question: Is this the testimony you give in the place where you work and live?

Do you know the worst testimony you can give in the world? It is to be lazy, to be complaining and finding fault with the system. There is always somebody who will complain about conditions. Often, on your first day in a new job, someone will come up to you and say, 'This is an awful place. You won't like the boss, this person or that person, they are awful.' Because you want to get on with everybody, you say, 'Well, yeah.' But you don't know what to believe or what to do. But if, as a Christian, you fall into the complaining spirit, what do you think it will do to your testimony?

Let me give you another example of giving a bad testimony. Are you a student? Don't say that the reason you are not going to make good grades and you are not going to pass exams is because you have been spending time witnessing for Jesus. 'I have been praying and fasting. That's why I'm going to fail my course.' Do you think everyone is going to clap their hands and say, 'Wow, what a wonderful Christian – he's failing, but he loves the Lord!'? No. That's the worst testimony you can give. So, if there's an anointing on you, you are going to be a hard worker; you are going to be good at what you do. That will impress others.

Jacob caused Laban to prosper because he had an anointing. There are many Labans today who have little interest in the true God but who are quite capable of appreciating what is genuine in others. The Labans of this world are not converted, but they can appreciate a good thing. There are people who may be church members, but they are not committed. There are those who attend church for social advantage but have little respect for Jesus Christ. However, they know it pays to be associated with God's people. There are many people who come to church because, they say, 'It feels good to have you around me; just to be there.' This borders on the superstitious. It is fairly well known that back in the days of the Vietnam War, when Lyndon Johnson was President, the most popular guest in the White House wasn't a military man, it wasn't a politician, it was Billy Graham. Not because President Johnson was asking Billy Graham for military strategy or political advice – he felt good to have Billy staying there. You see, there are the Labans of this world who just enjoy having someone round.

Many years ago, I was invited to the London City Mission to speak at their annual meeting. They had many high-powered people there. It was the one time of the year when they brought in their 'up-market' people to show them what the mission was doing. There was another speaker of whom I had never heard, but he was a very important man and everyone else there knew who he was. What disappointed me about this speaker is that, when he was explaining why the London City Mission was a good organization, he said it was good for London: it gets the drug addicts off the streets and, thus, cleans up the city. I see him being no different to a Laban who could see the advantages of having somebody like Jacob around.

2. The Deceptive Agreement

Jacob said, 'I want to go home.'

> But Laban said to him, 'If I have found favour in your eyes, please stay. I have learned by divination that the LORD has blessed me because of you.' He added, 'Name your wages and I will pay them.'

Jacob said to him, 'You know how I have worked for you and how your livestock has fared under my care. The little you had before I came has increased greatly, and the LORD *has blessed you wherever I have been. But now, when may I do something for my own household?'*

'What shall I give you?' he asked.

'Don't give me anything,' Jacob replied. 'But if you will do this one thing for me, I will go on tending your flocks and watching over them: Let me go through all your flocks today and remove from them every speckled or spotted sheep, every dark-coloured lamb and every spotted or speckled goat. They will be my wages. And my honesty will testify for me in the future' (Gen. 30:27–33).

Here was the proposition. Laban would have all the animals of one colour but Jacob would keep for himself the spotted and speckled sheep and goats.

'How's that, Uncle Laban?'

'You've got a deal,' agreed Laban.

So far so good. But it was sheer deception. Do you know what it is like to have someone look you in the eye and promise things they don't mean, and yet, because you are not very discerning or because you are just a little gullible, you believe them?

A few years ago, I went with a minister by the name of Jess Moody on my first visit to Israel. Every day we met this Arab who sold beads outside our hotel. There was something about this Arab. He was very endearing and he knew how to get on with the American Christians. He would say, 'You want to buy some beads? Jesus is coming soon! Hallelujah!' Well, on the following Sunday, we met in the Baptist Church there in Jerusalem, and the Arab turned up at the service. I thought, 'Oh, isn't that wonderful!' He sat through the service. Jess Moody preached, and at the end the Arab came forward to receive Jesus as his Lord and Saviour. I never saw Jess Moody so happy. But as soon as we got through the door when the service had ended, there he was again. 'Want to buy some beads? Jesus saves, Hallelujah!' He had only pretended conversion to make us feel good. It is so easy to believe that something has happened because a person does something which, on the surface, is honest.

Read these words from Matthew 21:28–31:

There was a man who had two sons. He went to the first and said, 'Son, go and work today in the vineyard.'

'I will not,' he answered, but later he changed his mind and went.

Then the father went to the other son and said the same thing. He answered, 'I will, sir,' but he did not go.

'Which of the two did what his father wanted?'

The answer to Jesus' question was 'The first son, of course.' So it's far more important that you don't come forward at an altar call to make everybody happy, but in your heart you embrace the truth. It's far better when you make a public pledge, to mean it. Don't do it because you think it's going to solve some problem: 'I've tried to do this, I've tried that, but God may honour that.' If something hasn't happened right there in your heart, then it won't do any good. You will be no different from Laban who said, 'Agreed.'

What do you suppose happened as soon as Laban agreed? Laban removed the very animals that he agreed to give to Jacob, put his sons in charge, and then put three days' journey between them. So after all this, we find that things go from bad to worse.

What do we know about Laban? We can say four things:

- He was controlling. There is nothing more exhausting than having someone around who wants to control you. There is no real fellowship. You feel that your relationship is based upon the degree to which you allow that other person to control you. If you are involved with someone who has a controlling spirit, remember that it is not genuine affection or respect. Laban was controlling.
- He was cruel. He was a bully who knew that Jacob was at his mercy. Jacob had no defence. He was alone in a foreign country while Laban was surrounded by sympathetic associates and sons who grew up feeling hostile to Jacob.
- He was a cheapskate. Jacob said, *'I worked for you fourteen years for your two daughters and six years for your flocks, and you changed my wages ten times'* (Gen. 31:41). He was cheap and Jacob was helpless.
- He was cold, detached, unemotional and insensitive. How else could a father treat his daughters like Laban did? Jacob was beginning to realize that this man Laban was not very nice and he was not going to change.
- Yet there was another side of the coin, and Jacob was beginning to see this. He was being hemmed in by God. He was being prepared by God. Jacob needed to be broken and there was something at work within him.

3. The Distinctive Anointing

Jacob, however, took fresh-cut branches from poplar, almond and plane trees and made white stripes on them by peeling the bark and exposing the white inner wood of the branches. Then he placed the peeled branches in all the watering troughs, so that they would be directly in front of the flocks when they came to drink. When the flocks were in heat and came to drink, they mated in front of the branches' (Gen. 30:37–39).

This is a mysterious scenario, rather like the mandrakes that we saw in an earlier chapter. There is no scientific correlation between mandrakes and fertility, but Rachel started eating mandrakes and she became pregnant. There was no scientific reason that this too would work, but it did. I think that the reason for this story is partly this. There are those who say, 'I will believe once you show me something scientific about the gospel. I want you to show me where science can confirm it.' There is no scientific reason that as you trust in the blood that Jesus shed on the cross it washes your sins away, takes away all your guilt and changes your life, but that is what will happen. It works.

The Apostle Paul said, *'If you confess with your mouth, "Jesus is Lord,"
and believe in your heart that God raised him from the dead, you will be saved'*
(Rom. 10:9).

- Before I close this chapter, I want you to see three ways in which Jacob coped with mistreatment.
- Jacob was careful not to pick a quarrel with Laban. He knew that what was happening to him was God's way of breaking him. Jacob could never forget that he was really getting his comeuppance, because he knew he had been a deceiver himself and now he had met his match. This is the way God may choose to break you: to let you meet your match.
- Jacob preoccupied himself with what he did best. He lived within his anointing and he was the best shepherd those parts had ever seen. He gave himself to what God had called him to do. You may have been mistreated, but God has given you a gift. Use it well. One day your time will come and God will say, 'Enough is enough.'
- Jacob didn't really break away until he had divine confirmation. *Then the LORD said to Jacob, "Go back to the land of your fathers and to your relatives, and I will be with you"* ' (Gen. 31:3). Until then, it had been Jacob's idea, but God had been watching and he said, 'Enough is enough. I am with you.'

God knows how much you can bear, and he is coming to your rescue at this moment to remind you that the one who was mistreated most was Jesus who died on the cross.

17

The God of Bethel

Genesis 31:1–21

I am the God of Bethel, where you anointed a pillar and where you made a vow to me. Now leave this land at once and go back to your native land (Gen. 31:13).

These are some of the most tender words in all Holy Writ. At the lowest moment in his life, God said to Jacob, *'I am the God of Bethel.'* When Jacob heard that, he knew that it was God who was speaking. He hadn't told anybody about that event 20 years previously. It was secret with him. Only God knew about that event.

There are things about you that only God knows. You have told nobody, but God has a way of getting inside your heart with a single word. This is the way he conquers the hardest heart and the greatest sceptic with his closed spirit.

Nobody but Jacob knew about Bethel. Bethel was a place so special to Jacob, and God knew exactly what to say. Jacob was so discouraged; he felt he had nothing to live for. And then God turned up with these words: *'I am the God of Bethel.'* God could have introduced himself by saying, 'I am the God of your father, I am the God of Abraham, I am the God of Isaac.' But he chose to introduce himself in such way that Jacob knew it was the true God.

The God Who Knows

I am reminded of when an American visitor, Jean Raborg from Arizona, asked to speak to my wife Louise at the end of a service in Westminster Chapel. They spent some time together and Jean told Louise her story. Her testimony went something like this:

I was brought up as a member of a Presbyterian church in Arizona. I am not sure my parents were Christians then. When I was eight years old, they sent me to a church camp. It wasn't all that spiritual. The leader said, 'Now, girls, I want you to take a pine cone and throw it into the fire and make a wish.'

I took my pine cone and threw it into the fire and said, 'God, I would like to know you personally.'

Many years later, I went to university, met my husband and became happily married. I was a school teacher. When I was forty years old, a student came to me with a problem. Instead of helping, I began shouting. They took me to hospital and called my husband to come from work. Things went from bad to worse, and they had to put me into a separate ward. Eventually, the hospital couldn't handle me and moved me to a private institution.

I'll never forget the day those iron doors locked. My husband wept and said, 'I am sorry we have to put you in here.'

I cried, 'Please *don't* put me in here!'

Four years later, my parents, who had moved to another church, were converted and went to hear an evangelist who had a gift of healing. His name was Paul Cain. When my mother went up for healing and he made ready to pray for her, she said, 'I am not here for myself. I have come for my daughter who is very ill. Would you pray for her?' The evangelist did.

That night, before he went home, the Lord said to him, 'I want you to go to that hospital and pray for that lady.' It turned out the hospital was five hundred miles out of his way, but he phoned home and got all my details and the name of the hospital. Even that was revealed to him in an unusual way.

Finally, he turned up at the hospital in California where I was a patient. He had to talk his way in because they told him, 'Mrs Raborg doesn't see visitors.' Having persuaded them to let him see me, they called me out of the mail room. My only duty was to seal envelopes because that was the maximum pressure I could take. I was doped up and glassy-eyed.

I looked at this man who said, 'I have come to pray for you, Jean.'

'There's no hope for me,' I replied.

'The Lord is going to heal you. In fact, I have told your little girl you will be out in three days.'

'There's no hope for me,' I repeated. 'I've been here for four years. It's so long.'

'Well,' he said, 'let me talk to you. I've been given a verse of Scripture for you. It is Isaiah 41 verse 10: "Fear not I am with thee. Be not dismayed." '

'That's interesting,' I said. 'That's the only verse I think about.'

'There's one other thing I have to tell you, Jean. The Lord said he's never forgotten the eight-year-old girl who threw pine cones into the fire and said she wished she knew him personally.'

I looked at him and said, 'I have never told anybody that. No one knows that.'

Then he prayed with me. I was totally healed there and then.

Next day the psychiatrist came and I told him I wanted to go home. He refused, but I persisted. They gave me a battery of tests and then let me go home for the weekend. I never returned to the hospital. That was twenty years ago.

What gave Jean hope was that God knew what nobody else knew. The Bible says that all things are uncovered and laid bare before his eyes (see Heb. 4:13). You've done things nobody knows. You have successfully swept dirt under the carpet. There are skeletons in your cupboard. No one but you and God know what they are. You have covered up, but the God of Bethel knows these things.

The God Who Sees

To Jacob, the words indeed meant God was a God who sees. In verse 12 God says, *'I have seen all that Laban has been doing to you.'* You may ask why Jacob waited 20 years to hear these words. I can't explain God's timing, but I know it is perfect. God sees the end from the beginning, but he knows we want answers now. It must hurt him to see our pain, and he longs for the moment he can speak to us. But it will be at the time when it is best for us and, when he finally steps in, we will have no complaints.

Some time ago, Colin Dye, the senior minister at Kensington Temple, came to preach at the Westminster Chapel. He told me of an unusual experience he had had when preparing for a service. He said that a wonderful sense of God came upon him. The feeling only lasted for about 15 seconds. He did his best to describe what it was like. After telling me what was conveyed to him, he said in that moment he had one thought: All he had gone through, all he had ever suffered was worth everything for those seconds. When God does speak, and when he unveils himself, he does so in such a way that you become at peace with him and with the past and all its disappointments. 'Those fifteen seconds,' Colin said, 'I would have gone through anything just for those.'

The God who sees. This was something of what Jacob felt. Jacob also saw Laban's change of attitude. Laban's sons were saying, *'Jacob has taken everything our father owned and has gained all this wealth from what belonged to our father.' And Jacob noticed that Laban's attitude towards him was not what it had been'* (Gen. 31:1–2). Jacob wanted to return home, and Laban, knowing his success was owing to Jacob, had said, 'Please stay.' But what about the change of attitude? Well, Laban's sons obviously mirrored his feelings and falsely accused Jacob.

Jacob was angry. Yet he cannot be excused for all he did. You can easily see Jacob wasn't being very generous to Laban now. *'Whenever the stronger females were in heat, Jacob would place the branches in the troughs in front of the animals so that they would mate near the branches, but if the animals were weak, he would not place them there. So the weak animals went to Laban and the strong ones to Jacob'* (Gen. 30:41–42). Jacob had said, 'Enough is enough. I have made this man prosper. I am not going to do anything more for him.' But the truth is that God was with Jacob. Laban's sons didn't have Jacob's ability and were unable to cope with Jacob's success.

We read this about Jacob: *'In this way the man grew exceedingly prosperous and came to own large flocks, and maidservants and menservants, and camels and donkeys'* (Gen. 30:43). This is what God did. He has it within his power to give or to withhold mercy, to make you prosper or to make you poor. God can do either one and be just. But God chose to bless Jacob, yet his prosperity was not anything he could enjoy. Maybe you are doing well financially, but you are not able to enjoy your wealth. Something is still missing from your life. As Blaise Pascal put it: 'There is a God-shaped blank in every man.'

The God Who Speaks

What was in Jacob's heart was a desire to go home. It turned out that what was in Jacob's heart was also in God's heart. He told Jacob, *'Go back to the land of your fathers and to your relatives, and I will be with you'* (Gen. 31:3). One of the most encouraging verses I know is Psalm 37:4: *'Delight yourself in the LORD and he will give you the desires of your heart.'* God saw Jacob's bondage. God saw that Jacob was virtually Laban's prisoner. He was living in a foreign land. He had unfriendly relatives and a cruel man for a boss. Jacob had endured these things for 20 years. Now, new conditions were imposed on him and Laban cheated Jacob again and again. Then God turned up and he said, 'I have seen what he has done.'

It could be that you are struggling with a situation which is very painful and you ask, 'Lord, can you see what they are doing?' You may think you cannot go on because of the pressure you are under. But the God of Bethel is the God who sees. He knows what you are feeling. He sees what they are doing.

Jacob now called a family conference. He sent word to Rachel and to Leah to come out to the fields, where he had flocks and where no one could eavesdrop. He needed to have a very delicate conversation since he was going to say things about their father that weren't going to be pleasant for them to hear:

You know that I've worked for your father with all my strength, yet your father has cheated me by changing my wages ten times. However, God has not allowed him to harm me. If he said, 'The speckled ones will be your wages,' then all the flocks gave birth to speckled young; and if he said, 'The streaked ones will be your wages,' then all the flocks bore streaked young. So God has taken away your father's livestock and has given them to me . . . The angel of God said to me in the dream . . . 'I have seen all that Laban has been doing to you. I am the God of Bethel . . . Now leave this land at once and go back to your native land' (Gen. 31:6–9, 11, 12, 13).

Why did Jacob do this? He needed the support of his wives, and it would be a big decision for Rachel and Leah, for they were at home and their destination was five hundred miles away in a land unknown to them. But their response was, 'Do whatever God has told you.' It was so wonderful. A united family, they closed ranks. The result was the great escape and Jacob left.

The God of Bethel, the God who sees, is the God who speaks. As Francis Schaeffer put it: 'God is there and he is not silent.' Hebrews 4:12 says: *'The word of God is living and active. Sharper than any double-edged sword, it penetrates even to dividing the soul and spirit, joints and marrow; it judges the thoughts and attitudes of the heart.'* God has a way of speaking at critical times.

Many years ago, when I took a stand against my old theology and thus displeased my father, there came a moment of what I could only call 'desperation'. Then, suddenly, the Lord spoke so clearly. He said, 'Philippians 1 verse 12.' I had no idea what that verse was. I pulled the car over, and got out my Bible and read, *'But I would ye should understand, brethren, that the things which happened unto me have fallen out rather unto the furtherance of the gospel'* (AV).

That message held me for years. I needed that word, I can tell you. God said, *'Never will I leave you; never will I forsake you'* (Heb. 13:5). The God of Bethel will speak and he will withhold nothing from you that is good. *'For the LORD God is a sun and shield; the LORD bestows favour and honour; no good thing does he withhold from those whose walk is blameless'* (Ps. 84:11).

The God Who Selects

He is the God who selects. He chose Jacob. Paul said to Timothy, *'God . . . saved us and called us to a holy life – not because of anything we have done but because of his own purpose and grace. This grace was given us in Christ Jesus before the beginning of time'* (2 Tim. 1:9). It is one of the greatest mysteries and I don't understand it. Every person who is converted sooner or later comes to see that their conversion was no accident. It was something that was planned for a long time. How long? God knew your name before the beginning of time. The most overwhelming feeling in the world is when you realize God chose you. You ask: 'Why me?' In the words of one hymn:

> Why should he love me so?
> Why should my Saviour to Calvary go?
> Anon.

We will never know the answer to that.

The God of Bethel is the God who surprises. He spoke to Jacob saying, 'I have seen what has been going on. Now, I'm telling you leave this land at once. Now! Get moving.' He does things suddenly. When he speaks, he means you to act now. *'I tell you, now is the time of God's favour, now is the day of salvation'* (2 Cor. 6:2). He has come now, and the God of Bethel is being as good to you as he was to Jacob. Why would he come to me again? I don't deserve it. None of us deserves it. But he is coming as tenderly as he did for Jacob.

18

The God Who Remembers

Genesis 31:1–21

God has a perfect memory, and yet, if we are to believe the psycholo -
gists, so have we. Psychologists say we never really forget. Well, you
could have fooled me, but that's what they say. We do forget, however.
There are many reasons for this. Jeremiah 17:9 gives us one reason: *'The
heart is deceitful above all things and beyond cure. Who can understand it?'*
You see, in our self-righteousness, we all remember the good we've
done. Suppose I were to ask a person this question: 'If you were to stand
before God, and he were to ask you, "Why should I let you into my
heaven?" how do you think you would reply?' Even if they tell me they
don't believe in a heaven, they would still say, 'Well, if there were a
heaven, I would tell God I have lived a good life and I haven't hurt
anybody. I think I would get in.'

When we look back on our past we remember things that were
pleasant. Yet it is one thing consciously to *remember* things, the sad thing
is there are some things we don't forget, especially if something is
pointed out to us. One of the things that will make hell, HELL, is that
you will have your memory in hell. In Luke 16:25, Abraham said to
the man who was in hell, *'Son, remember that in your lifetime you received
your good things, while Lazarus received bad things, but now he is comforted
here and you are in agony.'*

But even on this planet, sometimes even as Christians, our memories
have to be jogged. At the Last Supper Jesus said, *'Do this in remembrance
of me'* (Lk. 22:19). One of the reasons for the Lord's Supper is to jog
our memories, to remind us how we know we are going to go to
heaven. For when we eat the bread and drink the cup, there before us
are symbolized the body and the blood of Jesus.

The first time the word 'remember' appears in the Bible is in Genesis
9:15, where God said to Noah, *'I will remember my covenant . . . Whenever
the rainbow appears in the clouds, I will see it and remember the everlasting*

covenant.' In Exodus 3:7 the Lord said to Moses, *'I have indeed seen the misery of my people in Egypt. I have heard them crying out because of their slave drivers, and I am concerned about their suffering.'* Sometimes God seems slow to remember. Sometimes we come to him and cry, 'O God, remember!' Yet, when we pray with the deepest kind of burden as the Children of Israel did then, it's a good sign that he is at hand and about to set to work.

The question is, we ask God to remember but do *we* remember? On one occasion, Jesus simultaneously healed nine lepers. Just like that! But only one remembered to return and thank him. Jesus asked, 'Where are the nine?' (see Lk. 17:11–19). I have to tell you, there's one thing God appreciates, and I cannot stress this too much, he appreciates being thanked. Remember to thank him.

Let us return to Genesis 31:13. *'I am the God of Bethel where you anointed a pillar and where you made a vow to me.'* God hadn't forgotten the vow that Jacob made. I want to deal with this question: What is it that God remembers?

He Remembers Your Vows

Let me ask you a question. Have you ever made a vow to God? The Bible regards taking a vow very seriously. It's more than a promise. The word 'vow' and the word 'oath' can be used interchangeably. Some - times you will say to a person, 'I promise you I will do this.' You're not sure they will believe you, so you say, 'I swear I will do it,' because that would be stronger. And so when a person swears, it becomes doubly important. If a person who takes the oath in a court of law were to break that oath, they commit perjury; and it becomes very serious. The Bible says this about making a vow, which is the same thing as an oath.

When a man makes a vow to the LORD or takes an oath to bind himself by a pledge, he must not break his word but must do everything he said (Num. 30:2).

If you make a vow to the LORD your God, do not be slow to pay it, for the LORD your God will certainly demand it of you and you will be guilty of sin (Deut. 23:21).

When you make a vow to God, do not delay in fulfilling it. He has no pleasure in fools; fulfil your vow. It is better not to vow than to make a vow and not fulfil it (Eccl. 5:4).

Have you ever made a vow to God? It could be that in a time of deepest agony you cried out to God and said, 'Lord please help me! I'll do anything. Get me out of this mess!'

At Westminster Chapel, we invite people to confess Christ publicly. We call it a public pledge. Is it possible you have walked forward at a meeting somewhere, showing the whole world that you acknowledge Jesus Christ as your Lord and Saviour, and yet you have broken that pledge by the life you have led?

This takes me back many years to my boyhood in Kentucky. I grew up hearing a story about one of my uncles. My dad told me that many years ago my uncle developed a brain tumour, and he had only a matter of months to live. The church prayed for him, and my uncle told everybody that if he lived and his tumour was healed, he would give a large sum of money to the church. He *was* healed, and he lived for many years after that. But he never gave the church the money he had promised. No one asked him to. It was his vow. He stopped coming to church regularly and only showed up now and then. My last memory of that man is that he had become a mental case, in a far worse condition than he had been in many years before. He was the laughing stock of many. You talk about becoming a fool! You see, what you ought to know is that when you make a vow to God it's a serious matter.

'Well now,' you may say, 'just a minute – it's far better that we don't make any vows at all.' Now here's the interesting thing: it's better not to make a vow than to make a vow and not pay, but it isn't always wrong to make the vow.

Thinking of my uncle who died a 'cabbage' has taught me over the years to appreciate a clear mind. Romans 1:18–32 talks about those who, after repeated opportunities to acknowledge God, refused to put him first and were given over to sexual immorality, to idolatry and the worship of idols. God just gave them up. He gave them up to a mind void of judgement, so that they could no longer think clearly. In 2 Thessalonians 2:11, it says that God would send a powerful delusion, so that they would believe a lie and be damned because they did not love the truth.

Now what kind of vow is it that a person might have made? It could be a vow that he would serve the Lord if he got him out of trouble. In Psalm 66:13, we have these words: *'I will come to your temple with burnt offerings and fulfil my vows to you – vows my lips promised and my mouth spoke when I was in trouble.'* God does not condemn us for making a vow when we are in trouble. God may use the trouble to get our attention. What the Psalmist was doing was fulfilling that vow. Have you asked God, 'Please, help me in this situation?'

Do you know, back in 1982, during the Falklands War, we began to get thrilling reports of one soldier after another reading their Bible? During the Gulf War in Saudi Arabia and Kuwait, we began to hear the same story of soldiers reading the New Testament and becoming Christians. Where are they today? Perhaps you were not in a war situation, but you were hard pressed, you were in trouble and said, 'God I'll do anything if you help me.'

What we know about Jacob is that he made a vow. He said: *'If God will be with me and will watch over me on this journey I am taking and will give me food to eat and clothes to wear so that I return safely to my father's house, then the LORD will be my God . . . and of all that you give me I will give you a tenth* (Gen. 28:20–22). Twenty years later, God turned up and said, 'I am the God of Bethel. That was the spot where you made a vow to me.' The interesting thing is that when Jacob made a vow to tithe, he wasn't worth a penny; he didn't have anything. But we read in Genesis 30:43 that he grew exceedingly prosperous and came to own large flocks, maidservants and menservants, camels and donkeys. And now the Lord said, 'I remember your vow.'

Jacob could have said, 'Oh, I didn't think you took any notice of that!'

But I think as soon as Jacob heard the words, *'I am the God of Bethel,'* he knew exactly what that meant. Maybe, at this moment, God is taking your mind back to a vow you made to him. Maybe you took a vow to pray, and he took care of you. God remembers.

He Remembers Your Valleys

Before Bethel, Jacob was afraid, but God came to him. He was in the valley, but that became a mountain-top experience so great that Jacob anointed the stone that was his pillow, and said, 'This is a special place,' and he called it Bethel (see Gen. 28:18). Now, many years later, the Lord came again and said, *'I am the God of Bethel'* (Gen. 31:13). After his experience at Bethel, Jacob had spent a further 20 years in a valley. How long has it been for you? Perhaps, a long time ago, God spoke to you and you cannot forget it. You said, 'Lord, yes!' You didn't think he noticed. He did. He remembers your valleys.

He Remembers Your Vision

Listen to this: *'He saw a stairway resting on the earth . . . There above it stood the LORD, and he said: "I am the LORD, the God of your father Abraham and the God of Isaac" '* (Gen. 28:12, 13). What a sight it was! He saw the angels who were descending and ascending. Let me ask you this: Did you once have a vision? Do you remember that time when life was spread before you and the future was so bright, and people said, 'Ah, you're going to go somewhere.' But something has happened, something has gone wrong. You went astray. In Jeremiah 29 God says: *'I know the plans I have for you . . . plans to prosper you and not to harm you, plans to give you hope and a future'* (v. 11). *'You will seek me and find me, when you seek me with all your heart'* (v. 13). You say, 'Yes. That was once the case, but now the future looks so bleak; it doesn't look good for me right now.'

But God remembers your vision. He is saying to you, 'Come back to me! Renew that vow!'

That is something God shouldn't have to do, because when you break a vow that is a serious thing and, in so doing, you effectively release God from having to do anything for you. But God is so gracious and he is saying to you, 'Here I am again. Life is not over yet. There's still time, and if you will turn your life over to me, I will restore the years the locusts have eaten. I will forgive all that has happened, all the mistakes you have made and the sins you have committed. And not only that, if you will begin now, I will cause everything that you have done in the past, everything that haunts you, that leaves you terrified, to work together for good.'

Romans 8:28 says: *'We know that in all things God works for the good of those who love him, who have been called according to his purpose.'* I guarantee that if you return to him, you will find out that there was a purpose in everything that happened. God had not deserted you. There was a reason he let certain things happen. God meant it for good.

He Remembers Your Vulnerability

One of my favourite verses is this: *'He knows how we are formed, he remembers that we are dust'* (Ps. 103:14). God knows that we are weak. He knows that we are vulnerable. But this is why God sent Jesus who is actually touched by the feeling of our weaknesses. God comes and says, 'Look, I am still there and I care.'

19

The Great Escape

Genesis 31:17–37

The truth that I refer to is far greater than is portrayed in any movie like *The Great Escape*, because we are going to talk about the escape from bondage. For in this story of Jacob escaping from Laban, we have a picture of conversion and a picture of the Christian life, because conversion to Jesus Christ is the greatest escape there ever was. I want to compare Jacob's escape to conversion and to the Christian life. There are three things I want us to see: emancipation, expectancy and the enemy.

1. Emancipation

We read: *'Jacob put his children and his wives on camels, and he drove all his livestock ahead of him . . . to go to his father Isaac in the land of Canaan . . . crossing the River, he headed for the hill country of Gilead'* (Gen. 31:17, 18, 21). It must have been a wonderful moment. I suspect Jacob had to pinch himself every hour or so. 'Is it really true? Is it really over?' he must have wondered. He had 20 nightmarish years of being under the most tyrannical father-in-law that you can imagine. Not all that had happened had been bad. He was now a father and had a family, and God was with him in it all. He had been in bondage, but was now set free. I wonder if Jacob's situation rings a bell for someone reading this. You wouldn't want to tell anyone, but the truth is, what you feel inside could be best described as 'bondage', and you would love to be free.

Jacob was not only set free from bondage but also from bewilderment. Do you know what it is to be bewildered? You just cannot understand what is happening. It is as though you are in a nightmare although it is daytime. Have you ever been in a situation which is so awful, and where you feel what is happening is so bad that it is like a dream? You think, 'I just wish I could wake up and find that it is not true.' Yet you realize it *is* true, and you ask, 'Surely there is a better way to live? Surely there is more to life than what I've found?'

Jacob was also emancipated from beguilement. He had been deceived and tricked. The Bible says that the devil is the god of this world, who blinds people to the truth and thus tricks them (see 2 Cor. 4:4). Let me tell you how the devil tricks you. First, he convinces you that he himself doesn't exist because, as long as you can deny his existence, you will not be bothered to believe in anything beyond the level of nature. If you are reading this and you say, 'I don't really believe in a personal devil,' I have to tell you that the devil has already succeeded with you. Second, he wants you to be blind to the identity of Jesus Christ, to keep you from seeing that he is God's one and only Son. You see, the devil doesn't mind if you believe that Jesus was a good man. He doesn't mind if you believe that Jesus was the greatest teacher and prophet that ever lived. Do you know why the devil doesn't mind you believing that? It's so you will not see the beauty and the glory of the person Jesus really is. You know the phrase, 'damning with faint praise' – that is what the devil wants to do with Jesus. He wants you to be blind to the truth, and so he beguiles, he tricks, he deceives, he keeps you thinking that it's all going to be all right and you don't need to worry.

Jacob was also set free from blame. He heard Laban's sons saying, *'Jacob has taken everything our father owned and has gained all this wealth from what belonged to our father'* (Gen. 31:1). So it turned out that Laban and his sons were now blaming Jacob for everything. How does the great escape set us free from blame? The truth is that the blame that we deserve was put on Jesus.

2. Expectancy

There's one other thing from which Jacob made the great escape, and that was bleakness, the feeling that he had nothing to live for, because those 20 years were indeed horrible. In one respect Jacob didn't want to leave, because his brother Esau was after him and there was a sense in which he was safe there with Laban. But the time came when enough was enough. Something had changed. Jacob made the great escape because God told him to and had promised, *'I will be with you'* (Gen. 31:3). Now Jacob had something to look forward to. When God leads you to emancipation, he brings you to an expectancy that you do, indeed, have something to live for.

What then do you have to look forward to? Two things:

- When you die as a Christian you will go to heaven. We all have to die although we don't like to think about it. The Bible says, *'Man is destined to die once, and after that to face judgment'* (Heb. 9:27). What are you going to do when it comes to your time to die? Death is not the end, you live on. Do you know that, whatever else is true, one day *you* will go to heaven? I have one reason why I know I am going to heaven: it is that Jesus died for me on the cross, and I'm trusting totally in his death to get me there.

• Between now and the time you go to heaven God will be with you every day. Until now, Jacob must have felt like half a man; treated like he was treated, he didn't feel like he was a real person. Isn't it about time that you began feeling that you are a real human being – a real person? This is why the New Testament says that by faith you are made whole, complete. God said, *'I will never leave you or forsake you'* (Josh. 1:5). You will have a Bible and you can read it; it will become your most precious book. You will discover the thrill of talking to God, and you will reach the place where you just want to pray all the time. God listens and he will answer your prayers. He may not make you wealthy, but he will supply your every need (see Phil. 4:19).

3. Enemy

We read in verse 22, *'On the third day Laban was told that Jacob had fled. Taking his relatives with him, he pursued Jacob for seven days and caught up with him in the hill country of Gilead'* (Gen. 31:22). And so Jacob had pitched his tent in the hill country of Gilead when Laban overtook him. Do you know what this tells us? Your old enemy becomes your new enemy. You have a new enemy once you're converted – the devil. Laban was Jacob's enemy. Until now, Laban had Jacob where he wanted him – in his grip, but now Laban was on the attack. You need to know, that up until now the devil has been quiet because you have been in his grip, but once you profess faith in Jesus Christ, the devil doesn't like it, and the emancipation that gives you the expectancy will not come without conflict.

Before I end this chapter, I want to show you some things we learn about the devil from this story. The first thing is that when you are revived, the devil is revived. Jonathan Edwards used to say that when the church is revived, the devil is revived. And I can tell you now, the more that Westminster Chapel goes to pray, the more we can expect the devil to attack its leaders and deacons. The devil doesn't want us to pray, and the more we, as a church, are at prayer, the more conflict we can expect.

But the devil is under God's thumb. This is thrilling. Did you know that God talks to the devil? It says in verse 24, *'God came to Laban . . . and said to him, "Be careful not to say anything to Jacob, either good or bad."*' Elsewhere in the Bible we are told, God said to the devil, *'Have you considered my servant Job?'* (Job 1:8). That tells us that every single attack of the devil has already had a divine stamp of approval. I feel sorry for people who don't believe this, because they don't have a good theology of the sovereignty of God. It is wonderful to know that the devil is subject to God's authority. So whenever I sense a satanic attack, I think, 'Well, that's interesting.' But God knows I can take it. The devil can go so far, but *only* so far. I have discovered too that the devil always attacks me in an area of weakness. But this enables me to strengthen that area, so that the next time around he can't attack me in that place. I grow in grace because the devil attacks, even though satanic attacks are no fun.

Learn the secret that every satanic attack is with God's permission and has a purpose. Do you know what Job learned at the very end – it is so thrilling. Job said to the Lord, '*I know that . . . no plan of yours can be thwarted*' (Job 42:2). Indeed, no purpose of God can be threatened because God is more powerful than the devil. So that all that was happening now was that Laban was chasing Jacob rather like Pharaoh chased the children of Israel after they were set free. There is never emancipation without conflict. But it is always within the scope of God's permission.

Another thing about the devil is that he is an accuser. '*Laban said to Jacob, "What have you done? You've deceived me, and you've carried off my daughters like captives in war. Why did you run off secretly and deceive me?"*' (Gen. 31:26). The truth is that Jacob did all that God told him to do because earlier God said, 'Go, and go now!' You see, the devil will come along and accuse you, and he does this because you did the right thing. The devil wants you to feel stupid.

Furthermore, the devil is a liar. Laban said, 'I could have sent you away with joy and singing to the music of tambourines and harps' (see Gen. 31:27). Who believes that? But that is the devil. He will always lie to you. The devil will always make you think that you have done the most foolish thing by following Jesus Christ. This is the way he works. He always makes you think you have done something stupid.

Do you want to know *how* the devil attacks? The way it happens is always so surprising. The devil will use a close relationship to get at you. You would not have thought that the particular person that the devil will use would ever be capable of what they say to you, or do. He will use a relationship, and enter into your life, play upon your weakness. He will play upon the weakness of somebody you trust. And so we are told that Rachel, Jacob's wife, stole her father's household gods. She should not have done that. She was now a threat to Jacob and his future. Who would have thought that Rachel would do something like that? You will find that there will be somebody whom you respect, and to whom you may be close, and that person will do something they shouldn't. The devil will use that to discourage you. I tell you something that we are all learning: we must put our trust in

Jesus Christ alone, because even the best of God's people, and some - times those closest to us, will disappoint us sooner or later. In this case, Jacob was in difficulty because of what Rachel had done. She cleverly got out of it, but remember the devil will use a relationship to get at you.

There will be an enemy. Just know this: *'Greater is he that is in you, than he that is in the world'* (1 Jn. 4:4 AV).

20

When God Lets Us Down

Genesis 31:36–55

Why do I deal with this subject? Where will we find in this reading the subject of God letting us down? The answer is that it is the way Jacob felt. After 20 years of nightmarish bondage, he had made his escape only to have Laban overtake him. Why? After all, God told him to leave. He did, and thought that his troubles were over. At long last he was free of this awful man who made his life so miserable. But Laban had turned up with a vengeance and Jacob felt betrayed and let down.

Betrayed by God?

Perhaps you know the feeling of God letting you down. Do you know when it usually happens? Not only will it be at the worst moment that it could possibly happen, but it will be at the very time when you are doing your very best to get things right – the moment you seek to do God's will. Take the Christian who has strayed from the way or who has become lukewarm, who suddenly feels God talking to them, and they answer, 'Yes, Lord. I'll do what you say.' They fully expect God to say, 'Wonderful! Let me tell you what I am going to do to reward that act of obedience: I am just going to bless you; I am going to fill you with love, and you are going to feel my presence. I am going to cause all sorts of good things to happen to you because you are doing the right thing!'

Do you know, *that* is when God lets us down. Why? Well, it's always with a good reason. Always. For example, Paul couldn't go to Corinth when he promised the church there he would come. He let them down – but it was for a good reason (see 2 Cor. 1:23). Or take the time when Lazarus was ill and Mary and Martha sent word to Jesus, *'Lord, the one you love is sick',* and Jesus did nothing (Jn. 11:3). They were convinced that

Lazarus would be healed, just like that! They were certain that Jesus would stop everything and go like a shot and heal their brother. Instead, Jesus turned up four days after the funeral, and Martha said, '*Lord, if you had been here, my brother would not have died*' (v. 21). The Lord let them down. They felt betrayed, only to find out later that the Lord had a strategy in what he did. Jesus just turned up and said, 'Hey, I rather thought that raising Lazarus from the dead is a better idea than keeping him from dying.' So what God ended up doing was far greater than what they wanted to happen.

So God said to Jacob, 'Go! Leave at once!' But then Laban caught up. Jacob had unfinished business with Laban, and God decided the time had come that Jacob could say exactly what he had dreamed of saying for a long time. You can be sure that day after day Jacob would have said to himself, 'How can Laban treat me like this? It's not fair.' I dare say that Jacob had imagined conversations with Laban.

And if he had, he would have said something like this. Only now it was really happening.

I have been with you for twenty years now. Your sheep and goats have not miscarried, nor have I eaten rams from your flocks. I did not bring you animals torn by wild beasts; I bore the loss myself. And you demanded payment from me for whatever was stolen by day or night. This was my situation: The heat consumed me in the daytime and the cold at night, and sleep fled from my eyes. It was like this for the twenty years I was in your household. I worked for you fourteen years for your two daughters and six years for your flocks, and you changed my wages ten times. If the God of my father, the God of Abraham and the Fear of Isaac, had not been with me, you would surely have sent me away empty-handed. But God has seen my hardship and the toil of my hands, and last night he rebuked you (Gen. 31:38–42).

Jacob had long wanted to say that to Laban, but never had the courage to do it. Under different circumstances, he was able now to say it. He couldn't believe it was happening, but in God's timing Jacob was permitted to speak. I don't know if you have ever experienced a situation like this, where someone has hurt you: they've been cruel, maybe verbally, maybe physically, maybe they have manipulated you. It could have been a husband, a parent, the person you work for, or the person you have to live with. And you have imaginary conversations about things you would love to say.

Listen to these words of Jesus:

I know your deeds. See, I have placed before you an open door that no-one can shut. I know that you have little strength, yet you have kept my word and have not denied my name. I will make those who are of the synagogue of Satan, who claim to be Jews though they are not, but are liars – I will make them come and fall down at your feet and acknowledge that I have loved you (Rev. 3:8–9).

Time to Explain Yourself

Normally, we should never have to explain ourselves, but sometimes God presents us with the privilege. This is partly the meaning of Psalm 23:5: *'You prepare a table before me in the presence of my enemies.'*

Now, I have to tell you that we are not promised that God will deal with those who have hurt us in *this* life. Some years ago I was going through a pretty big trial, and I came across these words in 2 Thessalonians 1:5–7: *'All this is evidence that God's judgment is right, and as a result you will be counted worthy of the kingdom of God, for which you are suffering. God is just: He will pay back trouble to those who trouble you and give relief to you who are troubled.'*

I read that and I thought, 'Oh good, wonderful! Thank you Lord.'

And then the Lord said, 'Keep on reading.'

'This will happen when the Lord Jesus is revealed from heaven in blazing fire with his powerful angels.' I said, 'Lord, do I need to wait until then? Look what they're doing – look how they are treating so and so! Look, Lord – do something!'

I wish I could say it will always happen in this life, but what Jacob got to say to Laban would have come out eventually. Let me tell you why. God says, *'I, the LORD, love justice'* (Isa. 61:8). If you have been mistreated and have been hurt and you wonder if God sees it happening, I want you to know that God doesn't like it any more than you do, and one day he will correct the situation. It is only a matter of time.

Why Does God Let Us Down?

Why then does it appear that God lets us down? God said to Jacob , 'Go!' and Laban turned up. I said that Jacob didn't have the courage to tackle Laban, but there's another way of putting it. It may have been the opposite of that, that he wanted to say it, but God said, 'Leave it with me.' God appeared to let Jacob down so that Jacob could have his say.

The second reason he felt let down and God let it happen was that Jacob needed to learn something of God's timing. Listen to these words from Ecclesiastes 3:1–8:

> *There is a time for everything, and a season for every activity under heaven: a time to be born and a time to die, a time to plant and a time to uproot, a time to kill and a time to heal, a time to tear down and a time to build, a time to weep and a time to laugh, a time to mourn and a time to dance, a time to scatter stones and a time to gather them, a time to embrace and a time to refrain, a time to search and a time to give up, a time to keep and a time to throw away, a time to tear and a time to mend, a time to be silent and a time to speak, a time to love and a time to hate, a time for war and a time for peace.*

Ecclesiastes 3:11 says, *'He has made everything beautiful in its time.'*

Jacob must have asked, 'Is there no justice?' Why did he have to wait 20 years? You tell me. The answer, no doubt, is that there is justice and it is in God's timing. I suppose the hardest thing in the world we have to learn is just to wait. But I make you a promise, when God does step in it may not be to allow you to speak out as, at long last, Jacob was allowed to speak to Laban. But, in his own way, God will act because what he loves to do best is to vindicate the one who has been hurt. Wait for him to do it. It is only a matter of time.

William Carey

We must remember too that when God lets us down, he only *appears* to do so. At first it seems like betrayal. The greatest aviation breakthrough of this century was breaking the sound barrier. But you can do what scientists in their personal lives can't do. You can do what politicians and geniuses can't do: something that is greater than breaking the sound barrier, and that is breaking the betrayal barrier. Ten out of ten people in this world sooner or later feel that God betrays them. Nine out of ten shake their fists at God and say, 'Is that all the thanks I get? Forget it!' One out of ten are like Job, who could say, *'Though he slay me, yet will I hope in him'* (Job 13:15). And they press on and break through that betrayal barrier and they discover what's on the other side. They find out that when they said, 'God let me down', it was a rather hasty comment. God only *appeared* to let them down.

Did you ever hear of the story of William Carey, the first missionary of modern times, in the nineteenth century? Despite opposition from people in his own denomination, despite opposition from people all around him, he felt a burden to go to India to preach the gospel. He was opposed by his church, he was opposed by other Christians. Except for one or two who supported him, he stood alone. Well, he got on the boat at Southampton to go to India, but when the captain of the ship found out who William Carey was and why he was sailing, he put him off the ship in the Isle of Wight. How do you suppose William Carey felt?

And at first Jacob felt betrayed, and then God asked Jacob, 'Wouldn't you like to say a thing or two to this unjust man?' William Carey felt betrayed, but God asked him, 'Wouldn't you like to take your wife to India?'

'Oh yes,' he said.

So he went back to England and got his wife and they boarded a ship and sailed to India together.

God said, 'I wanted you to have her there. I only appeared to let you down.'

Carey had thought at first it wouldn't be best to take her. But God said, 'I want your wife to go with you.'

You see the little things that God does when we misread the signal, and too hastily say, 'Lord, how could you do that to me?'

God says, 'Lower your voice. I've got a plan.'

Eventual Clarification

The next thing to remember is that unjust people don't, ultimately, get away with this sort of treatment. They only appear to get away with it for a while. When you see injustice you will ask, 'Does God see?' Look at Isaiah 40:27: *'Why do you say, O Jacob, and complain, O Israel, "My way is hidden from the LORD; my cause is disregarded by my God"?'* And you think God doesn't notice! The truth is that Laban was now exposed before everyone.

A further reason God appeared to let Jacob down was because Rachel needed to be found out. She had stolen her father's household gods. What Rachel did was wrong. Rachel needed to be caught. She was spared being caught by her father and embarrassing Jacob, for she was a very clever woman and got out of the situation in a very shrewd manner. But Rachel, if she was to follow the true God, needed to know that it was wrong to have household gods, for such worship was demonic. Fortunately for Jacob and Rachel, Laban never knew; it was a narrow escape.

Perhaps God has spared you. Perhaps you know what it is to have come so close to getting caught for doing that which is wrong. Have you? Listen to me. God spared you. You should be so thankful that he would be so gracious to you. Jacob would learn later about his wife, and he needed to know that there was a serious defect in his beloved Rachel.

I want to bring this chapter to a close by showing you the most beautiful irony. Had this not happened, in all probability Laban wouldn't have come looking for Jacob. It was the way God overruled in the situation. It wasn't just that Jacob left suddenly. What angered Laban was his household gods were missing and that's what made him go looking for Jacob. You see, it just shows how the devil overreached himself, and it shows how God overrules that which is demonic and that which is motivated by false and satanic reasons to effect his purpose. Do you know this saying, 'The devil always overreaches himself'?

Supremely, this is what we learn about the crucifixion. Perhaps no one told you this before, but did you know that the devil was the architect of Jesus dying on the cross? It was the devil's idea. The Bible says that Satan entered into Judas Iscariot before he did that awful thing of betraying Jesus. Nobody could do what Judas did to Jesus except with the devil's help. And you wonder why there is evil today!

Do you want to know what happens when the devil is not stopped by the prayers of God's people? Look at what happened Rwanda in 1994, and you think that it can't happen to Britain? The time has come when the Church must intercede for this nation. Or if you think what you saw happening in Rwanda on television was bad, or what is available today in Britain is bad, 'you ain't seen nothing yet'. If the devil is not stopped (and it won't happen unless God's people intercede), you will be seeing a releasing of evil in this country such as you have never dreamed possible.

But when God's purpose is in effect, the devil always overreaches himself and that's what happened when Judas Iscariot betrayed Jesus and the chief priests took Jesus and ordered him to be crucified. What the devil didn't know is that this was God's plan all along. The plan was that Jesus would die on the cross for the sins of the world. *'For God so loved the world that he gave his one and only Son, that whoever believes in him shall not perish but have eternal life'* (Jn. 3:16).

Why did God let Jacob down? Rachel needed to be found out, and his way of doing it was to get Laban so angry that he came looking for Jacob. And God has now vindicated Jacob before everyone's eyes. God is the master of vindication.

One last point as to why it happened: God's word was at stake. You may recall that Jacob's father Isaac had given Jacob that blessing. *'May those who curse you be cursed and those who bless you be blessed'* (Gen. 27:29). Laban needed to be dealt with and, mark you, God doesn't forget his word. What I am asking you now is to believe his word. God doesn't let us down, he only *appears* to, and when we feel he has, it is just temporary.

21

When the War Is Over

Genesis 31:43–55

Jacob had spent 20 miserable years having to live with a man who had made his life a misery. It had been not unlike a war situation. In fact, Laban is a picture of the devil. So Jacob had been involved in spiritual warfare until, one day, God had said, 'Enough is enough. Go! Leave this land' (see Gen. 31:2). He had appeared to Jacob in a dream and the vision had united Jacob's family. So Jacob left. There was only one problem – Laban wouldn't take defeat. He came after Jacob. The war wasn't over.

It's interesting that whenever God does something powerfully then the devil tries to get in and will somehow use evil to parallel the good God is doing. As soon as Jesus was born, Herod sought to kill him. When God does something, the devil tries to stop it. So God had told Jacob to go, and now Laban had come after him. A similar thing had happened to the Children of Israel. Moses had told Pharaoh, 'Time is up. God says "Let my people go." ' And God's children were set free (see Exod. 12:31–50). You would have thought that would have been the end, but it wasn't. After three days, the Egyptians came after them (see Exod. 14:10–13). The devil won't give up easily. And now, Laban had caught up with Jacob – another confrontation.

There is a principle here. No war is won easily. Ever since the fall of man we have been engaged in a war with the devil. God could have finished off Satan long before. Have you ever wondered, since God has all the power and can stop evil – just like that – why he doesn't do it? Maybe you have asked why God allows tragic and evil things to happen. I don't know the answer, but one day we will find there has been a reason for everything.

You may wonder why God allows time to go on. Speaking person - ally, I'm glad he didn't end time before 1935 or I wouldn't have been born. I'm glad the Second Coming didn't happen before 1942 or I wouldn't have been converted. One reason why God allows history to continue may be that he would like you to be converted too. Do you realize what it would mean if the Second Coming of Jesus happened right now and for you to be in the state you are in? You think you've gone through hell. With the greatest respect, you haven't seen anything yet. When Jesus comes you will weep, you will wail, you will gnash your teeth and beg God for another chance. But after the Second Coming there will be no second chance. When Jesus comes – that is it. That is why the Bible says, *'Now is the time of God's favour, now is the day of salvation'* (2 Cor. 6:2). *'Do not harden your hearts'* (Heb. 3:8).

D-Day

D-Day was the day in the Second World War when it became certain the war would be won, although the fighting continued for another 11 months. Why then has God allowed time to continue? Ever since the fall of man we have been in a war with Satan and, for reasons I don't understand, God has decided to finish off Satan in two stages.

- Stage One: Calvary. Two thousand years ago when Jesus died on the cross it was D-Day, the beginning of the end.
- Stage Two: The Second Coming of Jesus. The war is then over.

Now we are looking at D-Day in the life of Jacob, when the victory was assured and never again would Laban bother Jacob, and never again would Jacob have to endure his cruelty. I want us to note three points.

First, we look at the question of obedience. Jacob was an obedient man: he wasn't perfect but when God told him to do something, he did it. God had said, 'Leave this country and go at once.' At the time, Jacob had two things going for him. (i) God was with him. (ii) He did what God wanted him to do. We all need to remember these things, for they apply to us as well as to Jacob. It brings to mind the old hymn 'Trust and Obey!'

> Trust and obey!
> For there's no other way
> To be happy in Jesus,
> But to trust and obey.
> J.H. Sammis.

Jesus was obedient to the Father and on the cross he cried, *'It is finished'* (Jn. 19:30). That meant the war was over as far as human history was concerned. That was D-Day because the work of Jesus was then com - pleted. It is all over as far as becoming a Christian is concerned. It doesn't mean there won't be a war. (Remember, fighting continued for some time after D–Day in the Second World War.) After Jesus died on the cross, the devil remained alive, but he is a conquered foe. He can only go so far (see 1 Jn. 5:18). The devil will tempt you, he will oppress you, he can get your attention. He will come as an angel of light, he will come as a roaring lion, he will come on you with fear, but the devil cannot harm you.

The Enemy Overreaches Himself

A second principle is that the enemy overreaches himself and becomes too ambitious. Let me put it like this. The worst thing Pharaoh ever did was to pursue Moses and the Children of Israel yet again. By doing so, he lost even more people. It was a stupid act. The worst thing Laban could have done was to pursue Jacob. Do you know why? Laban lost face before his daughters when, with all the family listening, Jacob gave him his opinion of how Laban had treated him during the years he had worked for him. Laban's response amounted to a tacit admission that everything Jacob said was true. He asked Jacob for a covenant. Why did he do this? It was because he feared Jacob's cleverness and ability. Laban feared Jacob's God. He feared the truth. He wanted to save face by making it appear that even he had a case. Jacob was a child of God, under God's protection, and this meant that he would be subject to a covenant devised by Laban.

Today we have the benefit of the death of Jesus but, as we have already seen, it was the devil who planned it, who inspired the chief priests in their jealousy and who entered into the heart of Judas Iscariot (see Lk. 22:3). Yet the worst thing that Satan could have done was to draw up a plan to get rid of Jesus of Nazareth because you can never take God by surprise. In 1 Corinthians 2:8 it says, *'None of the rulers of this age understand it, for if they had, they would not have crucified the Lord of glory.'* For what happened next had been the best kept secret in human history – and what God had in mind since the beginning of the world – that one day he would send his son Jesus Christ into the world to die on a cross. So he let the devil do what he thought was his own idea. God watched his Son shed his blood and Satan was doomed. His fate was sealed. Yes, he is still alive but Stage Two is coming. Read how John describes it in Revelation 20:10. *'The devil, who deceived them, was thrown into the lake of burning sulphur, where the beast and the false prophet had been thrown. They will be tormented day and night for ever and ever.'* Stage Two is just around the corner. *'You also must be ready, because the Son of Man will come at an hour when you do not expect him'* (Mt. 24:44). We are getting close to that moment when God will intervene.

The Oath

The third point to note is the oath, which is the heart of a covenant. Laban asked for a covenant. In this kind of covenant there are three things to note. (i) It's an agreement between two parties. (ii) Each takes an oath. (iii) It is sealed by sacrifice, by the shedding of blood.

'*Come now, let's make a covenant, you and I, and let it serve as a witness between us*' (Gen. 31:44). Here we see the agreement. '*So Jacob took an oath in the name of the Fear of his father Isaac. He offered a sacrifice there in the hill country and invited his relatives to a meal. After they had eaten, they spent the night there*' (v. 54).

God invites you to enter this covenant, and those who honour his Son, he will honour. You honour him in two ways: First, you honour the blood of Jesus shed on the cross and come to the place where you only trust in the blood of Jesus. Second, you honour Jesus by telling others of your decision to follow him. Jesus said, '*Whoever acknowledges me before men, the Son of Man will also acknowledge him before the angels of God* (Lk. 12:8).

One last thing, when Jacob took the oath, he took it in the name of the Fear of his father Isaac. Why? Well, whenever you take an oath, you swear by the greater to show you are telling the truth. So Jacob showed his respect for his father – his respect for his father's blessing. But there was more. It was an invitation to bring down the wrath of God upon himself if he violated the covenant. There is something here that has gripped me and that I have to share with you. Verse 52 says: *This pillar is a witness, that I will not go past this heap to your side to harm you and you will not go past this heap and pillar to my side to harm me.*' It was the end. Jacob and Laban could no longer interfere with each other.

22

Visiting Angels

Genesis 32:1–12

We are at the point in Jacob's life when he entered a new era. Laban was now behind him. The nightmare was over. And with Laban out of the way, Jacob suddenly remembered another problem that, for a long time, he had been able to keep at bay. He said to himself, 'Oh, no! I almost forgot – Esau!' Jacob had unfinished business with his twin brother, you might say. His last memory of Esau wasn't very happy. Remember, Rebekah, Jacob's mother, had told Jacob, *'Your brother Esau is consoling himself with the thought of killing you'* (Gen. 27:42). This was what had caused Jacob to leave home in the first place, but for 20 years he had been able to put it out of his mind. Now Jacob was gripped by the thought that he was returning to that area where he could run into Esau who, no doubt, knew something of his brother's whereabouts. Jacob knew that next he must face Esau.

Could it be you are like that? You are 'between the times', at the end of one era and the beginning of the next? You have the feeling something is at last behind you, only to find that facing you is a new challenge, and it is a great challenge indeed.

A Dramatic Experience

Unexpectedly, however, Jacob had an unusual experience with God, and we read, *'Jacob also went on his way, and the angels of God met him. When Jacob saw them, he said, "This is the camp of God!" So he named that place Mahanaim'* (Gen. 32:1–2).

1. It was a passive experience

It was not something Jacob planned or made to happen; he didn't expect it. It was something that happened to him.

One of the ways (but not the only way) that we can distinguish the truth from what is false is whether an experience just happened to you or whether it was something you made happen. You see, what makes an experience authentic is when it is something God does.

2. It was a pivotal experience

It came at the end of one era and the beginning of a new one. Sometimes, when you have come through an ordeal and are preparing to enter a new era, God will bless you in an unusual way. He did this with Jesus. Have you ever noticed that after Jesus was tempted by the devil in the wilderness, and after he had fasted for forty days, we read in Matthew 4:11: *'The devil left him, and angels came and attended him'*?

Why would God send angels to us? It's partly to reward us and partly to let us know he has been with us and will be with us from now on. Yet maybe the fact we have an unusual experience means there lies an unusual ordeal ahead. As far as I know God doesn't give unusual experiences like this because he wants us to have fun and say, 'Isn't this great!' In Jacob's case, he was going to experience an unusual kind of suffering and this is why God sent angels to him.

3. It was a preparatory experience

I recall a line of the well-known hymn by Charles Wesley:

Changed from glory into glory . . .

Do you know that usually a graduation from one level of glory to another is precipitated by trial? Whenever I am going through an unusual trial, an attack of the devil for instance, I know one thing beyond a shadow of a doubt, that when it is over it will be wonderful. I am going to be at such a high level spiritually, and I am getting to know God in an intimate way, tough though it is at the time. Listen. If God sends a measure of suffering to you, I don't say it's fun, but you have been marked as a vessel to be used.

This then was Jacob's experience. If Laban was a nightmare, Esau had become a symbol of something even worse. A great trial is usually preceded by a lesser trial but which seems great at the time. Laban was cruel, but at least Jacob's life had been secure. Now Jacob faced a life-or-death situation. God knew Jacob realized that and he sent angels. He didn't just send them – he let Jacob see them.

Visits from Angels

God has sent angels to me. I have no doubt about that. It happened on 16 January 1985. At the time I faced the greatest trial of my life. I was at the end of my tether and so discouraged. I looked at Louise, my wife, and we shrugged our shoulders at one another. It looked like the end. Suddenly, at my right hand, I could touch what I knew to be a presence. I couldn't quite see the presence, but I knew it was almost like a pillar. If the Lord had made it plainer, I sensed it would be golden. The Lord spoke; I won't say it was in an audible voice but it was just as clear. He said, 'Don't trust in your own understanding. Trust me.' And do you know, within an hour, the whole situation was turned around! When I get to heaven and see a video replay of all we went through, I guarantee I shall see it was an angel right there.

A few years ago, I met a lady who often sees angels. I asked her, 'Is it true you see angels?' She replied that indeed she did. 'What do they look like?' I asked.

'Well,' she said, 'they are different. I don't always see the same one. Sometimes one will come and eat at the table with us. Once, when I was in bed, an angel sat in the chair at the end of the bed.'

I asked her why she thought they visited her.

'I guess it's because I need them,' she answered.

I believed her, and knowing something of her situation, I could believe that indeed she needed their presence.

I recall my grandmother speaking about her experience of angels. It was at a time when her daughter, my mother, died. Just before she died, my Grandma McCurley said she knew an angel came into the room. She did not feel happy about it as she sensed it was the death angel coming to warn that my mother would be going to heaven. Two weeks after my mother's death, my grandma said that as she was lying on her bed (she couldn't remember if she was asleep, awake or halfway between the two), a big angel came into the room and hovered over her, giving her the greatest assurance.

The truth is we all have an angel with us. At least one. I can prove it. Psalm 34:7 says, *'The angel of the LORD encamps around those who fear him.'* How do you know you have an angel with you? If you fear God, the Bible says you do. Do you fear God? That means you want to please him. That means when you do wrong you feel sorry. On the other hand, are you able to do things that flagrantly go against what you know is right? It doesn't bother you? No fear of God there, well, no promise of an angel either. As surely as you fear the Lord, you've got an angel. In fact, sometimes more than one, because in Psalm 91:9–11 we read these words:

> *If you make the Most High your dwelling – even the LORD, who is my refuge – then no harm will befall you, no disaster will come near your tent. For he will command his angels concerning you to guard you in all your ways; they will lift you up in their hands, so that you will not strike your foot against a stone.*

If we could see clearly with our spiritual eyes right now, what a sight would meet them! If only for a moment we were able to penetrate what is really here. Apparently, Elisha was one who could see angels quite often. Once, there was someone next to him who was frightened by a particular situation, and Elisha said, 'I wish you could see what I see.' He then touched him and said, 'Now look.' His companion replied, *'Those who are with us are more than those who are with them.'* The truth is that we all have angels but not all of us can see them (see 2 Kgs. 6:15–17).

Jacob and the Angels

I want us to see three things about Jacob's experience:

1. The initiation by angels

The angels of God met him. He did not seek them. What makes an experience authentic is that God takes the initiative. To put it another way, the difference between natural religion and the Christian faith is who initiates what you do. You won't get to heaven by living a good life, for God demands *perfect* righteousness not your best efforts. Are you prepared to tell me your good works meet God's standards? Natural religion would make you think so – a kind of 50/50 situation where God does so much, you do so much, and you attain a certain level and you know you're in! Would you ever know for sure that you had reached that standard? The difference between salvation by works and the salvation described in the New Testament is who initiates what you do.

- *'He chose to give us birth through the word of truth'* (Jas. 1:18).
- *'But we ought always to thank God for you, brothers loved by the Lord, because from the beginning God chose you to be saved through the sanctifying work of the Spirit'* (2 Thess. 2:13).
- *'He who began a good work in you will carry it on to completion until the day of Christ Jesus'* (Phil. 1:6).

Do you really think you will get to heaven because of what you do? Then listen: you are going to have to reckon with this verse: *'For it is by grace you have been saved, through faith – and this not from yourselves, it is the gift of God – not by works, so that no-one can boast'* (Eph. 2:8–9). God doesn't want anyone to boast. He wants all the glory.

Jacob could never boast about his experience, saying, 'Look what I did!' Rather, he was humbled and in awe. He said, 'This is the camp of God.' He was so grateful. God wants to do something for you of which you could never boast. Isaiah 42:8 says this: *'I am the LORD; that is my name! I will not give my glory to another.'*

Speaking of angels, in Revelation 5:2 we read that the angel cried out, *'Who is worthy to break the seals and open the scroll?'*

John said, 'I looked in heaven, I looked on earth, but nobody was worthy. I began to weep' (see vv. 3–5). Do you know that when he said, 'I looked in heaven', that means he saw Abraham, he saw Daniel, he saw everybody in heaven and none were worthy. Then he saw an angel, who said, 'Stop crying, John. One is worthy, but only one – The Lion of the Tribe of Judah, the root of David.' He is Jesus Christ, the God-man who, alone, bore our sins at Calvary.

You have to come to the place where you affirm what God did for you by sending his Son to die on the cross.

So the angels took the initiative in Jacob's life. He now faced a trial so great that he needed an experience only God could provide. If you knew there was a tough ordeal around the corner, would you want anything else but what is authentic? One day, there will be an ordeal facing you: you are going to die. What will matter then is whether you have put your trust in God's word and in his Son.

2. The identification of angels

How did Jacob know they were angels? Well, he had seen them before and named the place where he met them, Bethel. When it happened again, he called the place *'Mahanaim'* meaning 'two camps'. You could call him a sentimentalist.

I am like that. I could never forget where I was in the USA, just ten miles outside Nashville, when the Lord met me so powerfully that I have never got over it (see Chapters 23 and 33). There have also been other times when I have had similar experiences. You may ask how I know such an experience is authentic. The Bible calls it the 'peace of God': it is warm, it is restful, it is sweet, devoid of fear and guilt. There are some reading this who have known this feeling and who have lost it. Others have never experienced it. They have never come to the place where they have said, 'This is Jesus and him alone.'

Jacob knew it was for real. He had had a taste and nothing less would satisfy.

3. The insufficiency of angels

The angels' visit didn't provide Jacob with a permanent peace because he was told, 'Esau is coming to meet you.' We read in Genesis 32:7: *'In great fear and distress Jacob divided the people who were with him into two groups.'* He thought that if Esau came and attacked one group, the other group might escape. This shows that his experience with angels didn't take away all his fears.

The reason for the insufficiency of angels is that God does not want anything to compete with what he alone can do. Angels don't compete with God. They are impartial and only want us to worship him. One difference between an angel and the Holy Spirit is that an angel cannot get inside you, but the Holy Spirit can. Angels are not God but the instruments of God.

Now Jacob needed more than an angel. He needed God. He needed to come to the place where he saw what God was able to do, in his own perfect timing, by his Spirit and by his power. In God's time, he will bring you to that place where his word will grip you and arrest you. You cannot shake it off. I've known some who, when God starts dealing with them, think they are losing their mind. It's called 'conviction'. And when God acts, it's out of your hands.

23

When Your Back Is Against the Wall

Genesis 32:1–21

In Jacob's life an old fear had been revived – the fear of Esau. Jacob decided to face the problem like this:

> *Jacob sent messengers ahead of him to his brother Esau . . . He instructed them: 'This is what you are to say to my master Esau: "Your servant Jacob says, I have been staying with Laban and have remained there till now. I have cattle and donkeys, sheep and goats, menservants and maidservants. Now I am sending this message to my lord, that I may find favour in your eyes" ' (Gen. 32:3–5).*

This mission to win the favour of the brother he offended was all he lived for now. You have to agree this was a noble thing to do. There is nothing better than to make up with the person with whom you have fallen out. And it is all the better if you have taken the initiative. Can you think of anybody who has anything against you, and you know it is within your power to do something about it? Maybe you don't have the courage or the honesty to admit you did something wrong. The Bible says if you know someone who has something against you, you are to go to them and put matters right.

Perhaps you fear someone who, if they told all they knew about you, could harm you or even destroy you. Yet there is something worse than this – the realization of what God knows about you. When was the last time you came face to face with the real problem, and that is your relationship with him? It is more important that you be reconciled with God than with a person you fear, because I have to tell you, you can make it up with them, feel better, and still lose your soul.

So now, Jacob sent word to Esau, and what do you think his reaction to Jacob's message was? Verse 6 says: *'When the messengers returned to Jacob, they said, "We went to your brother Esau, and now he is coming to meet you, and four hundred men are with him." '* Jacob was frightened. He could only think one thing: that Esau was coming to attack. He knew his back was against the wall. He had a few relatives; he had a few people working for him, but they were no match for four hundred armed men.

But then, I ask a question: What was God's purpose in all this? We know God was with Jacob, and because of his experience with God in his past, Jacob also knew this. Wasn't that enough for him? Why do you suppose he panicked like this? He had everything going for him. Are you like this? Do you panic at the drop of a hat? Like Jacob, you are without excuse. Jacob should have known he could not fail. First, he had the patriarchal blessing of his father Isaac; he had the oath of his grandfather Abraham. Then there was Bethel, the marvellous deliver - ance from Laban, and next the visitation of the angels. Why would Jacob be in a state of panic? Well, we know this: God allowed it. And I think I know why. Verse 9 says, *'Then Jacob prayed.'*

Jacob's Prayer

> *O God of my father Abraham, God of my father Isaac, O L ORD, who said to me, 'Go back to your country and your relatives, and I will make you prosper,' I am unworthy of all the kindness and faithfulness you have shown your servant. I had only my staff when I crossed this Jordan, but now I have become two groups. Save me, I pray, from the hand of my brother Esau, for I am afraid he will come and attack me, and also the mothers with their children* (Gen. 32:9–11).

When was the last time you turned to the Lord and waited before him and prayed with all your heart? The Bible says, *'If . . . you seek the L ORD your God, you will find him if you look for him with all your heart and with all your soul'* (Deut. 4:29). I'm not talking of a little prayer such as 'Bless me, Lord. Help me get me through this day.' There is praying and there is *praying*.

Let me tell you of my own experience. Many years ago, I was pastor of my first church, the Church of the Nazarene, in Palmer, Tennessee. I was on my way back to Trevecca College on a Monday morning and God seemed a thousand miles away. Yet I had such agony on my spirit, and I was praying, but I didn't think God was taking any notice. Suddenly, I sensed at my right hand that the Lord was there interceding for me. He was praying. And I began to realize God loves me more than I love myself. Not only was he near, he was more concerned for me than I was for myself. That day, when I was praying in such agony, I discovered God for myself. I had had Christian parents and had been brought up in a Christian home, but it was in that moment I found God to be so real.

Jacob might have had everything going for him. Yet there was one deficiency in his life and that was prayer. God does you a favour when he lets an Esau come into your life – someone who is out to get you when your back is against the wall. It is God's way of getting your attention so you will pray, and I mean PRAY!

There are four things I want you to see about Jacob's prayer.

- It was a heavy prayer. He was praying with a burden. He was desperate. Peter could say, *'You may have had to suffer grief in all kinds of trials'* (1 Pet. 1:6). Could it be you are like that – you are 'in heaviness'? Moses' back was against the wall. In Exodus 14, when the Egyptians were pursuing the Israelites, he found himself in a dead-end. There was no escape in any direction, and before them was the Red Sea. Moses cried out to the Lord (see v. 15). Have you come to that? When was the last time you were brought to tears?
- It was a humble prayer. Jacob said, *'I am unworthy of all the kindness and faithfulness you have shown your servant'* (Gen. 32:10). When is the time going to come when you stop blaming everyone else for your problem? Isn't it time you came to terms with the fact you are unworthy? You have lived all this time with a chip on your shoulder. You have blamed everyone but yourself for the situation you are in. I understand how you feel, but it is the wrong way forward. I'm asking you to climb down.
- It was an honest prayer. When Jacob said, *'I am unworthy of all the kindness and faithfulness you have shown your servant,'* he was surely right about that. He was not speaking out of false modesty, he was telling the truth. He had manipulated his brother out of his birthright, he had stolen his brother's blessing, but he was still being blessed by God. Could it be you know you've done everything that is wrong? Could it be that you know that God has been good to you and you are not worthy of that goodness?
- It came from the heart. Perhaps you haven't been converted because, although you have heard it all, the message has remained in your mind and has not reached your heart. You have never come to the place where your back is against the wall and your heart prays. This is what needs to happen. The apostle Paul said, *'If you confess with your mouth, "Jesus is Lord," and believe in your heart that God raised him from the dead, you will be saved'* (Rom. 10:9).

Jacob with his back to the wall was praying for two things. First, he was praying for a miracle; it would take a miracle for his brother not to kill him. Let's face it, it would take a miracle for anything to stop you from going on as you are, living as you do. Second, he was praying for mercy. Do you want to know how to be saved? You pray for mercy, knowing you have nothing to offer, no bargaining power. As long as you feel that you have something to offer God because you are pretty special, you will remain as lost as ever you were. You are not even close to salvation. A person who becomes a Christian is one who knows they have nothing to offer God. They just say, 'God, there is no reason you should save me unless you just want to be good to me. I need mercy.'

Remember how Jesus described two men who went into the Temple to pray, one a publican, the other a Pharisee. The Pharisee is the one who says, 'Lord, I thank you I am not like others, especially this publican here. I don't do this. I don't do that. Thank you that I am not like them.' The publican said only, *'God, have mercy on me, a sinner'* (Lk. 18:13).

That's what Jacob was praying for. It was for mercy.

24

Know Your Friend

Genesis 32:13–32

Genesis 32:24 says: *'So Jacob was left alone, and a man wrestled with him till daybreak.'* This term, 'to wrestle', appears significantly in both the Old and the New Testaments. In the New Testament it refers to wrestling with the devil; in the Old Testament it refers to wrestling with God. In this Old Testament passage, although, at first, Jacob did not know who it was, at some point he realized his opponent was his friend. That is what I want us to see about this remarkable story.

Now here is the question: At what point did Jacob realize that the one who had appeared to him to be an enemy was really his friend? Martin Luther used to say, 'You must know God as an enemy before you can regard him as a friend.' The only way you could ever like him is to see him as Jacob saw him – as one who was against him.

Life generally, also the Christian life, is made up of turning points. Jacob had had many of those. We are going to study now what was a major turning point in Jacob's life.

Whatever had happened in Jacob's life, the best was yet to come. For you too, the most wonderful experience you will ever have is to discover that the God of the Bible, who was your enemy, is really your friend. I want you to know that the very God of the Bible will send a particular situation along where you will feel everyone is against you – that *he* is against you. Whenever this happens, it is a sign he is wanting to bless you not, as it may first seem, to harm you. One of my favourite verses in the Bible is Psalm 84:11 which says, *'No good thing does he withhold from those whose walk is blameless.'* I live by that verse, knowing that God will not keep me from having anything that is good. When God withholds something from me, I know it is because he has something better.

Take Lazarus, for example, who, as we saw earlier, was a close personal friend of Jesus and who became gravely ill. His two sisters Martha and Mary sent word to Jesus, saying, 'Your friend Lazarus is sick!' They knew that Jesus would stop whatever he was doing and go to heal him. For Lazarus, Jesus would come immediately. But Jesus continued what he was doing. As a matter of fact, Lazarus died and Jesus didn't show up until four days after the funeral. Mary and Martha were hurt and Martha said, *'Lord, if you had been here, my brother would not have died'* (Jn. 11:21). But Jesus raised Lazarus from the dead and, as a result, God showed his glory.

Jacob had sent his family onto the other side. Maybe he would never see them again. God had deserted him. Now he was wrestling and struggling alone to survive. Yet this turned out to be the greatest experience of his life. God still leads people in the same way. Whatever he allows to happen, always happens on schedule and has a purpose. God has a great idea in mind. We may not understand; we may weep. When Lazurus died and Martha and Mary wept, Jesus wept with them (see Jn. 11:33–35). He didn't scold them or say, 'How dare you treat me like this! Don't you know I have a good idea for you?' Then, after they had this time of grieving, he said, 'Come here and watch.'

Similarly, this experience would turn out to be the greatest thing that could ever happen to Jacob. And he needed something to happen to him. Jacob could have said, 'Don't tell me something needs to happen to me: I'm God's chosen – that's enough.' Maybe he could have said, 'I don't need anything to happen to me: I had an experience at Bethel 20 years ago. I'm telling you that experience was good enough for me.' He could have added, 'I have even seen angels lately.' Yet Jacob needed something to happen to him.

Are you prepared to admit something needs to happen to you? Something needs to happen to all of us. Maybe the only way for us to see it is when God puts us into a wrestling match and when we don't understand what is happening. But he does this, not because he is against us, but because he wants to bless us.

How do we know that Jacob needed something to happen to him? Well, I will prove his viewpoint was governed by wrong assumptions. Up to this point, most of Genesis 32 describes Jacob planning a conversation with Esau which, as it turned out, never took place at all. He planned a reconciliation with his brother. *'He selected a gift for his brother Esau: two hundred female goats and twenty male goats, two hundred ewes and twenty rams, thirty female camels with their young, forty cows and ten bulls, and twenty female donkeys and ten male donkeys'* (Gen. 32:13–15).

Jacob held imaginary conversations with Esau and tried to guess how Esau might respond. It says in verse 19: *'He also instructed the second, the third [servants] and all the others who followed the herds: "You are to say the same thing to Esau when you meet him. And be sure to say, 'Your servant Jacob is coming behind us.' "* For he thought, "I will pacify him with these gifts I am sending on ahead." '

The word 'pacify' in the Hebrew language is the same one that means to 'atone'. It means to 'cover'. The blood of Jesus covers: it atones for our sins. Jacob thought the way to pacify his enemy was to appease him with gifts. I wonder if in your search for God you have thought, 'I will pacify God. I will give him money. I will give up that bad habit. I will attend church more regularly.' I need to tell you that if you are having such imaginary conversations with God (rather like the ones Jacob planned with Esau), thinking you can get on good terms with him this way, then this is as unnecessary as everything Jacob was doing. Nothing happened like Jacob thought it would. Nothing.

There is only one way to get right with God and that is to realize that two thousand years ago God's Son died on the cross and pacified God by shedding his blood. They nailed spikes through his hands and feet and pressed a crown of thorns into his head, and his blood flowed down. And God will not forgive sin except on the basis of the blood Jesus shed on the cross. That is the only way you can be saved.

Now why did this man come out of the blue and jump on Esau? It was because Jacob needed a new thing to happen to him; he needed to learn his real problem was not with Esau – his problem was with God. You may have thought that your problem is some enemy, some person, a particular situation, or habit. You imagine if this could be taken care of you would be set. 'If I could get that particular job, I'd be happy. If that person were out of the way, everything would be wonderful.' Not so. Your problem is with God.

We need to note three things about Jacob's experience:

- He was alone. You too need to discover the reality of God for yourself. You need to know that he is so real that even if no one else believes in him, you believe. You need to come to the place where you see how real God is, how faithful he is, and how much he loves you. You need to discover he's your friend. But, as with Jacob, God appears initially as your enemy.
- It was dark. Perhaps for you too, it is night. There is darkness inside you and the outlook is black.
- A man jumped on Jacob out of the blue. Perhaps, out of the blue, something has happened to you and you have lost control: you don't know in which direction your life is going.

So Jacob felt he was bridled, boxed in, controlled and bound. He felt betrayed and that God had let him down. He was alone and was wrestling for his life. There was no way forward. Sooner or later, every one of us will feel God has betrayed us. I speak as a pastor of many years experience. Sadly, nine out of ten resent it so much that they never find out God was their friend.

Something happened to Jacob in this process. We are not told what exactly. But when we get to heaven, we will be able to see it all through his eyes. Jacob started out wrestling with an enemy, but at some point during the night he began to realize this was his friend. *'The man said, "Let me go, for it is daybreak."*

'But Jacob replied, "I will not let you go unless you bless me" ' (Gen. 32:26).

For some reason, knowing this experience was the best thing that ever happened to him, Jacob begged for a blessing and received it.

Have you felt God was against you and all that has happened to you is proof he doesn't care? You can be like nine out of ten others and resent it, or you can be like Jacob, who said, *'I will not let you go unless you bless me.'* You can be just like that and go with God even if you haven't understood all that has happened. You can say, 'If Jesus Christ died for me on the cross and shed his blood, and all I need do is to receive him into my life, he can have me and my future.'

25

Struggling with God

Genesis 32:22–32

To come straight to the point, I want to identify your problem. Your real problem, or struggle, does not lie with other people, with your back - ground or culture, with your financial situation or even with yourself – your problem lies with God.

The Only True God

Many years ago, I read a book supposedly about God in an age of atheism. It was required reading for a seminary course in theology I was taking then. At first glance, I thought, 'Wow, this must be a wonderful book!' I was so aware we are living in an atheistic, secular age, and I thought that here was an author who was going to show us how to convince an atheist there is a God, and show us how to make God real to him. But do you know what the book was about? It was showing the atheist that his conception of God was not the God who is really there. To put it another way, the author brought God down to such a human level that the atheist suddenly discovers, 'Yes, I can believe in a God like that!' The book was a complete rejection of the God of the Bible, bringing God right down to the level of man.

Having read such a book, the atheist easily finds he has no problem with being a Buddhist, he could go along with Hinduism, and have no difficulty with New Age beliefs or any other religion. The only religion he would hate is that of the God of the Bible, and the belief that Jesus Christ, God's Son, is the only means of man's salvation. That is why Jonathan Edwards could speak about man being 'God's natural enemy' or of God being 'man's natural enemy'. Let me put it another way. To the person who has never been converted, the true God is distasteful, abhorrent, awful. People hate the God of the Bible. Then someone comes along and says, 'That's not God.' I have to tell you that the God of the Bible *is* the only true God.

That is your problem. That is why a person has to be converted – not to any other religion, because they are all natural religions. That means, by nature, you can just accept their beliefs. Every religion in the world has one thing in common: salvation comes through your own efforts. The difference between natural religion and the God of the Bible is who initiates what you do.

We naturally hate the God of the Bible. We hate every thing about him. There's nothing I could ever say to make you like him. A person has to be converted, and the way of doing that is not by the preacher trying to make God look any better, or reading a book which says, 'Look, we've just misunderstood. God is not quite so bad.' I want to tell you God is even worse than many have thought.

For one thing, this generation hasn't a clue what the wrath of God is like. Jonathan Edwards preached a sermon in Enfield, Connecticut, in 1741 that lives on in infamy, or in glory, depending how you look at it. When the sermon was printed it was called 'Sinners in the Hands of an Angry God'. Historians tell us that for about two hours the Spirit of God fell on that place and that there was such conviction that strong men literally held on to the pews to stop themselves from falling into hell. Many say, 'Well, in those days people were so emotional.' But Jonathan Edwards preached the same sermon two weeks later to those who had never heard it, in a place several miles away, and nothing happened at all.

In the New Testament we read that God gave a taste of this when John the Baptist preached the message, 'Flee from the wrath to come'(see Mt. 3:7). The Holy Spirit came with such power everyone was terrified.

You may hate this God, but he is the one with whom you are going to have to come to terms. You will never be converted when you bring him down to human level and say, 'Well, he's not so bad after all.' Conversion is something that happens to you inside and comes through what the Bible calls preaching. The God of the Bible can be summed up as the God of Glory, the God of Justice, the God of Wrath. 'Wait a minute,' you say. 'What about the God of Love?' I'll answer that. Martin Luther called John 3:16 'the Bible in a nutshell': *'For God so loved the world that he gave his one and only Son, that whoever believes in him, shall not perish but have eternal life.'* It means God loved the world so much, he gave his Son to die on a cross so that anybody can be saved, but only if they affirm his Son as being who he is.

Jacob knew the true God, but not very well. He accepted the God of his father Isaac. He accepted the God of his grandfather Abraham. He had discovered their God for himself, and God had given him small tokens of himself, but Jacob had a lot more to learn. This is a message, I think, that fits everyone. Many know God, but not very well, and they suddenly discover they have a lot to learn.

The Ways of God

The divine taste

Peter put it like this: *'You have tasted that the Lord is good'* (1 Pet. 2:3). This means that for the sake of Jesus, God, the true God (not the one whom you have imagined), will be gracious to you, and all the sins that you have ever committed will be washed away as though they had never been. I am convinced the greatest pain in the world is the pain of guilt. God will enable you to cope with the guilt that you felt. It is the most wonderful experience in the world.

Jacob had that taste. He discovered that. He felt so guilty, and indeed he had a lot to feel guilty about. He had done everything wrong and he couldn't imagine how, in the light of the way he lived, God would forgive him. And lo and behold, it turned out that God loved him. Jacob had a taste, but a taste was all it was. He had a lot to learn about God, and the learning came with a struggle. A real struggle. A struggle so great. A man suddenly leaped on him in the dark when he was alone, and Jacob wondered what was happening. He didn't know God was at work. Have you had a taste of the Lord? Have you found how gracious God is?

The divine toughness

Verse 24 says: *'So Jacob was left alone, and a man wrestled with him till daybreak. When the man saw that he could not overpower him, he touched the socket of Jacob's hip so that his hip was wrenched as he wrestled with the man.'* You see, Jacob needed to learn something more about the true God and it was going to be tough. God doesn't transport us out of the real world. The Christian life must be lived in a tough world. Take, for example, the eagle who forces her young out of the nest. God does that. And Jacob, who thought he knew God, is suddenly discovering something about God he had never seen before. God was being tough and he was unprepared for it. Every Christian finds out sooner or later God seems to desert them and appears in a way they fail to recognize. When things start to go wrong, we think, 'Oh, I am not pleasing the Lord. If I were, these things would not be happening to me. God is angry with me.' Here was Jacob, in the middle of the night, wrestling with someone who appeared to be stronger than he was. The same God was still at work with Jacob, but it appeared that Jacob was being deserted.

Christians and non-Christians alike have all asked the same question: 'Why does God allow unpleasant things to happen to me?' Well, it's a divine toughness, and this was what Jacob was having to learn. He needed to understand he could trust God when he didn't understand what was happening. Is your faith so weak that you can only trust God when you see you have a grip on events and everything is going just right for you? You may say in good times, 'Oh, isn't God wonderful!' Yet you will not know the real God until you have been deserted, when everything is wrong, and you still love him. That is what God wants to teach you and me.

The divine tease

Another thing to understand is something which for want of a better phrase I call the 'divine tease'. I speak of the playful, yet deadly serious way in which God provokes us. Let me explain. When the angel said, *'Let me go, for it is daybreak,'* he was teasing Jacob. He did not really want Jacob to let him go. What if Jacob had let him go? It would have been the worst thing he could have done. In your struggle has God ever said to you, 'Let go.' Have you ever responded by thinking, 'Lord, if that's what you want, I'll let you go.' Why would God do that? Well, he's teasing you. Now, let's be fair. It's a kind of deception. We meet then a new phrase – the 'tease barrier'. Have you broken it? Have you met with the angel who says, *'Let me go'*? If you answer 'OK', you have never discovered what could have been yours.

Let me give you some examples of the tease barrier. Jesus used it. The disciples were out on the lake in a boat while Jesus had remained on the shore. The Bible says, *'He was alone on the land. He saw the disciples straining at the oars, because the wind was against them. About the fourth watch of the night he went out to them, walking on the lake. He was about to pass by them . . .'* (Mk. 6:48). There they were, scared to death in the middle of the lake, and Jesus went out to them, for no reason but to help them. Imagine being out in the middle of the lake and Jesus turns up but *keeps on going!* Why did he do that? He was teasing them.

We find another instance in John 6:5. When Jesus looked up and saw a great crowd of people coming, he said to Philip, *'Where shall we buy bread for these people to eat?'* He was teasing them. John explained, *'He only asked this to test him, for he already had in mind what he was going to do'* (v. 6).

There is another example in Luke 24:28. The risen Jesus joined two followers on the road to Emmaus. They did not recognize him and, as they approached their destination, Jesus made as if he were going further. Why? He was teasing them. They said, 'Oh, don't go, please.' They broke the tease barrier.

What God wants to teach us to do, when he comes to us in that manner, is to break through the tease barrier because he loves us so much. But most people don't do it. I am challenging you to want God so much that nothing stops you, even if you feel he is saying, 'Now, it's all right. Let me go. It's enough.'

We read this passage in 2 Kings 2:1–2:

*When the LORD was about to take Elijah up to heaven in a whirlwind, Elijah and
Elisha were on their way from Gilgal. Elijah said to Elisha, 'Stay here; the LORD
has sent me to Bethel.'*

*But Elisha said, 'As surely as the LORD lives and as you live, I will not leave you.'
So they went down to Bethel.*

What was Elijah doing? He was teasing Elisha, because Elijah knew
Elisha wanted a double portion of his spirit. What had happened was
that Elisha discerned this divine tease.

I recall something that happened to me some time ago. I was praying.
My prayer list is quite a long one and I was so busy that week. I had
to finish a book I was writing, prepare two complete sets of notes for
a school of theology, and on top of that I had preaching engagements.
I felt Jesus would understand if I put my lengthy prayer list aside for a
later date. At that point, a wonderful thing happened. It seemed as if
Jesus was saying, 'I am just going to walk on by you.' I understood it
was like when Jacob was wrestling with the Lord. The Lord didn't want
Jacob to stop, and he didn't want me to stop praying because I was
busy. I said, 'Lord, I'll get everything done, but I am going to stay in
prayer.'

The Bible says if you want to know the Lord, if you seek him with
all your heart, you will find him (see Jer. 29:13). When the angel said to
Jacob, *'Let me go,'* he didn't mean it, and realizing this, Jacob said, *'I will
not let you go unless you bless me'* (Gen. 32:26).

This leads me to the divine touch. We are told when the angel
wrestled with Jacob, his hip was wrenched. I shall deal with this in detail
in the next chapter, but I would just like to say here that when God
blesses us it will have its effect on us and we will walk away with a
slight limp.

The divine tenderness

Now let's consider the divine tenderness for a moment. Let me tell you
something about the God of the Bible that people hate. James 5:11 puts
it this way: *'You . . . have seen what the LORD finally brought about. The
LORD is full of compassion and mercy.'* The Lord is so tender, so sweet;
he is wonderful. He tests us to see if we will accept him as he is, as he
is revealed in the Bible. It is true, he is the God of Justice, the God of
Glory. Ah, but he is so tender to those who break through the barrier
and affirm him and get to know him in the most wonderful, intimate
way.

The divine title

Finally we come to the divine title. We read in Genesis 32:26–28:

> *Jacob replied, 'I will not let you go unless you bless me.'*
> *The man asked him, 'What is your name?'*
> *'Jacob,' he answered.*
> *Then the man said, 'Your name will no longer be Jacob, but Israel, because you have struggled with God and with men and have overcome.'*

Perhaps, like Jacob, you have struggled with God. He has been the one behind your struggle and whom you have felt with you along the way. Commit yourself to him. Nail your colours to the mast. Recognize you have sinned against him and that God is the one with whom you have the problem. Acknowledge that he is the only true God and that Jesus is his one and only Son and that you need to be saved by the blood he shed on the cross.

26

Could This Be God?

Genesis 32:22–32

Having read from Genesis 32, we need to turn to another Old Testament passage:

> *Now when Joshua was near Jericho, he looked up and saw a man standing in front of him with a drawn sword in his hand. Joshua went up to him and asked, 'Are you for us or for our enemies?'*
>
> *'Neither,' he replied, 'but as commander of the army of the L ORD I have now come.'*
> *Then Joshua fell face down to the ground in reverence, and asked him, 'What message does my Lord have for his servant?'*
>
> *The commander of the* LORD's *army replied, 'Take off your sandals, for the place where you are standing is holy'* (Josh. 5:13–15).

We return to the subject of Jacob wrestling with the angel. This time, to see how it coheres with the angel who appeared to Joshua just before the Israelites entered the land of Canaan.

The Ever-New Ways of God

We never know exactly how God will turn up. I understand why this is. There comes a time when we all need to be confronted with the fact that we don't know God as well as we may think. God has a way of putting us in our place lest our preconceived ideas and our small way of thinking keep us from seeing him when he comes. Reading church history reveals God turns up in different ways. Take, for example, Hebrews 11. Not one of the people described there, Enoch, Noah, Abraham, Isaac, Jacob, David and Elijah could have the luxury of seeing God work as he had in previous times. They each had to accept that which was different to them and be regarded as a fool. That is what made faith, faith.

We have to come to the place where we see when God is at work for ourselves, and if no one else believes it, we do. That is how real God must become to us. The difficulty is, in knowing him a little, we assume we know God better than we really do. For example, in the sixteenth century God raised up men whom we call the 'Reformers'. John Wycliffe is known as the 'Morning Star of the Reformation' in Britain. There were others, including John Huss, Luther, Zwingli and Calvin. God was at work in the sixteenth century, and the world was turned upside down. Take the eighteenth century, the era of the Great Awakenings. God was powerfully at work. But if you thought the only way he could work was through Luther and Calvin, then you would have to say that what you saw with George Whitefield, John Wesley or Jonathan Edwards would be so strange, it couldn't possibly be God, because you would be judging by what God did in the sixteenth century. Or take what God did in 1904/1905 in Wales. It was unprecedented, and there was nothing quite like it.

But it is a fact that every movement of the Spirit in every age has been opposed by respectable Christians who felt they were following the Lord. The reasons they gave sounded good. In the Welsh Revival, for instance, there was very little preaching. So those who opposed it seemingly had a fairly solid reason for doing so. Yet God was at work in that revival. The point I make is that we all have our reasons for believing what we do, and we can back them to the hilt.

When we come to Jacob, we see he has come to know God, but not all that well. If you had asked him after Bethel, 'How does God turn up?' Jacob would have replied, 'In dreams.' If you asked him again after the nightmare of the Laban era was over, he would have answered, 'Well, it could be through dreams or angels.'

But the experience we look at now was so different. It was a totally different kind of manifestation. Without warning, a man leapt on Jacob. Jacob was alone. It was dark and he found himself wrestling with the stranger. He felt he had an enemy on his hands and fought in self-protection. Then, at some point, Jacob began to ask, 'Is this God?' By morning, he was convinced this was so. In the same way, what many of us have to learn is to recognize God when he comes.

Jonathan Edwards taught us that the task of every generation is to discover in which direction the Sovereign Redeemer is moving and to move in that direction. The worst thing Jacob could have done was to let go when the angel was wrestling with him or cry, 'Let me go!' On the contrary, Jacob said, 'Oh no! I am not going to let you go until you bless me!'

Did you ever let go when you had a struggle? Did you ever feel you were taking the right course of action, only to hear someone suggest otherwise, and so you gave up? One of the saddest stories I know is of the couple who came all the way from India because they had heard of the revival breaking out in Wales. They had arrived in London where they met an old Christian, and they told him of their plan to go to Wales to see for themselves what God was doing there. 'Oh don't bother,' replied this man. 'It's Welsh emotionalism. It's not of God.' The couple returned to India without bothering to go to Wales. They let their plan go.

Perhaps someone has persuaded you to abandon your principles and do things you know to be wrong and which will change your life for the worst. Maybe you are seeking God, and someone, perhaps a person whom you greatly respect, has persuaded you to give up. Perhaps you have prayed about something, and because God didn't answer you within a short time you gave up. Have you ever wondered what would have happened if you had held on? God graciously comes again. Seek God again with all your heart and you will find him.

Do you know the story of the importunate widow? Jesus told the story of a widow who went to a judge every day with her plea for justice until the judge granted her request (see Lk. 18:1–8). The point Jesus made was to keep praying and not to give up. Wrestling in prayer isn't all that much fun, and I wonder how many of us have given up too hastily, feeling God was not going to answer.

Breaking the Betrayal Barrier

There are several things we can learn from the story of Jacob wrestling with the angel: Jacob became a worthy successor to his illustrious grandfather in that he broke what we may call the 'betrayal barrier'. Everyone feels at some point that God has betrayed them, that he has let them down. They find he seems more like an enemy than a friend. Nine out of ten people say, 'Well, God, if that's how you want it to be, then I'll go my way and you go yours.' One out of ten, I reckon, breaks that betrayal barrier and holds on, like Jacob who wrestled with the angel and said, *'I won't let you go unless you bless me.'*

The same kind of thing happened to Abraham. We read in Genesis 22:2 how God said to Abraham: *'Take your son, your only son Isaac, whom you love, and go to the region of Moriah. Sacrifice him there as a burnt offering on one of the mountains I will tell you about.'* That made no sense to Abraham. He thought, 'How can God ask me to sacrifice my Isaac when he is my only son and the only way forward if I am to have offspring? It doesn't make sense.' But Abraham showed he was willing to obey God, and God honoured him for what he was prepared to do.

Sooner or later, God will ask you to do something that makes no sense at the time. We judge things by our keen analytical ability and by our knowledge, and we say, 'This has to match the expectations of my intellect.' Perhaps the barrier you have to break is the one that doesn't make any sense at the time, but you must give God the benefit of the doubt. Abraham obeyed God and was never sorry.

What was it, then, that Joshua discovered just before the Children of Israel were to pass into the land of Canaan? Joshua saw an angel. Standing in front of him was a man with a drawn sword. Joshua approached him and asked, *'Are you for us or for our enemies?'* (Josh. 5:13). The answer was *'Neither.'* What Joshua had to learn, what Abraham learned, what Jacob learned, is one of the most painful things we have to learn, and that is that God can be painfully neutral. It's rather like parents who have two or more children, and because they love them all they have to be neutral. God can be so impartial. We want God to be partial for us, but we have to come to the place where we allow God to be God. Would we affirm him if he were to work powerfully in another church, in another denomination? Would we say 'That is God'?

It brings to mind the story I heard of two churches in Alabama, one a Baptist, one a Methodist. They were just across the street from one another. They held missions. (We might term them 'revivals' but 'mis - sions' is a better term.) Sometimes these missions were held at the same time. After they were all over, one of the Baptists was heard to say, 'Well, we didn't have much of a revival. But, thank God, the Methodists didn't either.' Did you get the point? 'If God isn't going to bless me, I don't want him to bless you.'

In the American Civil War, someone came up to President Lincoln and asked, 'Is God on our side or on their side?' Lincoln's reply was, 'All I want to know is whether we are on God's side.' That is what Joshua had to be taught. It is the way forward when it comes to understanding God.

God's Unexpected Visits

Are you seeking God? How hard are you trying? Are you requiring that he meets your expectation? You say, 'If God turned up I would know him. I have read church history and I have spent so much time with him recently. Believe me, I would recognize him.' That is exactly the point I want to make: when we feel we know God so well, we are in danger of becoming so familiar with him that we think, 'Ah, I will be notified if he does something great in my country.' The way we must love the glory of the Lord is not that we affirm him because we see that which makes us feel comfortable, but that we know he is God and can manifest himself in unusual ways.

Israel missed the Messiah because they thought there would be no way the Messiah could turn up and *they* not recognize him. He came in the most ridiculous possible way. Mary and Joseph were engaged but not married. They lived with the stigma that everyone in Nazareth knew she was pregnant, but they were not allowed to tell them the truth – that she had the child of the Holy Spirit within her and had never known a man.

Sometimes, God puts us in a place where we can't give the reason we affirm him. He continues to work in this way, so there are times when we have to take a stand, where we know the truth, but we are not allowed to explain ourselves. Are you prepared to be committed to Jesus Christ to the extent that you just affirm him, even though you know you are not allowed to explain yourself except to say, 'Jesus is my Saviour. I am unashamed of him.'

When Jesus was 30 years old, he still had no reputation to speak of. He was the carpenter's son. He had no military background, he had no political background, he was not a member of the ruling council, the Sanhedrin, nor was he recognized by it. Jesus was neither a Pharisee nor a Sadducee. He wasn't a priest. He was a person of no account and he ended up being crucified. The people of Israel had no conscience about what they did. They said, 'This is what God is doing to him.' If he had been the Son of God, they felt they would never have got away with crucifying him. Remember, they said, 'If you are the Son of God, come down from the cross.' He didn't so they thought they were safe (see Mt. 21:41–44). When Jesus went to the cross, everybody was convinced he was a fraud. They said, 'This cannot be of God.' So they missed the Messiah altogether.

The angel was teaching Jacob that God could turn up in a different way. This was breaking the neutrality or detachment barrier whereby Jacob had to affirm God, even though he had not experienced anything like it before.

When we see God working in an unexpected way, we may fail to recognize him. Sometimes theologians describe the 'otherness' of God. He is different. He may turn up in a strange way. God may come with silence or by hiding his face and seeming not to answer. Sometimes the way in which he turns up seems silly. But God chooses the foolish things of this world to confound the wise.

Nothing could be more silly than Paul having to say to the people of Corinth, 'God wants to know you. He wants you to know him, and the only point of contact is that Jesus died on a cross. Before I came to you I determined to know nothing among you except Jesus Christ, and him crucified' (see 1 Cor. 2:2). Here was a message so strange, it seemed silly.

Joseph and Mary were put in their place 12 years after Jesus was born. They had taken him to Jerusalem and had missed him for three days. When they found him, they were angry with him and said, 'How could you do this to us? Your father and I have been anxiously searching for you.'

'Why were you searching for me?' he asked. 'Didn't you know I had to be in my Father's house?' (Lk. 2:49).

Our reaction is, 'How can God do this to me – if that's really God? This angel leaping on Jacob, how could that be God? This Jesus, dying on a cross, how can that be God? Why does God seem so detached from the way with which we are comfortable?' The answer is lest we feel too familiar with him and become presumptuous. The proof we love God is that we recognize he may appear in a way that feels strange and we are prepared to affirm him no matter how much it hurts and no matter how strange it seems.

27

The Greatest Victory in the World

Genesis 32:22–32

Then the man said, 'Your name will no longer be Jacob, but Israel, because you have struggled with God and with men and have overcome' (Gen. 32:28).

What would you say is the greatest victory in the world? Would you think of some military victory with some famous general, or would you think of D-Day, or when Germany finally surrendered to the allied forces? Would you think of the Gulf War? Would you think of a political victory or sporting achievement such as winning the World Cup? Maybe you are thinking in terms of a financial success or of an emotional breakthrough? What would you think in terms of personal achievement that would be a great victory? Suppose you could push a button and make what you want to happen. What would it be? I sometimes fantasize that if God ever came to me like he did to Solomon, and said, 'Name it and you've got it', I know what I would ask; I've thought about it a lot. I wonder if you know what it is you really want.

I'm going to talk about the greatest possible victory, and one God wants you to have. It was the victory Jacob had. You may think you know what you want to solve all your problems, but the truth is that God already knows. If you could press the kind of button that would allow you to decide, you would not even come close to what he would come up with and which would so thoroughly and totally satisfy you in the end. Our problem is we are so afraid that we are going to miss out on what would be thrilling and fun or what would achieve this or that, but what God himself wants for each of us is infinitely better than we ourselves could come up with if we were given the controls.

I live by Psalm 84:11: *'No good thing does he withhold from those whose walk is blameless.'* All the time I am having things happen to me, I ask, 'Lord, why did you let that happen?' or 'Why can't I have this?' I see others who seem to get what they want, or get away with doing things that I couldn't get away with. Then I fall back on this verse, and I know God's choice of victory for me is far greater than anything I could come up with. And I know that what God did for Jacob is what he wants to do for me and for you, because Jacob achieved the greatest victory he could ever have known. I want to say three things about it:

1. It Was a Double Victory

Notice how it is put: *'Your name will no longer be Jacob, but Israel, because you have struggled with God and with men and have overcome.'* So first, Jacob had a victory in his struggle with God, and he came to see that had been his biggest problem. Do you have an axe to grind with God? Perhaps you are one of those who say, 'I'm not sure there *is* a God, but if there is, I've got one or two things I would like to say to him.' Perhaps you are bitter over what he has allowed to happen, or perhaps you are disillusioned about the way your life has turned out, or perhaps you are filled with fear with regard to the future. God knows this. He knows about that bitterness and he knows about that fear. He wants to enter your life, so that you will find out that the very thing that concerns you most, concerns him even more.

The problem is that we are not usually prepared for the way he has of turning up. God's way of giving the victory to Jacob was that, out of the blue, a man leapt on him, and Jacob found himself in a wrestling match with an angel. The Bible says, *'Do not forget to entertain strangers, for by so doing some people entertain angels without knowing it'* (Heb. 13:2). 'But,' you say, 'Jacob wasn't entertaining a stranger, he was being jumped on.' Quite. But that is the way in which God often turns up. He comes in such a way that, at first, he appears to be our enemy, but it is his way of trying to become our friend. And if you feel bitterness towards God, you can see you are at enmity with him. What God will do is come alongside and enter into a wrestling match with you. I just hope that you see what Jacob saw because, before morning was over, Jacob somehow saw what very few see, that he had at his fingertips an opportunity to be greatly blessed. He said, 'I am not going to let this man go, for he has the power to bless me.' At daybreak, the angel said, 'Let me go. It's daybreak.' But Jacob replied, 'You are not leaving. You are not going to go unless you bless me.'

Jacob saw that God was in the whole situation. I promise you this: whatever you are going through at the moment, whatever the trial, the occasion of the bitterness, the nature of the hurt or the despair, if you refuse to give up, you will see that God is at the bottom of it. How many of us have had this sort of thing happen and we have let go, and as a result you have never known what could have been ours? The interesting thing is that this angel could have killed Jacob, for he had God's power. He could have done anything and would have had no trouble pinning Jacob down. Yet, somehow, Jacob had a grip on the angel so that the angel asked to be released. But that was God's kindness and symbolizes how we are in no predicament so great that we cannot escape.

You may say that you have come to the one trial in life so great that there is no way out. Wrong. In 1 Corinthians 10:13 we read: *'No temptation has seized you except what is common to man. And God is faithful; he will not let you be tempted beyond what you can bear.'* And 1 John 5:3 says, *'His commands are not burdensome.'* The angel could have had such a lock on Jacob that Jacob wouldn't have stood a chance, but instead he was given a certain freedom and flexibility. You could say that in a sense Jacob gained a victory over God. It doesn't mean that he defeated God, but rather, instead of God being his enemy, he saw God was his friend.

This is the thing you need to see: you don't just suddenly become friends with God until first you realize that your sin has made him angry with you. You think you have reason to be angry with God, but you don't seem to realize that God has something he wants to say to you. He wants to say, 'How dare you abuse that body I gave you! How dare you use the money that you have made like that! How dare you get away with lying and cheating! There are things that you have done and, apart from one or two others, nobody knows about them, but it hasn't bothered you. How dare you think this is going to please me!' The whole time you have been bitter against God, and you don't realize that he is angry about your sin. There is only one way of coming to terms with God and that is to realize, just like Jacob did before daybreak, that there is a way out. God planned it when he sent his one and only Son to die on a cross for your sins.

But Jacob had a double victory because he also won a victory in his struggle with others. There are those who say, 'I don't have a problem with God, it's people who bother me.' But I can tell you this: Get right with God and let him bring you to the place where you are delivered from the fear of people. The greatest freedom in the world is where you refuse to be governed by what others think and when you refuse to be governed by what they can do to you. Am I to believe that God wants me to live my life dominated by what people think and to live in fear because of what so and so can do to me? God wants to deliver us from that, and he offers us a double victory. But in this order (notice how it is put): *'Because you have struggled with God and with men and have overcome . . .'* In this order, you will have this victory.

2. It Was a Decisive Victory

Notice again how it is put: *'I will not let you go unless you bless me'* (Gen. 32:26). God gave Jacob the freedom to get the upper hand, and he will give it to you. Some, I fear, have let go when they could have held on, and have missed great opportunities. Some know that rather than dignify the trial that God gave them, they just got angry with him. That trial was God's invitation on a silver platter to know more of his grace. Yet some, instead of totally forgiving those who have hurt them, have preferred to wallow in bitterness and self-pity, and some perhaps, instead of taking a stand, chose to be cowards. But God is coming to you a second time, and you can win the greatest victory on the face of the earth, and that is to win God's approval. There is no greater feeling in the world than to know that you have God's approval.

There are many people who struggle with God but they don't overcome. There are a lot of people who struggle with others and they don't overcome. But this angel was impressed. And God authenticated Jacob and changed his name. The name Israel means 'he struggles with God'. It was a decisive victory: it was a permanent change of name. This is what God wants to do with you: he wants to give you a new identity. Jacob would never the same again. He would never feel the same way again about God or about other people.

By the way, all this blessing came without Jacob getting his big question answered. Jacob asked, 'What is your name?' The angel never would tell him. We are just told, *'He blessed him there'* (Gen. 32:29). You may say, 'When God tells me what I want to know, then I will do it his way.' Listen. Jacob didn't get his question answered, but he got the blessing. We've all got questions, and if you wait until you get answers to them all, you will never be blessed. Why must we keep asking God to answer our questions when the truth is he's already shown us so much? Jacob realized that, and he accepted the blessing without getting his question answered. St Augustine, a great saint of the fourth century, had this struggle with all his questions, and he then realized that the only way forward was to take God at his word. After that, Augustine was amazed at how question after question was answered. Don't think that you can play a game with God or say, 'Now look, I'll make a deal with you.' You will never be converted like that. The only way one can be converted is to bow down to him and ask him for mercy and acknowledge what Jesus did for you on the cross. Then you will be blessed, and you will discover that one by one God answers our questions.

3. It Was a Damaging Victory

In verse 25 it says, *'When the man saw he could not overpower him, he touched the socket of Jacob's hip so that his hip was wrenched as he wrestled with the man.'* As Robert Amess says, 'You don't get the blessing of God until he puts you out of joint.' You see, that limp would be a hallmark for life. I have to tell you that you will be given a limp. It means that in some measure you will forfeit things with which you have always been comfortable and what has seemed to be natural, as natural as walking. God says it has to go. The limp is an impediment; it's an inconvenience, but it's also a sign that God has touched you. I guarantee that Jacob treasured that limp he had. It was a daily reminder of the greatest thing that ever happened to him.

I remember that many years ago, when I was a student at Trevecca Nazarene College, I heard Dr Hugh Benner preach on Philippians 2:5. It was one of the most moving messages I ever heard. I got on my knees that day, and I asked God, in a way I had never asked him before, to make me like Jesus; I wanted that so much. I didn't know it but God said, 'All right. If that's what you want, I will make you a bit more like Jesus.' Little did I know, within 90 days of that moment, at the time when I was sitting on top of the world and I had friends and a future, everything – my world would collapse, and I would lose so many of the things that were so natural and seemed so right to me at the time. But God said, 'No, you cannot keep these things if you want my blessing.'

God wants to do that for you. You ask, 'What is it that I need to do?' Don't worry. He will put his finger on it in his own way. God doesn't lead us directly from A–Z, but from A–B and from B–C. God has a way of coming along and letting you know what it is he wants. Some of us would know exactly what to do if at this moment we were freed of those things which are impoverishing us and robbing us of dignity and joy. Yet giving this or that up won't save us, because the victory that was won was not the result of anything we did: it was Jesus who had the victory of victories.

Jesus had a double victory: he was able to please God by his perfect righteousness, and he was a substitute for man. Charles Spurgeon said that there is no gospel apart from these two things – satisfaction and substitu - tion. What does that mean? It means that Jesus took your place. He did it all for you. The most extraordinary thing in the world is to think that I am going to go to heaven because of what somebody else did for me.

It was a decisive victory. When Jesus said on the cross, *'It is finished'* (Jn. 19:30), he was saying that your debt is paid and God has bought you a ticket to heaven and he is willing to give it to you on the condition that you climb down and realize that the only way forward is to honour the blood Jesus shed on the cross. It will be damaging – yes. Are you willing to leave here with a limp, no longer Jacob, but Israel? What a word! God will do that for you, but you will limp.

28

Victory – But Only Just

Genesis 33:1–20

Jacob was a man of faith, but only just. We are going to look now at one of the most remarkable victories. You talk about dreading some - thing! Jacob was dreading a particular event more than you can possibly imagine. Are you dreading something at the moment? Are you dreading meeting somebody? Are you dreading a particular situation? The thing that Jacob was dreading so much was meeting Esau, his twin brother, whom he had deceived and manipulated to get the patriarchal blessing. Jacob had lived with this guilt for years, and the last word he had from Esau was that his twin was going to kill him. He had spent 20 years in hiding, but he couldn't hide any longer. He had to face his brother.

So we shall see how Jacob is such a disappointment to us, but no less than I am to myself when I consider how good God has been to me. Are you still struggling? Do you think, 'I ought to be stronger than I am'? Then Jacob's your man. He makes us all feel a little better. But he lets us down, not only because he was the world's greatest manipu - lator, but he was the type of person you would love to hate. He wasn't a very nice guy. What really gets me is that despite one marvellous experience after another with God he hadn't learnt a lot.

The greatest experience with God Jacob ever had was when he wrestled with God at a place he called 'Peniel', which means 'the face of God'. It was there God gave him a new name, saying, 'You are not Jacob but Israel'. The word 'Israel' means 'he struggles with God'. Did you know that the name Jacob occurs no fewer than 45 times in the book of Genesis, but Israel only 23 times, and although his new name was Israel, time and again, he was still referred to as Jacob? Have you ever noticed that both in ancient Israel and in the New Testament it always speaks of the 'God of Abraham, Isaac and Jacob'? Why does it not refer to the 'God of Israel'?

I want to give an example to show why Jacob is rather a disappoint -
ment. He wasn't a lacklustre person; on the contrary, he was a colourful
character, but he was lacklustre in his faith. Look at the situation: After
Peniel, one of the most stunning, spectacular and dazzling experiences
with God in the Old Testament, you would have thought Jacob would
have been totally changed.

Perhaps you are still waiting for something to happen, and you keep
saying, 'If only I could have this experience, then I'd be set.' The
possibility of God giving you an experience like he did with Jacob does
arise, and God could do that, but when you consider, you see how
little, apparently, it did for Jacob. I'm going to prove it. There are two
extremes that are to be avoided when we have an unusual experience
with God: one is to underestimate the experience and the other is to
overestimate it.

Approaching Esau

Jacob was in hiding, but the time came when he had to 'come clean',
and he knew he couldn't avoid Esau for ever. Look at verse 1: *Jacob
looked up and there was Esau, coming with his four hundred men.*' That was
quite frightening, for the men were probably armed. Perhaps Jacob
thought that the change of identity that God gave him would also
change the world around him. Perhaps God has met with you, and you
say, 'If I can have a great experience with God, I can then face life.'
Maybe you think that if God meets you in a wonderful way, then the
thing that's bothering you will just go away. Jacob had had such a
wonderful experience that he thought that he wouldn't have to see Esau.
But it says, *Jacob looked up and there was Esau, coming with his four hundred
men.*' This tell us that the greatest experience with God does not remove
that situation. It isn't going to take that problem away. Charles Colson
says that God doesn't promise to take us out of the fire, but he promises
to get into the fire with us. When you are converted, the next day you
will find the world is still there. You still have to get up, go to work
and return to the same old situation. Life goes on. Jacob looked up and
there was Esau. That's the first thing: the situation was the same.

When Jacob looked up and saw Esau coming, he divided the children.
'Oh, no! Jacob, don't do that! That's what you were going to do
yesterday.' That's what he had, indeed, decided to do the day before. He
was so sure that those men were going to kill his family that he divided
them into three different groups, so if one group was attacked the others
might have a chance to escape. That was his plan. Am I to believe that
he had had that great experience with God and he was still sticking to the
same strategy? The angel had already told him that God was with him
and that he had had a great victory (see Gen. 32:28). His father had already

told him, *'May those who curse you be cursed and those who bless you be blessed'* (see Gen. 27:29). He should have known that there was no way that Esau was going to kill his family. But he adopted the same strategy and prepared for the worst. What should he have done? He ought to have trusted God.

There are two ways of gaining the victory. One way is to recognize that God does change the situation around you, and the other is to realize the victory is in your heart. That is what I call the *real* victory, when you decide, 'I am going to face the world. I am not going to give in to that anymore. I am going to stop this self-pity.' You believe God so firmly that you say, 'I'm going to trust him no matter what.' What Jacob ought to have done was to have taken his family to meet Esau and his men and see what God would do. But no, he was still thinking like the old Jacob, before his name was changed to Israel.

But there is something else. We see the same servile manner that he had displayed the day before when he told his servants to go to meet Esau and say, 'Your servant Jacob is coming' (see Gen. 32:3). We find that when he does meet Esau, *'He . . . bowed down to the ground seven times as he approached his brother'* (Gen. 33:3). Now that was silly; it was 'over the top'. When Abraham saw an angel he just bowed once. Why did Jacob do that? He also called Esau 'lord'. He referred to himself as being Esau's servant (see v. 5), and yet God had said before the twins were born that the elder would serve the younger. That meant that the servant was Esau, not Jacob. Jacob grew up knowing this, but he did not affirm what God said. Jacob didn't need to grovel before Esau, but he thought he did.

Before his eyes was the most spectacular victory you can imagine, but he approached his brother with suspicion. I doubt there was never a day in the last 20 years but he wondered what meeting him would be like. Have you ever had imaginary conversations with people whom you were dreading meeting so much that the thought kept you awake all night? But Jacob had little to fear, for it says in verse 4: *'Esau ran to meet Jacob and embraced him; he threw his arms around his neck and kissed him.'* Esau was a changed man. We don't know why, or how it happened, but Esau had changed. It could be that God dealt with Esau like he dealt with Laban. Jacob saw all this, but what he said to himself was, 'Don't believe it. It's too good to be true.' Maybe you have seen God do something extraor - dinary, yet you say, 'No, I don't believe this. There is something suspicious here.'

Esau said, 'By the way, what are all these droves I met?'

'To find favour in your eyes,' Jacob answered.

'Well,' Esau said, 'I don't want them. I have all I need. Keep them for yourself.'

Still not convinced, Jacob insisted, *'No, please . . . If I have found favour in your eyes, accept this gift from me. For to see your face is like seeing the face of God, now that you have received me favourably'* (see Gen. 33:8–10).

Do you know why he kept begging, still afraid? He still didn't believe Esau was pacified. Do you know this gives us the picture of the gospel? The God who has been angry with you, and rightly so, has been pacified, but not by your gifts. Do you know why people keep doing things to try and please God? It's because they can't believe that God has been perfectly satisfied by what Jesus did on the cross.

A Better Way

The way Jacob should have approached his brother was by just believing God. Away with this nonsense of dividing his family. He could have met Esau with dignity instead of over-reacting, bowing down saying, 'O my Lord, I am your servant.' Jacob had been affirmed by God and he was without excuse. Not that Jacob denied the faith – he never did that. Not that Jacob fell into deep sin – he never did that. He was just weak. Do you remember that Jesus said to Simon, *'You are Peter, and on this rock I will build my church'* (Mt. 16:18)? Jesus gave Simon a new name, Peter, but sometimes Jesus would still call him Simon. In fact, before Jesus died on the cross, he said, *'Simon, Simon, Satan has asked to sift you as wheat'* (Lk. 22:31). Isn't it interesting that Jesus called him Simon then? You see, although we might wish that some experience would get us right, we all have that old nature with us. Jacob won the victory because God had dealt with Esau. It was a great victory, not because of Jacob's faith, but because what he had been dreading just didn't happen because Esau was quite happy. Jacob's victory did not come from within him. It was a victory – but only just.

An Explanation

What was the explanation? You may ask: 'Why can't I have more faith than this? Why is it that I am not stronger?' Well, I can't be sure about you, but I can tell you about Jacob.

- He had a nervous disposition. You find the words 'fear' and 'afraid' being used to describe Jacob's feelings (see Gen. 31:31, 32:7, 11). He was always afraid. There are people who are governed by a spirit of fear. There are two levels of fear: it can be at a natural level, where one is simply a nervous person, and there is another level, where the devil comes in and taunts a person. God understands when we have a nervous disposition. There are people like that. It goes back to childhood and feelings of rejection, or bad relationships, resulting in constant feelings of guilt. It's not a great sin, but it does militate against trust and faith.

- Jacob had a narrow sense of dignity. The past kept haunting him. All of us are affected by the past, and some people live with a sense of low self-esteem throughout their lives – like Jacob, in fact. You see, what he had done in tricking his brother to get the birthright, then deceiving his father to get the blessing, backfired on him. As a result, when he thought of seeing Esau, he didn't feel right: he didn't have any sense of worth or dignity, and he went 'over the top'. God didn't want him to feel that way, but that's the way he felt. The reason God gave him a new name was that Jacob might regain his self-esteem and see himself in the way God saw him. And maybe, for a moment, after his encounter with God, Jacob thought, 'This is wonderful!' even though he limped away. But the moment he saw Esau, his nervous disposition and his narrow sense of dignity returned.
- Jacob had a natural sense of deceitfulness. It characterized his behav - iour, and now once again he was being deceitful towards Esau. He was predisposed to be deceitful. He was not being honest. He could have walked up to Esau and stood beside him with dignity because God had affirmed him, and in his heart he knew that. But in his weakness, Jacob lived just below the level of the great victory that he could have had. The victory was there – God arranged it. But in his heart, Jacob missed it.

Jacob came through in the end. The last verse of this chapter says, *'He set up an altar and called it El Elohe Israel.'* Do you know what that means? He did affirm his real identity. And that's what we must do. God has chosen us although we don't deserve it. One of the most wonderful things about the Bible is that the worse you are, the more God seems to love you.

29

Letting God Love Us

Genesis 33:8–20

Some time ago, in Florida, someone told me that they had picked up enough of my preaching to be able to say that my main theme could be summed up in one word, 'vindication'. I didn't know what to think of that, but there is a thread that holds together everything I preach, summed up in the words 'letting God do it'. Then I realized something: I wished it could be said that the thread that held my preaching together was summed up in this phrase: 'letting God love us'.

There is a connection between the principle of vindication and the principle of letting God love us. 'Vindication' means to have your name cleared. God alone wants to do that. You may want to do it, but he will do it in his time and in his way. The moment you and I start to clear our own names, God backs off and says, 'OK! Now you do it!' And immediately we are in trouble, and we see the folly of trying to do it ourselves. So unless we let God do it, it won't really happen in the right way. The same is true when it comes to this principle of letting God love us. In much the same way, we do not allow God to vindicate us but try to sort things out for ourselves; we don't let God love us. Instead, we compete with him by trying to perform for him so that we can feel worthy of that love. This message is intended for those who feel that God doesn't love them because they haven't matched his standards and feel, therefore, they don't have his approval.

Affirming What God Has Done

How do we learn this from the story of Jacob? It says in the Bible, *'There he set up an altar and called it El Elohe Israel'* (Gen. 33:20). What did Jacob do when he did that? First, he affirmed his change of name. You will recall that God told Jacob he was no longer Jacob but Israel. And it was

a wonderful thing when, at long last, Jacob said 'All right,' and he built
an altar to the God of Israel, affirming what God had done. There are times
when we need to affirm what God has done for us. There are some
Christians who don't enjoy the Lord's Supper because they don't feel
worthy. They are looking to *themselves* the whole time, wanting to feel good
enough about *themselves*, so that they can enjoy the communion. But
what God wants them to do is affirm what *he* says about them. For the
bread and the wine are God's symbols that say, 'You are all right. My
Son died for you on the cross.'

So it is a wonderful thing to affirm what God has done. That is what
Jacob did. He affirmed his change of name, and second, he affirmed the
God who made that change. *'He set up an altar and called it El Elohe Israel.'*
Yet how dare Jacob do that – after he had behaved so pitifully! In the
previous chapter we saw how disgracefully he had behaved towards Esau.
God had given Jacob a stunning victory on a silver platter, and suddenly
we found that Jacob was behaving like an unbeliever. Despite the high
watermark in his life when he wrestled with God and God gave him the
change of name, Jacob had been so weak and cowardly. But the next
thing I learn is he set up an altar. I think to myself, 'Jacob how can you
involve yourself in such an act of worship? You aren't worthy to build
an altar to God.'

Yet do you know what Jacob was doing? He was letting God love
him. Surely he had to realize that he had been a poor example of God's
grace. If he didn't know it, it proved it all the more when he went on
and built this altar to God as if nothing was wrong. It's exactly how
you and I have continued in our worship of God, and then, years later,
God puts his finger on something in our lives and we think, 'Oh, Lord,
have you loved me all this time and you knew about that?'

And he says, 'Yes. But don't worry. I know everything about you and
still love you.'

You see, there is so much wrong with all of us, and if we knew just
how much we wouldn't hold our heads high. How is it that we manage
to get through the day? How do we manage to come to the Lord's Table
when we are all so unworthy? It's because Jesus shed his blood on the
cross, and that means infinitely more to God than our getting it right. At
the end of the day, despite all our obedience and our efforts to please
God, nothing matches the blood that Jesus shed on the cross. Any one of
us can hold our heads high in the presence of God, not because in
ourselves we have come up to standard, but because of what God has
done for us.

Recently, in Florida, we came across a man who struggled as to
whether God loved him because of a particular weakness he had. This
weakness was neither illegal nor immoral, but, because he had it, he had
no assurance that he was saved; he had no assurance that God loved him,
faithful though he was in attending church. We all have weaknesses, and

this particular chap felt that if only he could deal with his and put it behind him, then God could love him. Do you know what I said to him? 'If you became perfect first, you would rob God: you would cheat him of just loving you like you are.' Most of us feel that God cannot possibly love us like this! Yet, you see, that is what makes God, God. He's different. It's a wonderful thing when we come to the place where we just let God love us without our having to perform. So, at the end of this chapter in his life, when Jacob had been such a pitiful example, he built an altar to God and it didn't bother him one bit.

Jacob Runs From Esau

What exactly then had Jacob done in showing less than a good perform - ance with Esau? Despite his wrestling with God and having the change of name, Jacob behaved as though he hadn't even met God at all. Perhaps you think that if you had an experience with God like Jacob had, you'd be set, for you've heard of these great saints who have had wonderful experiences with God. But I'm going to tell you, they don't necessarily change your life permanently. You know people criticize what has been happening at Holy Trinity Church, Brompton, and in other churches where there is a movement of the Holy Spirit. They say, 'If it's a blessing, why doesn't it last?' Well, a bath doesn't last. You have to take another bath in a day or two. A meal tastes good, but you have to eat the next day. You may think that you will need to have some experience that will cause you to coast and sail from now on, but you'll be the same person.

We have seen the silly way in which Jacob over-reacted when he met Esau. Have you ever acted in a way that was not becoming? Maybe you thought, 'I can't believe I said that. I can't believe I acted that way. I can't believe I had that thought. I'm horrible. I'm so awful.' Look at Jacob. He continued to be manipulative, controlling and deceitful, even when it was obvious that Esau was a changed man, held no grudge and wasn't going to kill him. You would think that by now Jacob would believe it, but he still couldn't grasp it.

Here's what happened. Esau was much happier to see Jacob than Jacob was to see him. Esau thought that he and Jacob were going to be friends. Esau was reconciled and suggested, 'Well, now, let's just walk together.'

'No, let's not do that,' said Jacob. 'Look here, my cows and ewes are nursing their young, and if they are driven hard they will die, and we'll have to go really slowly.'

'Oh, well, I'll walk with you then.'

'No,' replied Jacob. 'You run on.'

Esau said, 'In that case, I will have some of my men walk with yours.'

'No, I wouldn't want you to do that. Let them go on!' (see Gen. 33:12–15).

Esau was assuming that Jacob wanted to be his friend, when the whole time Jacob was still scared to death, and he wanted Esau gone. Can you believe that this is the same man who 24 hours earlier had had this wonderful experience with God? He hadn't changed. Funda - mentally, he was still a weak, cowardly person, motivated by a spirit of fear, and with a negative outlook that was not becoming. The truth is that Jacob had no intentions of seeing Esau ever again. Probably Esau could see this. He said, 'All right. I'll see you in a couple of days.' So Esau headed south and, as soon as he was out of sight, Jacob headed west. It was so sad.

Why is this chapter important? It is because here was a man who, at the end of the day, still worshipped and affirmed God, and this was important enough to be included in God's Holy Writ. Do you have the need to perform before you can feel that God can love you? Maybe you are rather like me. I grew up with one difficulty that could have affected me for life were it not for the grace of God: I have difficulty in believing that God can love me just like I am. My father was so demanding and such a perfectionist that no matter what I did, in his view, it could have been done a little better. It was almost as though my dad was afraid to compliment me lest I should slip back and think everything was all right. I remember crying virtually all the way home one day. I had my report card, and on it were straight A's, except for two grades which were A minus. I knew those would be the first thing my dad would see. He wouldn't say, 'Oh wonderful! Straight A's!' He would say, 'If you worked a little harder, you wouldn't have those A minus grades.' What, then, do you suppose my dad said when he saw that report card? 'Well done, son. But those two A minus grades – work a little harder; you won't have those next time.' So I grew up, never coming up to his standard. I don't hold it against my dad. He couldn't help it. Maybe that's the way *he* was brought up.

What grips me is, the more I get to know the God of the Bible, the more I see that he wants to vindicate us without our help; he wants to love us just like we are. I want you to know something: there is a standard that God requires and it is beyond our reach. It is sinlessness. That's God's standard. He looked high and low over the earth for someone who was sinless, and he got up one day before breakfast and said, 'I'm going to send my Son into the world.' So Jesus of Nazareth came to this earth. He never sinned, not even once – he was perfect.

Letting God Love Us

I want to give some reasons why we should let God love us:

1. God loves us because he does

That is, as I said, part of what makes God, God. And to keep the friendship going we all need to be reminded of this. You see we do things for one another, but God just keeps on loving us. There is no earthly frame of reference to measure what his love is like. Jacob didn't trust Esau, for he didn't trust himself. Jacob didn't trust Esau because he thought Esau was really like *he* was. He didn't trust Esau because he didn't really trust God. It turned out that *Esau* was really the gracious person. Have you ever noticed that sometimes in the parables of Jesus it was the most surprising person who was gracious, for instance, the Good Samaritan rather than the priest or the Levite? (see Lk. 10:25–37). Here was Jacob who *ought* to have been gracious because he had had an experience with God. But no, it was Esau. Yet I have to tell you, I'm afraid I'm like Jacob, I've let God down. However, it has really gripped me that at the end of this chapter in his life, after the way he'd been, Jacob set up an altar and called it El Elohe Israel. 'All's well that ends well.'

One of the weakest, if not the most wicked, men was King Henry VIII. He's the skeleton in the cupboard for the Church of England as he was the cause of the Church of England coming into being. If Henry VIII had had a son by his first wife, there probably wouldn't have been a Church of England. He killed his wives off to get a son. When he was dying of syphilis, it is said, the priests prayed with him and asked, 'Your Majesty, if you can hear me, and you have hope in the blood that Jesus shed on the cross, and all is well with your soul, will you just squeeze my hand?' He did. That's the same thing as setting up an altar. Henry didn't deserve that chance, but neither do we. Who is worthy among us? The King could do nothing as he lay dying except let God love him. That's what I want you to do whenever you go to the Lord's Table – just let him love you.

In 1 Kings 19, God was trying to have an intimate relationship with Elijah who kept saying, 'No, I'm no better than my fathers' (see v. 4).

It's as though God replied, 'Whoever said you were!' He just wanted Elijah to know that he loved him just as he was.

We all feel that we have to break new ground, to do something that no one else has done and do it better. We can then ask, 'Lord, how am I doing? Do you love me now?' That's not what God wants. He wants you to let him be God, for no one else is like him who can love you as you are, because his Son paid the price. We should let God love us because he does.

2. God wants us to enjoy his loving us

Paul told the Corinthians, 'You are a letter from Jesus' (see 2 Cor. 3:2). Did they deserve to hear that? You could say that they certainly did not.

But Paul said, 'It is true. You are a letter from Jesus.' This is why I am gripped by Psalm 103: *'He does not treat us as our sins deserve or repay us according to our iniquities . . . As far as the east is from the west, so far has he removed our transgressions from us . . . For he knows how we are formed, he remembers that we are dust'* (vv. 10, 12, 14).

You may have a particular weakness that you wouldn't want to admit to anybody, apart from one or two who are close to you, who already know it very well. The Bible says that Jesus is touched by the feeling of our weaknesses (see Heb. 4:15). He is *touched* – he is not turned off. That's our heavenly Father. We can know God loves us because he wants us to enjoy his love. How would we know God loves us if we got everything perfect first?

If we did manage this, we would say, 'Lord, I am enjoying your love now.'

He would reply, 'You don't realize that I would just love you anyway.'

We don't let him love us. We continue to just try to perform, but God says, 'I wish you would let me love you just as you are.'

When we get to heaven, I guarantee you are going to see how much you were loved the whole time. You are going to think, 'If only I had realized it then.' But it's all there in the Bible: *'How precious to me are your thoughts, O God! How vast is the sum of them! Were I to count them, they would outnumber the grains of sand'* (Ps. 139:17).

3. God chose us

He chose us before we were even born. He chose Jacob, knowing exactly what Jacob was like. Do you see the marvellous thing about the love of God? He knows what the future is, yet he still loves us now. Jesus could say to Peter, *'Before the cock crows, you will disown me three times'* (Jn. 13:38), and addressing all his followers, he continued, *'Do not let your hearts be troubled. Trust in God; trust also in me.'* (Jn. 14:1).

I could love all of you, but if I knew that tomorrow morning you were going to betray me, I don't know if I could say, 'Don't worry about it. I know you love God.' I'm not so sure I could say what Jesus said to Peter, but he did say it. Why? Because that's the way God is. He knew everything when he chose us. I don't understand the rationale of God's choice; all I know is that it had nothing to do with our works but everything to do with his purpose and grace. So when we let God love us, we dignify his choosing us. 'Why did you choose me, Lord? Why did you save me? I don't understand it. But you did. Thank you.'

We should let God love us because his grace and his plans take into account our failures, our unbelief, our self-righteousness and fear. There are two things to understand: (i) The sacrifice of Calvary dealt with it all. The blood of Jesus saves. (ii) God has his own secret way of dealing with us at his own pace. He didn't look down at Jacob and say, 'I can't let you build an altar to me. You really disappointed me, Jacob, after that wonderful experience I gave you. I changed your name, and yet you were silly with Esau. You ought to be ashamed. I am not going to let you build an altar to me.' No! God allowed Jacob to build an altar to him, and God affirmed him. It was a great moment.

You may wonder about some people and you may ask, 'Why are they like that?' But God is gracious to you, and he is gracious to them. Sometimes he deals with one person at an earlier stage than he deals with another, but to some degree we are all in his will. If I haven't got a particular area of my life right, he may let me get away with it for years. Then, maybe, just before I die, he might put it right. But with some, God may act the day after they are saved. God doesn't want us to stop that good feeling that comes from his love by checking our spiritual pulses every day. He says, 'If only you could know that I love you just as you are.' We desperately need the kind of love that only God can give. Can you let God love you as you are?

30

Are Some Sins Worse than Others?

Genesis 34

The Bible doesn't cover up the faults of its heroes, and although Jacob, who became known as Israel, was in a sense the most popular, colourful and, in some ways, the greatest man of the Old Testament, he wasn't perfect. There was so much about him that was undesirable, as we shall see in this chapter. We also see the 'bad guys' were those within the family of faith, and although there is no way we can justify what the Shechemites did, they turned out to be quite respectable people.

Jacob's Daughter

Jacob, who had been chosen, and who had everything to live for because of the promises of God, once again became bogged down with painful family problems, this time with his daughter Dinah. We didn't know he had a daughter until now. Maybe Jacob himself was hardly aware of her; maybe he didn't concern himself with his daughter. I'll give you one little 'throw-away' comment: if you don't spend time with your children now, they will take your time later.

Here we have a story of a daughter who was able to do the unthinkable. Surely caring parents would not have allowed this to happen? Apparently bored with country life, she went to the city. One translation simply says that when Dinah went to the city, *'Shechem . . . took her and defiled her'* (Gen. 34:2 AV). The New International Version has translated it this way: *'Shechem . . . took her and raped her.'* However, many commentaries have not regarded this as rape but rather that Dinah lost her virginity, and this was the disgraceful thing. Now, while the entire chapter does not revolve around this point, I have assumed that it simply meant she lost her virginity. The context suggests that because there is no hint that she wanted to leave the place where she had been living. After a person has been raped, they don't usually want to stay there, and the rapist doesn't usually want that person for his wife. But Shechem was a man who was in love, and this is why I question whether 'rape' is the right word to use. Shechem's family showed themselves to be very respectable, and clearly he loved Dinah and wanted to marry her. So his father came to persuade Jacob to allow this marriage.

Revenge

What happened was that behind their father's back Jacob's sons made a deal with Shechem, his father and the whole family. It was all very deceitful. They said, 'Look, we cannot allow one of our family to marry an uncircumcised person. It's just not a part of our religion. But if he becomes circumcised, together with all the males in your family, then we can allow it.' They talked it over and reached agreement. But it was a trap because they knew the physical effect circumcision would have on all the men. On the third day, when the Shechemites were in the greatest pain, and presumably at their weakest, Levi and Simeon, two of Jacob's sons, went in and attacked the unsuspecting city, killing every male. They put Hamor and his son Shechem to the sword, took Dinah from Shechem's house, and left. It shows they had no need to rescue her from Shechem, for there's no hint but that she was very happy to stay with him. However, the point is that the city was plundered. And when he found out what had happened, Jacob reacted like this:

> 'You have brought trouble on me by making me a stench to the Canaanites and Perizzites, the people living in this land. We are few in number, and if they join forces against me and attack me, I and my household will be destroyed.'
> But they replied, 'Should he have treated our sister like a prostitute?' (Gen. 34:30).

Learning from Dinah

1. Looking for friendship and fun outside the Christian family means problems

Dinah wanted to go to the city, and she went there, obviously alone. How could this have happened? How could anybody be so foolish? But it happened, and her life changed totally because of this. We are told that Lot, who was Abraham's nephew, pitched his tent near Sodom which had a reputation of being very wicked. But Lot decided to live near there (see Gen. 13:12). There are those people who want to see how close they can get to danger and still be kept safe. How close can you get to the world and still not give in? If we use this kind of rationale, it shows how little sense of the fear of God we have in us.

We know that Jacob had been a deceitful man, and that all his family knew it. So it is possible that the reason Dinah could do what she did was that she had seen her father do what he did. Only days before, he had been deceitful towards his brother Esau who had been ready to 'kiss and make up' and become friends. His children saw that. This is a message for parents: our children watch us, and what they see in us gives out certain signals that they interpret as freedom.

2. Marriage outside the Christian family is unbiblical

Here was the big problem: Jacob could not allow his daughter to marry a Shechemite, and they were trying to work out a way whereby it could be possible. But there is a principle running right through Scripture that believers should not marry non-Christians. I will go further than that. It is a risky thing to keep company with a non-Christian of the opposite sex if you are thinking romantically. I know of happy endings, and I know of stories where this happened and the man, or the young lady, has been converted to the Christian faith as a result, and we thank God for that. But it is risky. I would urge anybody reading this to be very careful. The first thing you will want is to have a wife or a husband who is converted.

3. Worldly people don't understand Christian ideals

It says in verse 8: *'Hamor said to them, "My son Shechem has his heart set on your daughter. Please give her to him as his wife. Intermarry with us; give us your daughters and take our daughters for yourselves. You can settle among us; the land is open to you. Live in it, trade in it, and acquire property in it."'* That sounded reasonable, but that's the way the worldly person thinks. As Christians, we live by a different code of ethics, a code of morality and principles that the world doesn't understand. You see, the people of God are to be a *separated* people. They are different; their ideals are different. So Jacob faced a dilemma because there would have been a high price to pay so that Dinah could have had the respectability of a marriage. For had that taken place, it would have meant that the whole of Israel would have lost their distinct identity.

Using Sacred Ritual to Cover Sin

The sons of Israel, Simeon and Levi, went to Shechem and Hamor and said, 'Now look, we have a little problem here: we just couldn't allow our sister Dinah to marry an uncircumcised person. But we'll make a deal with you – if all the men get circumcised, we'll agree to the marriage.' That was the abuse of a holy, sacred ritual. Circumcision was the sign that you were a part of Abraham's covenant. Circumcision in itself didn't do anything except send a signal that this body of people was different. Yet it was the way in which they were distinguished from all others. But the brothers weren't the slightest bit interested in the Shechemites getting to know the true God. It wasn't the case of Simeon and Levi saying, 'Our God is the Creator of heaven and earth; our God is holy; our God is wonderful. He wants to have fellowship with you, and we want you to know him. You have to be circumcised.'

You know this is the same thing that can happen whenever, to get a quick conversion, a person says, 'All you have to do is to join the church and be baptized.' Perhaps you have had some idea that all I want to do is to be part of the church, or I want to be married in a church, or I just want some token of religion because it makes me feel better. But you would do me no favour to imply that being baptized will make me a Christian.

The Cause of the Trouble

I wish this were not true, for it is so sad. This problem with Dinah, going to town, losing her virginity, and all the problems that resulted in her brothers trying to make everything right by killing the Shechemites, could have been avoided if Jacob had done what God told him to do in the first place. He said, *'I am the God of Bethel . . . Now leave this land at once and go back to your native land'* (Gen. 31:13). When we don't obey, there is a sense in which God's hand is lifted and he just lets us go, and we can get into all sorts of trouble. It doesn't mean that we lose our salvation, but it does mean that we lose an anointing, an ability to think clearly and a sense of what is right. Sadly, Jacob was now seeing the consequence of disobedience.

Categories of Sin

I deal now with the question of various types of sin:

- Predictable sin. Dinah went to the city, acted very foolishly and got into trouble. Have you done something that when people hear about it they say, 'Well, what did you expect?'
- Avoidable sin. This whole situation could have been avoided if Jacob had obeyed and Dinah not gone into the city.
- Hypocritical sin. In using religion as Simeon and Levi did by abusing the rite of circumcision, they abused something that is most holy.
- Presumptuous sin or planned sin. The Bible talks about presumptuous sin as opposed to being overtaken in a fault. What's the difference? Well, here's a person who loses his temper and says things he wishes

he hadn't said. Thirty minutes later, he asks himself, 'Why ever did I do that?' Or here's a person who had not planned a sexual encounter but, perhaps, is momentarily overcome with lust and is so sorry afterwards. But what we are talking about is deliberate, planned sin, where Simeon and Levi had purposefully set out to connive and use the sacred ritual of circumcision to hoodwink the Shechemites. Presumptuous sin and planned sin is where you justify what you do to make it look good. So what Simeon and Levi did in killing people and then abusing this ritual was wicked.

- Blindness to sin. What partly makes sin, sin, is that we lose all sense of objectivity about ourselves and what is going on around us. I refer now to Jacob and his comment when he heard about dozens of men and women being killed and his sons plundering the whole town and taking the women captive. Jacob said, ' *You have brought trouble on me* ' (Gen. 34:30). Which do you say was worse, the possible rape, the attack of Simeon and Levi, who killed and plundered the whole town, or Jacob's reaction? His first thought was, 'Look, what you've done to *me.* ' It showed Jacob's heart and the deceitfulness of his heart.

- The sin of self-justification. 'How could you have done this to me?' Jacob asked. And his sons replied, *'Should he have treated our sister like a prostitute?'* (Gen. 34:31). Was that supposed to make it right? In other words, they excused themselves. I wonder if that's you? What you have done is wrong, but you have excused yourself. What you have done cannot be justified, and yet you have justified it.

Are Some Sins Worse than Others?

How serious is sin? Is all sin equally reprehensible and wicked before God? Now, this is important because there are people who say, 'Any sin is sin, so if you are going to sin, do it well and enjoy it.' I've known of people who, in order to justify what they wanted to do, have said, 'Well, we have sinned already and it's not going to change anything, so let's carry on.' What kind of reasoning is that? Don't assume you have nothing to lose if you sin more seriously. Don't be a fool – that would be the devil trying to get you into serious trouble. However, some sins *are* worse than others, depending upon the effect they have on people and society. The proof of this is that the law does not exact the same punishment for every crime. But all sin needs to be dealt with. All sin needs to be forgiven. The wonderful thing is that one drop of the blood of Jesus will wash all your sins away. Some of you have sinned grievously, some not so grievously. But whatever you have done, whatever is in your past, know that God will give you a new beginning.

31

Hope for the Backslider

Genesis 35:1–15

Jacob was God's chosen one and he was a backslider. That ought to
encourage you. Have you proceeded at a particular point beyond what
God wanted? Joseph and Mary, we are told, went a whole day's journey
and left Jesus behind them assuming that he was in their company. They
had to retrace their steps and go back (see Lk. 2:41–50). That is exactly
what Jacob had to do. What God told him to do he should have done
earlier, and that was to go to Bethel. Bethel was a sacred spot: it was there
he met God and enjoyed an intimacy with him. Now he was in such
trouble. He had lost all sense of objectivity – he was in a pitiful state of
mind – everything was going wrong. But God stepped in and said, 'Go
back to Bethel!'

Returning to Bethel

And that is what he is saying now. Bethel is a symbol of the place where
we can meet God. The difference between you and Jacob is that you
don't have to go two hundred miles out of your way. Bethel comes to
you – it can happen in your heart. The heaviness and confusion you feel,
the lost intimacy with God, and loss of hope for your future, that can all
change. Bethel comes to you. I want you to know that there is hope for
the backslider.

The word 'backslider' means a believer who got 'off the rails' – who
proceeded beyond the point where God said it was all right. So I want
to make this clear, a backslider is a Christian, a person who is saved, a
believer. You say, 'I thought a backslider was a person who doesn't
hold on to their faith.' That may be true, but God never lets you go.
If you have been converted at one time in the past, you are still a
Christian. You say, 'I just can't believe that is true.' But it is. God says,

'I am married to the backslider.' When God accepts you into the family, he treats you with the same dignity as if you were his very own Son. What is the likelihood, in your opinion, of Jesus, who is the Son of God, being dislodged from the Godhead, from the Trinity? That's not possible. There is no way that God would turn his back on Jesus and say, 'You are no longer my Son!' The Bible says that when we are converted we are put in Christ so that we are as secure in him as he is in God. The Bible says we are co-heirs with Christ and what is his is ours (see Rom. 8:17). What happens then when a person gets converted and backslides? They don't cease to be Christians, and it doesn't mean that they will go to hell when they die; they will go to heaven, but there's a lot that they lose.

The Sleepy Backslider

Now what do we know about backsliders? They are set in their own ways. That means that they are unteachable – almost unreachable. People tiptoe around them; they can't talk to them; they can't reason with them. It's very hard to talk to a backslider; they are full of self-pity; they don't think clearly.

Yet I have to say before I go further that sooner or later all of us backslide to some degree, on a scale of one to ten. Ten being the score of the worst and most wicked, overt, obvious type, who bring disgrace on the name of Christ. Reaching one on the scale perhaps is someone whose backslidden state is not obvious to others. A backslider is a person who is spiritually asleep. When Jonah ran from God, he was asleep in the sides of the ship (see Jonah 1:5). He is a symbol of any person who has not obeyed the Lord and who has become spiritually asleep.

Let me tell you some things about people who are asleep:

- They don't know they were asleep until they wake up. When they are asleep they are not conscious of it. In the same way, backsliders are spiritually asleep. They are not conscious of the problem until something happens to jar them, to wake them, and they say, 'I can't believe I was like that.'
- They do things in dreams that they wouldn't do if they were awake. According to Freud, dreaming is an unexpressed fear or wish. Would you want everybody to know your dreams? I wouldn't want you to know things I have dreamed of. You would say, 'And I thought I had problems!' It's only after you wake up that you can't believe that you were in that state.
- Sleepers hate the sound of the alarm. Don't you love it – especially on Monday mornings!

Does somebody ask, 'Is there really hope for me?' Let me tell you there is hope for you. Yet there *are* such people as backsliders without hope. For now that's true. It doesn't mean that they are going to go to hell, but it does mean that they cannot be rescued in this life, for they are unreachable, unteachable to the point that nobody can get to them. You see there are two kinds of backsliders. (i) Those for whom there is hope. (ii) Those for whom there is no hope.

The Backslider Who Cannot Recover

You ask, 'How do you know the difference?' Backsliders who are beyond hope have become stone deaf spiritually. They no longer hear God speak. One of the most difficult passages in the Bible is Hebrews 6 which speaks of true Christians who fall away but cannot be renewed again unto repentance. That means that God doesn't renew them. They are never again to be changed from glory to glory. They don't hear God any more. They have lost their intimacy with him and will never be used by God again. They will have no reward in heaven and, here on earth, no sense of God's guidance. Now, in some cases God isn't talking to them. It is like the case of King Saul who said, *'God has turned away from me. He no longer answers me'* (1 Sam. 28:15). But then there are those cases where the person is stone deaf. I have seen people like this. I have a cousin who I believe is *exactly* like this. If he came to Westminster Chapel, he would listen to me and look up at the ceiling and say, 'This is a beautiful church.' He would see all the lovely things, the way the banisters are made, the organ, he would note the size of the congregation, but he wouldn't really hear a word. I know a little about him, how something happened to him a long time ago, and now he doesn't hear God speak. It is so sad for he had a genuine conversion.

The Backslider Who May Recover

Jacob's story was different. God spoke to him and Jacob heard. The story tells us how to recover from our backsliding ways.

1. Hear God's voice

God said, 'Go back to Bethel!' (see Gen. 35:1). Then Jacob said to his household, 'Let's go. We're going to Bethel.' It's so wonderful when you hear God speak. How do you know it is God speaking? The answer is, when you are gripped, when inwardly you know that God is on your case. That's God talking. There's more: God spoke, and Jacob heard and obeyed. There is a Hebrew word, 'shamar'. Any Hebrew knows that word 'shamar'. The word 'shamar' means to 'hear'; it also means to 'obey'. The Hebraic way of thinking is, if you hear, you obey. It's not possible to hear and not obey.

What amazes me is that Jacob heard God despite his disobedience in the first place (see Gen. 31:3). I wonder if you have looked at this passage and asked how Jacob could have got away with his sin? Do you remember when his beloved Rachel had stolen Laban's household gods, and when Laban came looking, she very cleverly concealed that she had them? Why didn't Jacob say something to her? He should have known this went completely against anything that he believed. But he loved Rachel so much she could get away with anything. So there he was tolerating that which was demonic, occultic. There was also his unbelief after God changed his name. There was his hypocrisy with Esau and his lack of clear thinking after his sons had slaughtered a whole family. Jacob should have been angry with his sons for doing such a thing. He should have had a heart for the women and the children who lost husbands and fathers, yet the only thing he could say was, 'You have got me into trouble! I am going to be a stench to the Canaanites!' (see Gen. 34:30).

That's a backslider, a person who's not right with God and who immediately thinks, 'Well, if I don't get caught, I'll be OK.' There is no conviction of wrongdoing. The proof somebody is not a backslider is they think, 'If I sin, what will God say?' The marvellous thing about Joseph when he refused to sleep with Potiphar's wife was that he said, *'How then could I do such a wicked thing and sin against God?'* (Gen. 39:9). You see a person who wonders, 'Will I get caught? What will people think? What will happen to me?' is a person who is not right spiritually. But now, when God spoke, Jacob heard and he obeyed.

2. Trust in the blood of sacrifice

Another thing I want us to see is the provision of hope for the backslider. We read: *'Then God said to Jacob, "Go up to Bethel and settle there, and build an altar there to God" '* (Gen. 35:1). Why build an altar? What's an altar? I suppose the most popular kind of altar is an ornate affair that would have gold trimmings, a place for the Eucharist, the Lord's Supper. But that isn't what was meant here when God said, *'Build an altar.'* In those days an altar was the place for the sacrifice of an animal. That was because a sacrifice recognized that you needed to have something to take your place because of your sin. The animal sacrificed was a substitute for the sinner. That was what happened here. If you are coming as a backslider to Bethel, you should know the provision for your hope is the blood that Jesus shed for you on the cross of Calvary. It is your only hope. You need to come back and ask for the forgiveness of your sins because of the blood Jesus shed. I want you to know the only thing that is required of you is to put all of your trust in a substitute – that's Jesus. He was God's offering, he was your sacrifice, he took your place.

3. *Purify yourselves*

Then there was something that happened quite spontaneously. The interesting thing is that God didn't tell Jacob what to do, but Jacob *knew* what to do. When you hear God speak, the Holy Spirit will convict you. What do you suppose he did then? At long last Jacob said to his household and all that were with him, 'Get rid of those foreign gods' (see Gen. 35:2). Jacob was so partial to Rachel that when she stole her father's household gods he just blinked at what she did until then. Perhaps you are so partial to somebody, and you love them so much that you tolerate what they are doing. But it is quite wrong and it has an effect on you. If you get right with God you must know that he is impartial. Jacob now had to tell his beloved Rachel that the gods had to go. God is no respecter of persons, so, if there is something in your life that has come between you and him, it must be put right. What is wrong with a 'foreign god'? For one thing it is demonized. I don't understand it, but those who have been involved in these things and have escaped from them will testify the devil gets in. They can describe it more graphically than I can.

When I was a young pastor at a church in Tennessee, a young man who was around 15 years old came to me and said, 'I need to talk to somebody. I have never told anybody this before. I've got a coin that somebody gave me a year ago. The person who gave it to me said, "This will solve all your problems." After I took it, I found that I didn't need to study for my exams. The answers were just there, coming into my head. In fact, because I wasn't an A student, the teacher thought I was copying somebody else's work. So I would intentionally get some of the answers wrong so I wouldn't have a perfect paper. But I could have got a hundred per cent every time. I've had a funny feeling since I have had this coin.'

I said, 'There is only one thing to do. You must throw it into a river.' He promised me he would do it.

And so we read Jacob said: *'Get rid of the foreign gods you have with you, and purify yourselves and change your clothes'* (Gen. 35:2). Verse 4 continues, *'So they gave Jacob all the foreign gods they had and the rings in their ears, and Jacob buried them under the oak at Shechem.'* You may have wondered why he didn't sell them. I would have thought that the little coin that kid had would have been worth a lot of money if anyone found out about its intrinsic powers; people from Las Vegas would have given him a million dollars for it. If you have been playing with anything which was originally dedicated to that which is evil, a good luck charm, perhaps, *don't* play around with it – throw it in the river – get rid of it. If you have been playing with the Ouija board, throw it away, burn it. If you have been reading books that are dealing with the occult burn them. If you have been reading the astrology chart, stop it – don't look at it, even out of curiosity. Anything that would draw you into the occultic world – cut it off.

Notice how Jacob put it: *'Purify yourselves and change your clothes.'* God wants you to look different and keep company with the people who aren't going to hurt you. When you are converted, you are given a robe of righteousness; Jesus Christ is your substitute, and he pleads your case in heaven, but you are expected to live lives that honour him. But when you have the Holy Spirit, you *know* what is right. And when Jacob heard God speak, he knew what he had to do. He said, 'Get rid of the foreign gods, we are going to Bethel.'

So what does hope for the backslider mean? It means four things: (i) God will use you again. (ii) There will be renewed intimacy with God. He'll be close to you. (iii) God's guidance will return. (iv) There's time to build up treasure in heaven. Heaven is your destination. Build on gold, silver and precious stones. It's not too late.

32

The Return to Self-respect

Genesis 35:1–15

Everything was falling apart for Jacob. His family was in disarray and he had lost his self-respect. The best thing that could happen to him was to hear God speak to him once again. God did. He said 'Go back to Bethel.' It was there that Jacob had discovered God for himself. What we learn is that a sense of repentance and conviction so gripped Jacob that he said to his household, *'Get rid of the foreign gods you have with you, and purify yourselves and change your clothes. Then come, let us go up to Bethel'* (Gen. 35:2). What grips me is verse 5: *'Then they set out, and the terror of God fell upon the towns all around them so that no-one pursued them.'* Imagine that – someone so unworthy as Jacob being forgiven and then God coming alongside to affirm and authenticate him, so the fear of God fell wherever he went! It just shows that when we are forgiven we can face anybody and God will use us.

Perhaps you are feeling so distraught and demoralized that you have given up believing God will ever use you again, and you have lost that sense of self-respect – it's a horrible feeling. I want us to see in this story that you can regain your self-respect.

The Sense of God's Presence

Every time I look at these words in Genesis 35:5, I am reminded of something that Jonathan Edwards wrote 250 years ago. At that time, the Great Awakening was taking place in America. America had never seen anything like it. Jonathan Edwards was mightily used by God, and as revival had broken out he did a very wise thing by writing about it. Almost as fast as he could write, a book would come off the press. Much of what he wrote was to speak correction into what was happening, and much of what he wrote was to justify what was taking place. In one book he wrote this: 'The whole town was filled with talk of God.' It was the same thing as happened when Jacob set out to return to Bethel: *'The terror of God fell upon the towns all around them so that no-one pursued them.'* In Acts 5:13 we read a similar account: *'No-one else dared join them, even though they were highly regarded by the people.'* I shall return to this, but it shows, when there is a fear of God upon the people, respect is shown for believers. Now with due respect, although I affirm it, I don't think the Toronto Blessing has done this. But it may lead to this, and I pray it does, and we shall see a fear of God falling on places. That is what happened in Genesis, and to someone as unworthy as Jacob.

When Simon Peter preached on the Day of Pentecost he had so much power that when the fear of God fell on the people he knew it had nothing to do with him. I sometimes think that those of us who try to get it right may be passed over lest we think, 'Now God can use us.' I believe that if God is to use us, there must be an element where we feel devoid of worthiness, self-righteousness and a sense of having prepared.

Jacob hadn't even reached Bethel, but because he had got it right in the sense that he had obeyed the Lord, God honoured him. Yet he knew there was no reason God should do so, for he had acted badly of late. I think that when a church gets totally right with God that can happen and God will honour it.

It brings to mind a service back in Ashland, Kentucky, some years ago, when there was such a sense of the presence of God that a haze filled the premises, and for several minutes those on one side of the room could not see across to the other side. It was the glory of the Lord. It was the way God manifested his glory just for a short period of time. I recall this incident because one of the men involved in the service, a layman who gave his testimony, had such a sense of the fear of God on him that no one in the service forgot it. Apart from the haze, they remembered the almost traumatic effect his testimony had. He ran a little restaurant a block away from the church, and for several days he himself had such power that he witnessed to his customers. You would say everything was wrong in the way he testified. He would go up to a customer and say, 'John, I've known you for a long time. You are lost. You are going to hell.' You would think John would take his business elsewhere, but he broke down and wept, kneeling there on the restaurant floor. The result was that more people than ever came to the restaurant. My friend lost his anointing after a week or two. It didn't stay. My point is that we often think that something that seems 'over the top' is going to scare everybody off. But, as we read in the previous chapter, Jacob buried the demonic, and now God put his seal on what he did. The terror of God fell on the towns around him. What Jacob regained was his self-respect, and God affirmed him.

Gaining Self-respect

Let's consider this for a moment. What had God given to Jacob? What has he given to you? Has he been gracious to you? Has he been good to you? God was gracious to Jacob. He gave him a new nobility. Let me tell you what it means to have self-respect.

You like yourself

Have you ever heard someone say, 'I hate myself?' People who hate themselves don't like other people and they are miserable. But saying this also gives them a certain kind of self-righteous feeling, as if people will excuse them. But when you have real self-respect you like yourself. You may say, 'Oh, I don't think God wants us to like ourselves.' Wrong. The Apostle Paul said that no man ever hated his own body (see Eph. 5:29). Jesus told us to love our neighbours as ourselves, and that is part of being human. But, when you don't appreciate yourself, something has gone badly wrong.

You have confidence

The opposite of being confident is being fearful. Are you governed by a spirit of fear where you don't have confidence? Are you always looking over your shoulder thinking, 'Look who's here! What are they saying? What will they think of me if I do that?' Have you ever wanted publicly to confess Christ but have been afraid of what someone would think if they heard about it? Confidence is lost when you lose self-respect.

You are unashamed

The gospel of Jesus Christ was designed to give you self-respect. Jesus will never lead you to do anything that would prevent you being true to yourself. If you want to regain that feeling of self-respect, of liking yourself and feeling confident and unashamed, you need to come to the foot of the cross and get right with him. Once you put your faith in Jesus you are given the Holy Spirit. He will be with you and will guide you. The Bible will become the most precious book you have ever known, and you will know through the Spirit and the word how to live your life. You will begin to like yourself and to have confidence, and you will not live with feelings of guilt and shame.

New Name, New Nature

One other thing, Jacob was given a new nature. That means God put within him a desire to please him. This is what happens when you invite

Jesus Christ into your life. The Bible says *'If anyone is in Christ, he is a new creation; the old has gone, the new has come!'* (2 Cor. 5:17). It happened to Jacob. It can happen to you.

Jacob returned to self-respect. God called him back to Bethel, the place where he had first experienced God. God had said, *'Go back to Bethel.'* But there's more. We find he had a change of mind. He told his household to get rid of the foreign gods, to change their clothes and purify themselves in preparation for the return to Bethel. And so the real blessing was that his family listened to him. Jacob repented and was given respect, and the terror of God fell on towns all around them.

When you think something is 'over the top' you are afraid the world will no longer respect the church. Let's return to Acts 5 which I quoted earlier. Ananias and Sapphira, who were husband and wife, began playing games with the church and they lied to be part of the crowd. Now if there hadn't been a revival situation and such power, they would have got away with that. Perhaps you have got away with things until now that you never would have got away with if power were present. The trouble was that then power *was* present, and the Holy Spirit revealed to Peter what each of them had done. When Peter rebuked Ananias, Ananias was struck dead right on the spot. Three hours later, his wife came in unaware of what had happened. She too lied to the Holy Spirit and was also struck dead. Humanly speaking, one would say, 'Well, there goes any respect we are going to have. This will ruin the church.' But do you know what we learn? The Bible says, *'Great fear seized the whole church'* (Acts 5:11). It had a salutary effect. Non-Christians no longer tried to join the church in a light-hearted way, tiptoeing into the worship. They now had too much respect for believers to do that. In fact, more and more people believed in the Lord and were added to their number. So what happens when a church gets right with God? The fear of God falls on the neighbouring communities.

God gave Jacob a word of encouragement as Jacob returned to self-respect. God repeated what he had said when Jacob wrestled with the angel, *'Your name will no longer be Jacob, but Israel'* (Gen. 32:28). I think Jacob wanted to hear that but had thought it too much to hope that God would say that again. Perhaps you have known that tender touch of God, yet you have become a backslider, you have not been true to yourself, and you think God will never speak again. Renewal – it's so wonderful! *'If we confess our sins, he is faithful and just and will forgive us our sins and purify us from all unrighteousness'* (1 Jn. 1:9). You'll hear him speak again. You say, 'Surely God won't come back again?' He will, as surely as you are reading these words. He is not mocking you. He will come.

Have you lost your self-respect and your confidence – and you feel so ashamed? (It may not mean you have done anything disgraceful. It could be you have a very sensitive conscience.) If in your heart there is a resolve to honour God and honour what Jesus did on the cross, if you are willing to let everybody know you are putting Jesus Christ first in your life, you will hear him speak again, tenderly and clearly. Bethel has come to you.

33

When God Speaks a Second Time

Genesis 35:8–22

I find such encouragement at the thought of God coming a second time. We don't find it mentioned all that many times in the Bible, but there are times when the Scriptures explicitly say, 'The Lord came a second time.' For example, in Jonah 3:1 we read:

> *Then the word of the LORD came to Jonah a second time: 'Go to the great city of Nineveh and proclaim to it the message I give you.'*

The Bible says of Solomon:

> *When Solomon had finished building the temple of the LORD and the royal palace, and had achieved all he had desired to do, the LORD appeared to him a second time, as he had appeared to him at Gibeon* (1 Kgs. 9:1–2).

Speaking of Abraham, the grandfather of Jacob, the Bible says:

> *The angel of the LORD called to Abraham from heaven a second time and said, 'I swear by myself, declares the LORD, that because you have done this and have not withheld your son, your only son, I will surely bless you and make your descendants as numerous as the stars in the sky and as the sand on the seashore'* (Gen. 22:15–17).

What Is Not Meant

'When God speaks a second time.' There are certain things I *don't* mean by this phrase. Let me give you three examples. I *don't* mean what some would call 'two-step salvation'. I was brought up in a particular denomi - nation where they talked about two works of grace: one when you are saved, and one when you become sanctified and, supposedly, live without sinning from then on. I used to go back to the altar again and again to get sanctified so that I would never sin again, but I always did. I know of some who say they have received such sanctification, but as I get to know them better, it becomes apparent this isn't the case. There is no one who lives without sinning. So when I refer to God coming a second time, I am not referring to what some would regard as a second work of grace.

The second thing I *don't* mean by this subject is daily communion, when the Lord speaks to you through his word. I am thinking of something more definite than that. After all, God speaks to us in some degree every time we read the Bible, although sometimes we feel it more powerfully than others. I read four chapters of the Bible a day, and God speaks to me objectively in every verse, although I may not feel it subjectively. So I could say that he has spoken to me thousands of times. But when I refer to God speaking to you a second time, I do not mean when he communes with you at a spiritual level when you feel that intimacy with him.

The third thing I want to say is that I am *not* particularly referring to the baptism of the Holy Spirit. It could be that does have relevance for some, but I am not dealing with that subject here.

Experiences with God

What we know is that Jacob had some wonderful experiences with God. He had known a degree of intimacy with the Lord, and God had spoken to him. The first major experience he had was at Bethel, and that was so special and, as he was in a backslidden state, God said to him, 'Go back to Bethel!' (see Gen. 35:1). So it was that God came to him at Bethel.

But, strangely enough, Bethel is not what I mean by the first time God spoke to Jacob. Now this could be a little confusing because certainly God did speak to him there. You may think it was the first time, but it wasn't, because the first time God spoke to Jacob was when he was at home. But the first time to which I refer when I compare *this* experience (see Gen. 35:9, 10) is found in Genesis 32 when we find that Jacob wrestled with that angel. You will recall that in verse 28 the angel said, *'Your name will no longer be Jacob, but Israel.'* That was the big moment, the turning point in Jacob's life, when God stepped in and wrestled with him and spoke so powerfully. On the second occasion, the Bible says, *'God appeared to him again and blessed him. God said, "Your name is Jacob, but you will no longer be called Jacob; your name will be Israel"'* (Gen. 35:10). And so it was the mountain-peak experience that stood out above all else.

As I have shown, there is a little confusion here as to when was the first time God spoke to Jacob. Perhaps at this moment you are asking yourself, 'When did God speak to *me* for the first time?' It could have been at your conversion. I expect there are some who can say, 'I have no problem in identifying the time and the place when God "zapped" me, when a laser beam went straight into my heart. I can never forget it.' But there may be others who would have to say, 'I'm not sure when it happened to me.' There are some who are converted but their conversion was so gradual that they couldn't tell you the exact time or the place it happened. Augustus Toplady put it like this: 'You may know that the sun is up, although you were not awake when it arose.'

People who have been brought up in the church, born of Christian parents, sometimes find it especially difficult to pinpoint the moment of their conversion. I myself could say that there is a sense in which I have been a Christian all my life. And yet, at the age of six and a half, on an Easter morning in 1942, I knelt at my parents' bedside and confessed my sins to God. I would say that was the moment of my conversion.

However, I have to tell you it was many years later when I would say it was the first time I really heard God speak to me so powerfully and in such a way that I was never the same again. So I return to the wonderful experience I had one morning whilst driving when I was a student at Trevecca College (see Chapter 23). Something so extraordinary happened that the glory of the Lord filled my car. It lasted for about 45 minutes or maybe an hour. How I was able to drive I will never know, because I was in another world. I was carried up into the heavens and I have never been the same since. God became so real that if every one of you deserted the faith, I would not. If my father deserted the faith, I would not. If all the people I admired said, 'I no longer believe in Christianity', it would not affect me. If I were the only believer in the world, nothing could ever change me. I *know* that Jesus Christ has been raised from the dead, that his death on the cross assures me that I am going to go to heaven. Right now, Jesus is at the right hand of God making intercession for me – I don't think that, I *know* that. So that's what I would mean by the first time God spoke powerfully to me.

How was it for you? Perhaps it was that time you were utterly astounded, and you will never forget it. My old friend Rolfe Barnard, now in heaven, used to say he didn't want to hear people talk about when they were saved. He used to say, 'Tell me about when you knew you were lost.' Do you remember that moment when it hit you that you were in trouble, when you were gripped with the fact that you had offended God and he was really angry with you, and you were ashamed and greatly afraid? You thought then there would be no hope for you at all.

How Does God Speak?

How does God speak? His primary way is through his word, the Bible. As far as I know how, I only preach what the Scriptures ask me to preach. I don't make up things or come up with ideas; I just follow the Bible and let it speak for itself. It means that when I speak the Holy Spirit can use my words, and thus they are not merely *my* words. At some stage, you become conscious that God himself is speaking. A number of times after the service people have asked me, 'How did you know I was there tonight?' I would reply, 'I didn't know you were there, but God knew.'

Sometimes God will speak in a particular context. You may be in a situation where you are suffering; perhaps something traumatic has happened to you; maybe, you have gone through a particular kind of trial, and you happen to be in the service and, lo and behold, the word that is spoken is so relevant and so intimate that it's almost embarrassing. You think that the preacher knows all about you, but it's only the Holy Spirit applying the word. There is another way of putting it: when God speaks, is when the penny drops. Here is the person who hears the same old gospel week after week, and they say, 'I have heard it before and I know all of that.' Then suddenly, the truth hits them and they say, 'Oh, I see it! I see that Jesus lived on this earth, kept the law for us and, because he did, he is our righteousness. I am actually saved by what someone else did. Jesus died on the cross as my substitute, and God punished him instead of me. The blood he shed satisfied God's justice.'

'You've got it. Well, you've heard it a thousand times.'

'Ah, but tonight, I heard it for the *first* time.'

Someone has said that no one has the right to hear the gospel twice until all have heard it once, which is a fine statement. But a truer statement would be that nobody hears the gospel once until they have heard it twice, and suddenly they realize that God is speaking to them. You see, only the Holy Spirit can make you understand the gospel.

What does it mean if God does speak to you like that? It means that he loves you and that you are chosen. You ask, 'Doesn't he love everybody?' Indeed, the Bible says that *'God so loved the world that he gave his one and only Son, that whoever believes in him shall not perish but have eternal life'* (Jn. 3:16). So God loves everybody in the sense that he loves the world. Yes. But when you believe on him, it happens that God loves you in a special manner, and only those whom he has chosen see this. When the light is turned on, you see it. That's the Holy Spirit. And the Holy Spirit only applies the word to the ones whom God has chosen. So when you know God has spoken to you once, and you realize that he's with you, it means that God loves you, he has chosen you.

Hearing God's Voice

What is it like if God speaks to you a second time? We're talking about something that is very unusual. It is as unusual as the first time. God doesn't always pay a second visit to those to whom he has spoken before. He doesn't have to; he doesn't need to. What is it like when he does?

- It will be very real. Just as real as the first time. When God speaks a second time in the manner I refer – when he came to Jonah, to Abraham, to Solomon and as when he came to Jacob, it would have been a very real experience. In fact, let me show you how it is put: *'God appeared to him'* (Gen. 35:9). How did he appear? Was it in a vision? Maybe – I don't know. All I know is that God turned up and Jacob said, 'I will never forget this.'
- It confirms what God said the first time. Now what did God say to Jacob the first time? *'Your name will no longer be Jacob, but Israel'* (Gen. 32:28). What was it God said the second time? *'Your name is Jacob, but you will no longer be called Jacob; your name will be Israel'* (Gen. 35:10). Sometimes a person needs to hear the same thing again. When God came to Abraham the second time, he said the same thing as before. *'I will surely bless you and make your descendants as numerous as the stars in the sky and the sand on the seashore'* (Gen. 22:17).
- It is often in a context of special circumstances. Jacob had suffered great tragedy. First, there was the death of his mother's nurse Deborah. Second, was the death of Rachel, his beloved wife. Third, was the gross sin of his first son Reuben, and finally his father's death. So when God speaks a second time, it's because you especially need to hear him speak to get you through whatever lies ahead. I can tell you this: if you want God to speak to you a second time – if that's what you need – that's what you will get. *'No good thing does he withhold from those whose walk is blameless'* (Ps. 84:11).

What does it mean then when you are one of those to whom God comes a second time and when he speaks powerfully again?

After Jonah was swallowed up by the great fish, God said to Jonah, 'Go to Nineveh and preach' (see Jonah 1:1). But Jonah said, 'I don't think I like that idea. I don't think I am going to do that.' So he got on a boat to Tarshish. God sent the wind, he sent a storm. Jonah was thrown overboard and he was swallowed up by a fish. He was in the belly of the fish for three days and three nights, and he prayed like he never prayed in his life. Then, mercifully, the fish spat him out, ejecting Jonah on to dry ground. There was no guarantee that God would come to Jonah again. He didn't have to send the wind and the storm after Jonah disobeyed him. He didn't have to overrule in the mariners casting their lots so the lot fell on Jonah, but he did. God didn't have to send the fish, but he did. He didn't have to speak a second time, but he did. What do you suppose he said? 'Go to Nineveh' (see Jonah 3:1). So if God speaks to you the second time, you heard him correctly the first time; the orders haven't changed. What does it mean? Note four things: (i) God cares a lot. (ii) He wasn't speaking aimlessly the first time. (iii) You are special. You are earmarked for something special. (iv) He wants you to believe what he has said the first time and never forget it.

If you are reading this and you are a Christian, and God has spoken to you a second time, you know what you have to do. You should know you are special and his message is the same. God really wants you to believe what he has said.

If you have never been converted, you should know how serious it is if God speaks a second time and you do not respond. God has come again and you have been given special attention. Don't disregard God this time. Obey him.

34

Coping with Sudden Change

Genesis 35:8–29

Did you ever wake up one day only to discover nothing is like it was? Everything has changed. You have different surroundings, different people around you and a different outlook – and it happened almost overnight. It is as if the bottom of your life dropped out without any notice. You are having to cope with sudden change. Nothing prepared you for it, and you are now in a new world. A new, strange, lonely world. That happened to Jacob.

Now there's more than one kind of change. There can be an unforeseen change for the better and you are glad that nothing is like it was – you couldn't be happier, and also voluntary change – you made it happen. The change in Jacob's life was involuntary and it was not pleasant. Yet, even though the change for Jacob was caused by external factors and he didn't ask for it, no doubt it had the inevitable effect of changing him inwardly in certain ways, and that for the better. When we are living within the purpose of God the trauma of unwanted change will improve us, and the day will come, sooner or later, when we will thank God for all of it, although at the time we couldn't be convinced that was possible. But man is born to trouble as sparks fly upwards, and change – sudden change – comes to most people, and it is inevitable. But for the most part, we don't like it, especially if everything has been going along fairly well.

Four things happened to Jacob in a very short period of time. Three were deaths, and one was a family tragedy. There was the loss of his mother's nurse Deborah, and I will explain in a moment why that was hard for Jacob. Second, there was the loss of his beloved wife Rachel. Then came the death of his father. On top of that, came the tragedy of his son's unthinkable wickedness when he slept with Bilhah, his father's concubine. The result of all four things coinciding so traumatized Jacob that, for him, nothing would be the same again.

There are four things I want us to see about what happened to Jacob, and Jacob having to face and cope with sudden change.

1. A Change of Place

Jacob moved twice during this time. Psychologists say that the second greatest trauma in life is moving house; the first is the death of someone close to you. Here, Jacob was experiencing both: coinciding with the deaths of three people very close to him was a change of place. It says in Genesis 35:21, *'Israel moved on again and pitched his tent beyond Migdal Eder.'* Now he had been on the move before that, because it says in verse 19 that *'Rachel died and was buried on the way to Ephrath'* which was near Bethlehem. Then we read, *'Jacob came home to his father Isaac'* (v. 27), and *'Jacob lived in the land where his father had stayed'* (Gen. 37:1). The change meant new surroundings, and wherever he was then, until eventually he came home, nothing seemed right. It seems to me that whenever something very significant or precious happened to Jacob, he would erect a stone that was very special. But there was no memorial erected on this journey because everything that happened was awful, and it was as though he wanted to put it out of his life.

We are told in Hebrews 11:9, *'By faith he [Abraham] made his home in the promised land like a stranger in a foreign country; he lived in tents, as did Isaac and Jacob, who were heirs with him of the same promise.'* But what kind of home was that? You may know what it is to want a home where you can just say, 'This is home – here's where I stay.' Maybe you are in a situation where you don't know what to call home, and maybe you are receiving a calling not unlike Jacob's, who was not allowed to feel just then that anywhere here below was home. It may be that God is trying to tap you on the shoulder and hint to you that this world is not all there is, lest you get too attached to anything here below.

2. A Change of Perspective

What do we know about Deborah? The Bible says Deborah, his mother's nurse, died and was buried under the oak below Bethel. She had come to live with Jacob. The scholars tell us that Rebekah had probably died, and obviously Deborah preferred to live with Jacob then. I think that having his mother's nurse living with him would have reminded Jacob of his childhood home.

I recall how, shortly after Louise and I were married, my Grandma McCurley came and lived with us a number of times. It was like having my mother back. You will remember I told you earlier that my mother died at the age of 43 when I was only 17 years old (see Chapter 22). Her mother, my Grandma McCurley, lived until she was 91. But when she died that was the end of an era. This is what it meant for Jacob – the end of an era. He had a new perspective, facing life without any prop from the past. At about this time his father died too. Everybody who had been special to Jacob, his father, his wife Rachel, his mother, and now Deborah, had gone. He had no one who was important to him with whom he could share things. Sadly, Leah was the wife he never appreciated.

Why did all these things happen to Jacob? God brings us to the place that we have to face life without any tie to the past, so that we will get our pleasure, not from knowing who finds out about this or that, but from knowing that God is pleased with us.

3. A Change of Priorities

Rachel died giving birth to Benjamin. There is no hint as to how Jacob took it until you read Genesis 48:7, where Jacob lets you know something of the sorrow he felt. Rachel's departure came suddenly, and early in life, but not before she got right with God. Even though she was Jacob's wife, she had a worldly bent, a leaning towards that which was quite wrong – I mean the occultic – for, as you will recall, she carried with her a household god. How do we know that Rachel became right with God? When Jacob went back to Bethel the second time, he himself had been in a backslidden state, and he said to his household, *'Get rid of your foreign gods.'* They all obeyed him. Rachel got right with God before the end.

There is something else about Rachel. (I say this reluctantly, because I wouldn't want to send anyone on a guilt trip.) Bible commentaries have noted that maybe Rachel asked for this. In Genesis 30:1 she threatened Jacob: *'Give me children, or I'll die!'* It was an unwise remark. Jesus said, *'I tell you that men will have to give account on the day of judgment for every careless word they have spoken'* (Mt. 12:36). We ought to be careful when we say things like 'I would rather die than do that.' Maybe there is something in this and we should watch what we say. As Grandma McCurley used to say to me, 'Mean what you say and say what you mean.'

You may know the expression 'When it rains, it pours.' It must have seemed that way to Jacob. Reuben, Jacob's firstborn, did an unthinkable thing: the Bible tells us that he slept with Bilhah, who was the handmaid to Rachel, and his father's concubine. Sometimes the Bible is given to brilliant understatement, and it just says, *'Israel heard of it'* (see Gen. 35:22). That's all. But later on, when Jacob was on his deathbed, he turned to Reuben and said, *'You are my firstborn, my might, the first sign of my strength, excelling in honour, excelling in power. Turbulent as the waters, you will no longer excel, for you went up onto your father's bed, onto my couch and defiled it'* (Gen. 49:3–4). And so, Jacob's priority changed with regard to his own firstborn. Reuben was special and nothing could grieve Jacob more than the son, for whom he had these great plans, bringing about a family tragedy – incest.

In the New Testament church of Corinth was a man who slept with his father's wife; speaking of that, Paul said in 1 Corinthians 5:1: *'Such fornication is not so much as named among the Gentiles'* (AV). But what Paul didn't say was that the sin wasn't named even in Israel because here was a skeleton in the cupboard of the ancient Jews.

4. A Change of Pace

The time came when Jacob had to slow down. It says in verse 27, he came home to his father. Genesis 37:1 says, *'Jacob lived in the land where his father had stayed, the land of Canaan.'* For a long time he would remain in one place. And it may be that when God brings sudden change into our lives, it means an inevitable change of pace for us. A close friend of mine was taken to hospital some time ago, and he was told that he was in the early stages of congestive heart failure. It shook me up for he is a very close friend and he is younger than I am. He had to change his whole pace. God has a way of getting our attention to slow us down, and this is what happened to Jacob. Is God saying that to you?

There is something I haven't mentioned. Until now, all of these sad events took place directly after Jacob had that great experience with God when he came to Jacob a second time. Let me put it to you like this: Do you want a great experience with God? How much do you want it? One reason God gives an unusual spiritual experience is that person is being prepared for a long haul, or an enormous kind of suffering. God doesn't give unusual experiences just to tickle someone and say, 'Isn't that nice?' No. These are serious things. And so Jacob was given a mighty visitation. It was the last time he was to hear God speak powerfully for 22 years. He was now to undergo the greatest suffering he had ever known. These three deaths and the tragedy of Reuben were to pave the way for what would happen to his beloved Joseph, for God took Joseph from him. What did Jacob have in his favour? He met God in a powerful manner. If you want a great experience with God, you need to know, he gives it for a purpose: it's to prepare you. But for Jacob it also meant a change of pace.

You need, and you can have, not an involuntary but a voluntary change of place. Jesus said, *'In my father's house are many rooms; if it were not so, I would have told you'* (Jn. 14:2). You can know that wherever you live below you are going to go to heaven one day. But you need a change of perspective, a change of priorities, and perhaps a change of pace to get out of the fast lane and make you realize that there are things that are more important than success and all that has been driving you.

35

A Child of an Imperfect Father

Genesis 37:1–11

Do you feel betrayed by God that he chose the particular parents you have, or had? Do you blame your parents for all your problems? A further proof that Jacob was an imperfect father was Joseph. Joseph was the product of a father who wanted to show this son how much he loved him but who went to extremes. Now some see Joseph as a model of perfection, but this is a hasty judgement and far from true. In fact, a close look at Joseph reveals that he is like the rest of us. I want us to look at the life of Jacob and see what we learn about Jacob as a parent.

Three Mistakes

What we know is that in verse 3 it says, *'Israel loved Joseph more than any of his other sons, because he had been born to him in his old age; and he made a richly ornamented robe for him.'* When I was a small boy, my dad told me Bible stories, and I treasure that memory. My favourite story was the life of Joseph, partly because it was so long and meant I had my dad with me a little while longer. But I remember hearing my dad justify Jacob for giving Joseph this coat of many colours (as the Authorized Version describes it) by saying that Jacob loved Joseph so much that he wanted to show it by this gift. Many today don't see that as particularly wrong. However, I want you to know how wrong it is.

Jacob repeated his father's error

Genesis 25:28 says that Isaac loved Esau and preferred hm to Jacob. Now, I don't know about you, but I think that if my dad preferred another in the family and I felt that he did not approve of me, it would be pretty hard to take. I am certain that Jacob resented that and that he was hurt by it. I don't know whether Jacob vowed that if he ever became a father he wouldn't be like that, but it is often the case that when we feel our parents abusing us in some form or other, whether mentally, by neglect, by being insensitive, or by preferring someone else – whatever the form of abuse – we grow up saying, 'If I have a child one day, I am not going to be like that. I am going to be different.' My father told me that as he grew up he was so bitter about the way his father treated him that he determined that when he grew up and had a family he wouldn't be like his own father. And when I grew up, I said much the same thing.

It is a sad fact that statistics show that those who are bitter about the way their parents treated them tend to repeat the very same mistakes. Abused children make poor parents. Yet we should all remember that our parents are like they are because of how they themselves were brought up. The trouble is we all tend to repeat history. The German philosopher Hegel was famous for his saying that the only thing we appear to learn from history is that we do not learn from history.

I love my dad. I honour him and I feel blessed, but if I had to put a finger on his weakness as a father, I would have to say he did neglect me. For example, what I wanted to do more than anything as I grew up was to go fishing. Now, it was my mother's father, Grandpa McCurley, who would do that with me. Every summer, when we went to Illinois, he would take me fishing. I'll never forget the day I caught my first fish in Lake Springfield; it was a little blue gill. I was so excited, and I went back to Kentucky wanting to go fishing again. But, over the years, my dad took me fishing only twice, and even then it was when my mother made him do it. Then, when we did go, he was bored. Looking at his watch, he would ask, 'How much longer do you want to stay here, son?' But *his* father did not know how to be a father to him. My dad, though, was a good father in so many ways. But that is the area in which I felt the most deprived.

Several years ago, the Billy Graham organization approached me: they wanted to make a video to be shown worldwide, and they wanted to interview two or three church leaders in London. I remember that they interviewed me for about an hour, asking questions such as, 'How do you prepare your sermons? What is it like to be where you are?' There were a couple of minutes left when they said, 'Now tell us about your role as a parent and about your family relationships.'

I looked at them and said, 'You can roll the tape if you like, but you are not going to use this because you are looking at a man who wishes he could turn the clock back. If only I had spent as much time with my children as I should have done!' Later, they wrote me a letter saying that was the only part of the tape they *were* going to use because it might encourage pastors around the world.

We are all so sure that we are going to be better than our parents, yet we repeat history. I want to tell you to stop blaming your parents.

You may say, 'I am like I am because of the way my parent treated me.' That is true in many ways, but, although your parents are a major influence on you, they are not the only influence. It will not do for you to go on blaming them endlessly. The time has come when you must say, 'The buck stops with me.'

In Exodus 34:7 we read these words God said through Moses: *'He does not leave the guilty unpunished; he punishes the children and their children for the sin of the fathers to the third and fourth generation.'* Do you know what that is saying? That I am being punished because of the way my great-grandfather was. I don't think that's fair, but that is what it says. Am I to believe then that my great-grandson or great-granddaughter will suffer all manner of emotional problems, or whatever, because of me? It's an awesome thing. We should pray that not only do we no longer blame our parents but also, by the grace of God, that we break the cycle of this sad legacy and we do not repeat history.

Jacob justified his favouritism

The Bible says, *'Israel loved Joseph more than any of his other sons, because he had been born to him in his old age'* (Gen. 37:3). As if that makes it right! But Joseph was the firstborn of his beloved Rachel, and Reuben, who was his eldest son, disappointed him as we saw in the previous chapter. So it's obvious that Jacob was not now going to give to Reuben the rights of the firstborn. He wanted to transfer those rights to Joseph. Leah was still alive, the wife he never wanted. Perhaps he resented having to be a father to her children, especially to the firstborn Reuben. He had loved Rachel so much that giving all his affection to Joseph was, perhaps, a way of showing his love for her.

So he gave Joseph this robe. Scholars tell us the robe symbolized a different kind of lifestyle: it represented an easier life. It showed that Joseph wouldn't have been expected to be a shepherd and work hard – he would 'have had it made'. There was a silver spoon in his mouth. Perhaps Jacob was thinking that if he had been an absentee father with Leah's sons he would compensate with Joseph, and he was going to ensure that Joseph was now treated like a father *should* treat a son. He was going to be so good to Joseph and see that his firstborn to Rachel would turn out to be a wonderful person. He was going to guarantee it by giving Joseph a lot of attention. We call this 'smother love'. Some think that 'smother love' is a good thing. Let me tell you something. This story shows that too much attention is as detrimental as too little. Never think that the child you prefer is going to be better off if you say, 'I am giving this child a wonderful break because I love them more than any of my other children.' You would be wrong. But, whatever the reason, Joseph became Jacob's new priority. As I said there was an explanation for Jacob's behaviour; but it doesn't make it right.

Jacob was slow to rebuke Joseph

It's the only time we ever hear that he rebuked him – but it was a bit late for Joseph was now 17 years old. It says in verse 10: *'When he told his father as well as his brothers, his father rebuked him and said, "What is this dream you had? Will your mother and I and your brothers actually come and bow down to the ground before you?" '* Here's the story. Not only did Jacob love Joseph best, but Joseph had been given a special gift from God which had to do with dreams. There was no doubt about it – Joseph had an anointing that would follow him for the rest of his life, and one day it would be the chief reason why he would be made Prime Minister of Egypt.

The trouble was, Joseph told his dreams. His brothers already hated him because he was their father's favourite. Nevertheless, he gathered them all around him and said, 'Hey, guys, listen to this dream I had last night. We were binding sheaves of corn out in the field when suddenly my sheaf rose and stood upright while your sheaves gathered around mine and bowed down to it. What do you think of that?' You didn't need to have Sigmund Freud around to interpret that dream. His brothers said to him, *'Do you intend to reign over us? Will you actually rule us?'* (Gen. 37:8). They hated him even more because of this dream.

Then he had another one. (You are talking about one spoilt, insensitive teenager, strutting around with his coat of many colours.) Now Joseph said, 'Hey, I've had another dream! Do you want to hear this one? This time, the sun, the moon and eleven stars were bowing down to me.' At long last Jacob was waking up to see the kind of son he had produced, and he finally rebuked Joseph. But it was rather late in the day. The trouble is, like Jacob, we all want to try and correct our children when it is too late.

Three Results

Now, let's look at the result of this kind of parenting.

Joseph was a 'tattletale'

The first thing we see is that Joseph was a 'tattletale'. Verse 2 tell us that Joseph brought their father a bad report about the sons of Bilhah and sons of Zilpah. Not a very nice thing to do, but that's the first thing we learn about Joseph: Jacob had brought up a son who was encouraged to be like that. Suddenly, he was no longer one of the boys; he was different, and he was encouraged to spy on his brothers.

Jacob brought up a son who caused such jealousy

Verse 4 says: *'When his brothers saw that his father loved him more than any of them, they hated him and could not speak a kind word to him.'* This was not Joseph's fault; it was Jacob's mistake in spoiling him.

Jacob created an insensitive child

Joseph would tell his dreams to the brothers who already hated him. It was a stupid thing to do, for a child can grow up so spoilt that they lose all sensitivity to what other people are thinking.

God Gets Involved

But now something interesting, although it rather adds insult to injury: God stepped in. And who do you think that he had chosen to be the future Prime Minister of Egypt? Was it Leah's firstborn? No, it was Joseph. Preparing the way, God had sovereignly given Joseph a gift of interpreting dreams. Does that make you angry with God? Why would he give such a gift to a child who was already spoilt rotten? Why didn't God spread his favours and give something to Reuben, something to Levi, or something to Simeon? Why give it to Joseph? He already had everything.

Yet sometimes God *will* take a spoilt child who doesn't deserve it and give them a special gift. But let me tell you something else: before that child can be mightily used by God, they will go through a period of intense suffering to compensate. No one would have wanted to be in Joseph's shoes: he would be betrayed by his brothers, falsely accused by Potiphar's wife, and then put in a dungeon with nothing to live for. Maybe you are a spoilt child and you know it. You are loved; you are favoured, and God has been very good to you. Nevertheless, God has a way of dealing with you.

Perhaps you have a gift and there is nothing wrong with it; it is unimprovable. But maybe there *is* something wrong with you, and you can't be used yet because of what you're like. Do you say, 'I wonder why God is not using me? I have this great intellect, I have this high IQ, I have this particular technique, I have this voice and talent, but God is not using me and I don't understand it.' That's because there is something wrong with you. There's nothing wrong with your mind, your technique or your talent, but you aren't ready. In not letting you succeed, God is being gracious to you.

The Perfect Father

No parent is perfect. Hebrews 12:10 says, *'Our fathers disciplined us for a little while as they thought best; but God disciplines us for our good.'* Notice how it is put: *'Our parents disciplined us as they thought best . . .'* That's the most we are ever going to get from our natural parents – they do as they think best. You may want to go to your mother or your father and say, 'You really made a mess of bringing me up!' Yet that's the way parents are. They do as they think best, punish when they lose their tempers, and scold their children in front of other people.

But only God is the perfect Father. God disciplines us for our good, and he doesn't make mistakes. Many of you have had an imperfect parent. Some of you can't call God Father because your only frame of reference for a father is that the man who fathered you wasn't very nice. Let me tell you something: If we have to have a perfect father in order to address God as Father – then no one would be able to do it. We are not supposed to look to our natural parents for the perfect frame of reference of what a father is supposed to be like. Let me tell you at whom you are supposed to look. Jesus himself said, *'Anyone who has seen me has seen the Father'* (Jn. 14:9). If you want to see the perfect father, look at Jesus who will accept you like you are. When he disciplines you, he will get it exactly right; he will love you like you are; he will never desert you, and he will give you all the time in the world. Look to Jesus. He is your frame of reference.

Despite Jacob, Joseph was a sovereign vessel. He was a special person in the sight of God to be given a special work to do. There was nothing wrong with Joseph's gift, but a lot wrong with Joseph. Yet God had his own plan for him, and it wasn't going to happen with Jacob breathing down his neck. God saw what he had to do, and he removed Joseph from Jacob's life.

Let me say this: you and I need to remember that God has a plan for our children as well as for us. The time comes when we have to release them. Maybe, after they are too old to discipline, we still want to point the finger and straighten them out, as Jacob was belatedly doing with Joseph. But God said, 'Jacob, I am going to take Joseph. I am going to show you what I can do with him when I have him all to myself.' Perhaps you who have children need to join me in releasing them to God.

One last point, Jacob hung on to one thing. After Joseph told his brothers all these dreams in such an insensitive manner, the Bible says, *'His brothers were jealous of him, but his father kept the matter in mind'* (Gen. 37:11). I think that's profound. It meant that despite Joseph saying what he did, Jacob thought, 'There's something here.' I don't doubt that even after Jacob thought Joseph was dead, he looked back on that moment and said, 'Just maybe . . . ? Two dreams – and they both said the same thing.' Perhaps you have had a prophetic word about a son or daughter, or God has given you a promise about your child or about someone else dear to you. At the moment, it doesn't look as though it's going to come about, but you have something to hang on to. Just maybe . . . ?

36

The Brilliance of God's Providence

Genesis 37:12–36

We have reached the point where all that happened to Jacob was partly because of Joseph, and their stories overlap from this point. Jacob had lost his beloved Rachel and he now poured all his affection on Joseph. Because of the disgraceful behaviour of his firstborn Reuben, Jacob transferred the rights of the firstborn to Joseph and gave him the coat of many colours – the ornamented robe – that not only was beautiful to look at, no doubt, but symbolized a different lifestyle from that of his brothers. Jacob was going to make life easier for him.

The problem was that Joseph was a spoilt 17-year-old teenager, and all this went to his head. It also caused jealousy and surprise among the other sons. Yet behind all of this was God's own plan for them all. We call it providence. The word 'providence' means God's overruling ways in the affairs of his people. As William Cowper wrote in his famous hymn:

> God moves in a mysterious way
> His wonders to perform;
> He plants his footsteps on the sea,
> And rides upon the storm.

We sometimes refer to it as God's inscrutable providence. It means that you can't figure it out until it's all over. You don't know what's happening; you don't know what God is doing, and you don't see how all of this could possibly work together for good. As Paul put it in Romans 11:33: *'Oh, the depth of the riches of the wisdom and knowledge of God! How unsearchable his judgments, and his paths beyond tracing out!'* You can never work out in advance what God will do, and you can never predict what will happen next.

Now I want to deal with three things. First, I want to explain how Jacob lost Joseph and what followed. The second thing we are going to look at is the inseparable connection between suffering and being a sovereign vessel. Finally, we are going to look at certain principles of God's providence.

These things are important for the following reasons:

- The providence of God is one of the main fringe benefits of being a Christian. It's a *fringe* benefit; it's not the main benefit. The main benefit of being a Christian is that you know that you will go to heaven when you die. Don't let anybody ever divert you from that fact. God's providence means that if you are a Christian, you will *always* be a part of God's purpose because he has a plan for your life.
- What was true regarding God leading Jacob and Joseph is true for you. St Augustine told us that God loves every person as though there were no one else to love. God will pour out all of his affections on you. The same God who made the stars and the planets in his vast universe has a plan for you.
- This message should help us never to question God again. We are never sure what he is up to, but as we see how he rules and overrules in our lives, we realize that 'All's well that ends well.' God is determined that everything that has happened to you will work together for good – that's his plan, that's his promise. So rather than question him, if you will lower your voice and wait on him, you will be so glad.

How Jacob Lost Joseph

Jacob had twelve sons in all, and ten of them were out tending the sheep. (Benjamin would have been little more than a baby.) One day, Jacob sent Joseph to check on the other ten. They had decided to go to Shechem where there were green pastures, but Shechem was some 60 miles away. Now it may have been a questionable thing for him to do, sending a 17-year-old boy on a journey of that distance. It meant Joseph would take more than one day to get there. No doubt, for years to come, Jacob would blame himself for sending Joseph because it would be the last time Jacob would see him for at least 22 years, and during that time he thought that he would never see him again. So doubtless Jacob would relive the story: *'I said to my son Joseph, "Go and see if all is well with your brothers and with the flocks and bring word back to me"'* (Gen. 37:14). Maybe it was a routine thing that Joseph had done before, but, no doubt, Jacob constantly asked himself, 'Why ever did I allow him to do that?'

Perhaps you took a decision, and as a result something happened and your life was changed, or someone else's life was changed, and you wonder, 'Should I have done that?' What happened here was God at work, because Joseph was a sovereign vessel, although there was no way Jacob could see God's hand in it at the time.

When his brothers saw Joseph coming, they conspired. Plan A was to kill him. Plan B was to throw him into a cistern and let him die. But Reuben spoke up and said, 'No, let's not kill him. Leave him in the cistern' (see Gen. 37:21, 22). He had every intention of going back to rescue Joseph and delivering him to his father. No doubt, it was Reuben's hope to do something that might compensate for the disgraceful way he himself had behaved. The problem was that Jacob would never know that Reuben tried to do something right, for plan C emerged. It was spontaneous. The brothers saw some Ishmaelites coming, and they sold Joseph to them for 20 pieces of silver and never expected to see him again. Then, verse 31 says, *'They got Joseph's robe, slaughtered a goat and dipped the robe in the blood. They took the ornamented robe back to their father and said, "We found this. Examine it to see whether it is your son's robe." '* Notice how they put it: *'your son's robe'*, they didn't say, 'our brother's robe'. Everything went according to plan because Jacob recognized it and said, *' "It is my son's robe! Some ferocious animal has devoured him. Joseph has surely been torn to pieces." Then Jacob tore his clothes, put on sackcloth and mourned for his son many days. All his sons and daughters came to comfort him, but he refused to be comforted. "No," he said, "in mourning will I go down to the grave to my son." '* Jacob's world came to an end.

Suffering and Sovereignty

Now I use this phrase 'sovereign vessel'. Let me explain what I mean by that. A sovereign vessel is someone chosen by God for a special work. In a sense all Christians are chosen vessels, because a Christian is a person chosen by God from the foundation of the world. But there are those Christians raised up for a *very* special work, and we call them 'sovereign vessels'. I think of Nelson Mandela, a modern-day Joseph if ever there was one, raised up by God for a part of the world which has never been the same as a result of God having his hand on him. But here's the catch: the more special the work, the more specialized the suffering.

In Acts 9:11, God told a man by the name of Ananias, 'Go to Straight Street where you will find a man named Saul. He has just become one of my children.'

Ananias replied, 'Lord, that couldn't be. I have heard many reports about this man.'

'But the Lord said to Ananias, "Go! This man is my chosen instrument to carry my name before the Gentiles and their kings and before the people of Israel. I will show him how much he must suffer for my name" ' (vv. 15–16).

So a sovereign vessel is someone chosen by God for special work, and the more special the work, the more specialized the suffering.

Jacob was a sovereign vessel, and we have already seen how he suffered – but he was undergoing the greatest trial yet. All that he went through in running from Esau, all that he endured through having to be with Laban over those 20 years, and all he suffered in losing Rachel, all of that was eclipsed when he saw that bloodstained coat of many colours. Not knowing that it had been dipped in the blood of a goat, he concluded his son Joseph was dead and he would never see him again. It was the trial of trials.

Perhaps you know great suffering, and just when you think you can't take any more, lo and behold something happens which turns into the worst ordeal you have ever undergone. Listen. It is a hint from God – you are a sovereign vessel – he doesn't do that to no purpose. Deep suffering is a strong hint that God has chosen you for a very special task. It's an honour to be a sovereign vessel. But if you want to volunteer to be a sovereign vessel, don't do it until you're ready for God to deal with the sore spots in your life, for you do have some. Some have sore spots, and it seems as though they have them forever, and nothing is ever done about them. But, if you have been raised up for a special work, God is going to refine you by dealing with the sore spots in your life. You may volunteer to be a sovereign vessel – but don't do it until you are ready to pay the price. The connection between suffering and a sovereign vessel is inseparable.

Joseph was a sovereign vessel. Jacob planned a life of ease for this son, but God had a greater plan. The fact that Joseph was being sold to the Ishmaelites was part of God's purpose. There may be things God has allowed to happen in your life that you don't understand, but if you will wait I guarantee that one day you will look back and see the hand of God in everything.

The Ishmaelites sold Joseph to an Egyptian officer by the name of Potiphar. The Bible says that the Lord was with Joseph and Joseph blessed everybody wherever he went. Potiphar trusted him totally and exalted him in his household. Joseph lived there in total charge. Potiphar had a wife whom he couldn't trust, and she was physically attracted to Joseph. We read that Joseph was handsome and well built. Potiphar's wife found him very attractive and began flirting with Joseph day after day. And day after day he refused her. No doubt he did it politely, but she could only take so much rejection. When she finally made a set for him, Joseph said, 'No, I can't do it.'

Victor Hugo said, 'Hell hath no fury like a woman scorned!', and this seems to be the case here. When Potiphar got home from work that evening, his wife said, 'The servant you hired tried to rape me!' (see Gen. 39:16). Whether he believed her, we don't really know. Someone has said that if he did, Joseph wouldn't have got off with just a prison sentence. What we do know is that Joseph was now put in a dungeon where he remained for a number of years.

One day he got company – the cupbearer and the baker from the house of Pharaoh. Joseph interpreted their dreams and said to the cupbearer,

'You are going to get your job back in three days, and when you do, remember me because I don't deserve to be here. My name is Joseph. J-O-S-E-P-H!' (see Gen. 40:14).

I think God looked down from heaven and said, 'Oh, Joseph, I wish you hadn't said that. You are going to need a couple of more years here yet.' And it was during that time that Joseph learned to forgive. God was not about to exalt Joseph to be anybody of significance until his heart was free from bitterness. God would exalt some of you to high places if you were not so bitter. You are like Joseph who said, 'Remember me. I don't deserve to be here.'

And God says, 'You're not ready yet.'

Someone asked Nelson Mandela how he had changed after he emerged from 27 years in prison, and he replied, 'I came out mature.' That's not all: we learn from Mandela's own lips that in prison he came to understand that bitterness would achieve nothing and would leave him no closer to his goal. So the truth is that Nelson Mandela learned to forgive. After he was released, not once did he express bitterness towards the white community responsible for his ordeal, but instead, he called for a generosity of spirit on the part of the black people to allay their fears. That's the man that God used to change the face of South Africa. Yet look how he suffered! 'Twenty-seven years – these long lonely wasted years!' he wrote in 1985. But perhaps that's how long it took for him to be refined.

Maybe you are in the equivalent of a dungeon, and you can't understand why God would allow you to be in that situation. You ask questions such as 'Why can't I be promoted? Why doesn't God use me?' It may be because you cannot forgive and you are bitter. One would understand why Joseph might have felt bitter. Who could help it when your own brothers sold you into slavery and planned to kill you?

The Providence of God

The first principle to consider is that vindication is what God does best. Vindication means that he clears the name of those who deserve to have their names cleared. Vindication is where the truth comes out. God does everything well, but if you had to come up with one area in which he excels, it is in vindicating. Yet some people never find out how brilliant God is because they can't wait for him to do it his way. The Bible says, ' "It is mine to avenge; I will repay," says the Lord' (Rom. 12:19). That's a promise. God wants to carry out that promise for you, and he wants it more than you do because he loves to show he can vindicate.

Providence means that God overrules. He sets aside something to take over. He works through evil and through our weaknesses. Do you know why he does it? It is so he receives all the glory and honour. In

Joseph's case, God had a perfect opportunity to receive these, because Jacob was a pitiful father, while Joseph was an insensitive, spoilt teenager, and what the brothers did was wicked – it was inexcusable. What God wanted to do through this story was to put a family in a situation whereby, humanly speaking, there was no way out. Are you in a situation like that? God says, 'Give that one to me.' Are you trying to make it easy for God? He says, 'No, I want a difficult case. I want something that humans cannot possibly do. Leave it to me! I'll do it!' Will you let God do it, or do you have to pull a string here and there and say, 'Remember me? My name is . . .'

Humanly speaking, there was no way this situation could turn out for good, but God loves to work when everything looks absolutely bleak. That's where the gospel of Jesus Christ comes in. *'While we were still sinners, Christ died for us'* (Rom. 5:8). Jesus had been betrayed by someone who was close to him, and Joseph, without knowing it, became a *picture* of Christ. And the ten brothers were a picture of Judas Iscariot who betrayed Jesus. One day, Joseph would be able to look at those ten brothers and say, 'Yes, you meant it for evil, but God meant it for good.'

The second principle is that God's providence sorts out the sore spots in our lives. Joseph's sore spot – what was that? It was that coat of many colours. I have often said, 'The only thing worse than giving a coat of many colours was wearing it.' How could anybody wear that thing around? You would think Joseph would have been too self-conscious, but it didn't bother him at all – he strutted around in it. God looked down at that coat of many colours and said, 'That's got to go.' And it went. It was the first thing to go. When the brothers saw Joseph coming, they said, *'Here comes that dreamer!'* and they took that coat. They hated it, but so did God.

Have you got a sore spot? Of course you have. Could it be your pride that's getting you into trouble all the time? Are you hypersensitive? Is it your jealousy? Is it your negative spirit? Is it that you love gossip? Could it be sexual lust or some addiction? Have you stepped on people to get where you are? Do you have an inability to handle money? God has to deal with you. Do you want to be exalted? That's all right. There's nothing wrong with that. God wants to exalt you – in his due time – but the sore spot will have to be dealt with first.

Jacob had a sore spot. Do you know what it was? He was the arch-deceiver. You are talking about a 'con artist', about someone who could 'sell refrigerators to Eskimos', someone who really could manipu - late people. He deceived his brother, his father, and his uncle. The day had come when he himself was deceived. The brothers dipped that coat of many colours in blood and pulled off the greatest deception ever. Jacob had the ultimate comeuppance.

The Lord has a way of dealing with our sore spots. If vindication is due, you will receive it, and if it isn't, you will not. God will know. He will make that decision. Remember this: vindication will always have reference to the honour of God's name and the truth.

The day would come when those ten brothers would be very sorry. In Genesis 42:21, we learn they said to one another, *'Surely we are being punished because of our brother.'* Twenty-two years had passed and strange things were happening. They realized that God was dealing with them. And God will have to deal with you. If you have hurt someone and you are not a Christian, you may get away with it; God may simply send you to hell. If you are a Christian and you have hurt somebody, God may take his time, but you come to realize that you are the one that needs to put things right. The greater the hurt, the greater the honour – that's the principle of vindication.

Talking of honour, I was interested to hear that it was said that Nelson Mandela's moral stature stands out all the more in an age bereft of political morality. His natural authority and charisma are evident to all those who know him; foreign leaders have been only too keen to be seen in his company to enhance their own respectability. One major newspaper said that he is the last authentic hero. The greater the hurt, the greater the honour.

The third principle is that the longer it takes, the greater the outcome. Have you been suffering for a long time? You have seen injustice and you have dealt with the problem of bitterness. The longer it takes, the greater the outcome. Joseph waited for 22 years; the modern Joseph, to whom I have been referring, waited 27 years.

Joseph was snatched away from Jacob without notice. There was no hint that this was God at work. Yet one day, Jacob would see Joseph again, but not until he had lost control and had given up completely, because God wanted to show Jacob what *he* could do. And look what God did with Joseph! Maybe God is speaking to you about someone precious to you, and he is saying, 'Leave it to me.' Once our hands are removed, God's brilliant hand begins to work.

37

Having to Cope with Guilt?

Genesis 37:19–36

In the darkest moment in his life, Jacob had to cope with feelings of guilt. In Genesis 37 are classic illustrations of two kinds of guilt: true guilt and pseudo-guilt, namely, the feeling that you are to blame but which has no valid basis in reality is pseudo-guilt – you shouldn't feel guilty, but you do. The sad thing is that pseudo-guilt can be just as painful as true guilt, if not more so.

Two Kinds of Guilt

Let us look at two kinds of guilt. Consider first the true guilt in the case of the ten brothers who sold Joseph to the Ishmaelites and who had to come to terms with that. The truth is that they did not come to terms with it for a long time. But we read in Genesis 42:21 that they said, *'We are being punished because of our brother. We saw how distressed he was when he pleaded with us for his life.'* Now, they were admitting their wrongdoing; what they had done had come home. That was true guilt.

Jacob experienced pseudo-guilt. When his sons showed him a bloodstained robe, they didn't actually say whose it was: 'We found this. Tell us, could this possibly be Joseph's robe?' The Bible says: *'He recognised it and said, "It is my son's robe! Some ferocious animal has devoured him. Joseph has surely been torn to pieces." Then Jacob tore his clothes, put on sackcloth and mourned for his son many days. All his sons and daughters came to comfort him, but he refused to be comforted'* (Gen. 37:33–35). That final sentence shows that he felt guilty. Any person who didn't have this burden of guilt would have said, 'Thank you so much. I appreciate your comfort. Thank you for standing by me at this time.' But no, Jacob refused to be comforted and continued, *'In mourning will I go down to the grave to my son.'*

There is a simple difference between these two kinds of guilt: True guilt is where *God* says you are guilty; pseudo-guilt is where you blame yourself. Jacob could not forgive himself because he sent Joseph on that errand – a 17-year-old teenager to look for his brothers. Neither could he forgive himself for showing such affection for one son and disregarding the others. Jacob was a man who felt guilty all his life, but his wasn't a case where God said, 'You are guilty.'

First, I address the person who has a sense of guilt which, in fact, is pseudo-guilt. You blame yourself and you feel horrible. It's awful. The feeling is very real and sometimes you feel it worse than others. But, with the help of the Holy Spirit, if I can help you see that what you are feeling is not from God, it could set you free and be the beginning of a new era. However for some, be they those who have never been converted or those who, though Christians, are backsliders, the problem is true guilt.

I want to show the irony of both true guilt and pseudo-guilt. Why use the term 'irony'? Well, irony means what appears to be contradictory but is true. And there is irony concerning true guilt. I am going to deal with this first.

The Irony of True Guilt

1. The first irony is this: You can experience true guilt when you ought to feel guilty and you justify what you do. That's why I call it irony. You would think that if a person feels true guilt they would be ashamed of what they do. They would say, 'Oh, this is awful!' But, you know, the irony is that you can be truly guilty and still justify everything you are doing. *'Here comes that dreamer!'* the brothers said (Gen. 37:19). You see, they were so angry they felt justified. Joseph had told his dreams to his brothers, dreams which didn't need a brilliant interpretation to see they meant that his brothers would bow down to him. He should never have told them that. It just added fuel to the fire and they hated him even more. So when they saw him coming and said, *'Here comes that dreamer!'* it didn't bother them one bit. Anger has a way of hiding sin. Anger has a way of making you do silly things, making you feel justified in what you do. So here is the irony of true guilt: you can do bad things and it doesn't bother you.

2. That brings me to the second irony. With true guilt, you can deny your real feelings. True guilt is often repressed guilt. You avoid pain and simply refuse to admit there is a problem. Our minds have a way of playing games with us, so that we switch off before we even think about something, because it is so painful. But you haven't come to terms with how you really feel. I heard a psychologist say that if he could get clients to come to terms with their real feelings he could cure

any psychopathology in ten minutes. That may have been an overstate -
ment, but what it means is that we tend to dismiss how we are really
feeling.

I may ask you, 'How are you?'

'Very well, thank you.'

'How are you *really*?'

'Very well, thank you.'

'Oh, come on. Tell the truth! How are you?'

'Fine.'

After we have talked 30 minutes, I ask, '*Are* you all right?'

'Well, there *is* a problem.'

'Tell me about it.'

And then, an hour later, you break down. I have had that happen time
and time again. It takes a while for us to come to terms with how we are
really feeling. The irony with true guilt is that you allow yourself to do
that which is against God's will and it does not bother you.

For example, in the Old Testament, a man by the name of Samson
had unusual strength (see Jdg. 13–16). It would not be an exaggeration
to say that Samson had such an anointing that if he wanted he could go
to any of the posts in Westminster Chapel and just pull them down, one
after the other, with his bare hands and then bring the galleries down too.
He did that sort of thing. He had that kind of strength. There has been
no one like him since. People wanted to know the secret of his strength.
He was in a covenant relationship with God, and he had that anointing
as long as he didn't give away the secret. The Bible says, *'The secret of the
LORD is with them that fear him'* (Ps. 25:14 AV).

I have long suspected that God would do so much more for us, and I
include myself, if we would be willing to be quiet about what we know.
We are too quick to blab everything to the world. Samson was doing
pretty well until the woman with whom he was in love wore him down
and he finally revealed the secret of his strength. Here's my point: when
he did this, he didn't feel a thing, but now he was guilty before God. I
mean he had to reckon with true guilt, but he didn't feel it. The irony
of true guilt is that we do things and they don't bother us. Repression is
a defence mechanism to avoid pain, and it lets you get away with murder.
That's what Joseph's brothers had planned – until the last minute they
were going to kill him.

The Bible says that when Samson did what he did, he didn't know
that the Lord had left him. But he had grieved the Spirit of God. The
defence mechanism enables our minds to switch off anything that we
don't like when the pain would be too great to bear. This is why you can
have true guilt, yet feel nothing. Where guilt is concerned, there are only
two things that will cause that defence mechanism to dissolve.

The first of these is the conviction of the Holy Spirit. That's when, in
the mercy of God, his Holy Spirit seizes you, and you come to your

senses. Nothing people can do to make you see your guilt will work. You can be involved in the most ridiculous things, and people can go up to you and say, 'You ought not to be doing that.' You may be involved in an affair, you may be involved in drugs, you may have an addiction to drink, you may have a sexual weakness – or whatever. Everybody but you can see that you are hurting yourself. People tiptoe around you, and they wonder, 'How can I get them to see it?' They want to shake you and say, 'Stop it! Don't you realize what you are doing to yourself? Don't you know what you are doing to people around you?' But the only thing that will make a difference is where the Holy Spirit does what human persuasion can't.

There's one other thing that will take away this defence mechanism, and this is awful – I wish it weren't true. But if you lose your soul you go to hell. That's the only other place to go if you don't go to heaven. I return to the story Jesus told in Luke 16 where two men died and one went to heaven and the other went to hell. In hell, the man lifted up his eyes in torment and the word came to him, 'Remember what you did in your lifetime' (see v. 25). In hell you will have no ability to deny your feelings. I think the pain of guilt is just about the worst feeling in the world. It is so painful that we will do anything to avoid it. If you get a migraine headache, you take a Paracetemol or an aspirin, or anything else that might cure it. But what do you do with guilt? You repress it – you just switch off. It doesn't bother you until the Holy Spirit comes alongside. But if that doesn't happen when you are alive, know that in hell there will be no ability to repress your guilt and you will have to live with the consequence of your sin throughout eternity.

3. Another irony of true guilt is this: you usually get away with it for rather a long time. I can prove it. In the Bible we read: *'They said to one another, "Surely we are being punished because of our brother. We saw how distressed he was when he pleaded with us for his life, but we would not listen; that's why this distress has come upon us"'* (Gen. 42:21). Do you know how long it took them to acknowledge that? It was 22 years before they came to terms with their guilt! I've sometimes said that authentic spirituality is closing the time-gap between the moment you sin and the time you repent; for some, it takes years; for some, it takes only seconds. Look at this: *'We saw how distressed he was when he pleaded with us for his life.'* Can you imagine looking at your own brother, who is probably screaming and shouting, begging, 'Please don't do this to me. Please!' For 22 years they lied. You ask, 'How were they able to do it?' The answer is that it was a case of true guilt and they got away with it for a long time. That's the irony. Sadly, people expect that if it's true guilt, you will feel shame. Wrong. King David committed adultery with Bathsheba, then tried to cover it up and ended up murdering her husband (see 2 Sam. 11). The scholars tell us that it was approximately two years before he came to terms with his guilt, and

that was because Nathan the prophet came to him (see 2 Sam. 12). He was going on fine until then. These ten brothers managed 22 years.

4. The fourth irony of true guilt is that it enables you to cover up as though you did nothing wrong. Look how the brothers did it. It says in verse 31 that they took Joseph's robe, slaughtered a goat, dipped the robe in the blood, and took the ornamented robe back to their father saying, 'We found this robe. Is there any chance this could be your son's?' Yet, strictly speaking, they didn't lie; they simply never told their father what happened.

When David slept with Bathsheba, he felt nothing. She came back a few weeks later and said, 'David, we have a problem. I'm pregnant and my husband has been away for some time' (see 2 Sam. 11:5).

'Oh, no problem. We'll bring him home and he can spend a weekend with you.'

David assumed that if Uriah slept with his wife and she had a baby, he would always think it was his. It didn't bother David at all. Some of you are in a backslidden state, and you have done things that are wrong, but it doesn't bother you. That's the irony of true guilt.

The Irony of False Guilt

1. The first irony is this: with pseudo-guilt you feel it at once, and there's a reason for that. The devil doesn't *mind* you experiencing pseudo-guilt. The devil wants to camouflage true guilt: that's where he comes in and blinds a person to their sin. Paul says that the god of this age has blinded the minds of unbelievers (see 2 Cor. 4:4). And so there's a reason why you could be involved in that which is wrong and everybody sees it but you. The devil is at work; he has got in and has convinced you that there's no problem. The Bible says that the backslider is filled with his own ways – so you just can't reach him (see Prov. 14:14 AV). Jacob's was a case of pseudo-guilt – he felt it immediately.

2. The second irony about pseudo-guilt is that it is very difficult to deal with someone having this. With true guilt, if a person comes to terms with it, you can easily deal with it. The Bible says, *'If we confess our sins, he is faithful and just and will forgive us our sins and purify us from all unrighteousness'* (1 Jn. 1:9). With pseudo-guilt, the person wallows in self-pity and becomes self-righteous and says, 'I know God forgives me, but I can't forgive myself.' And so when Jacob's sons and daughters came to comfort him, he refused to be comforted.

Your not forgiving yourself is blaming yourself, and that doesn't make God very happy. Yet the subtle irony is that then you *are* truly guilty after all but not for the reason you think. You are truly guilty because not forgiving yourself is sin, for you are competing with God. He's forgiven you, but you think you are smarter than he is and you can't forgive yourself. If you know that God forgives you, then, in his name, forgive yourself, otherwise you offend him. He wants you to forgive yourself. He wants you to be free.

3. The third irony of pseudo-guilt is that it has no objective basis in reality. How do we know that in Jacob's case? Because Joseph was alive. It was Jacob who said this, and that illustrates how a person can assume something to be true when it is not. What I want you to understand is that if God forgives you of all your sins because you have confessed them, you can *know* that you are free, you can *know* that you are saved. Psalm 103:12 says: *'As far as the east is from the west, so far has he removed our transgressions from us.'* But pseudo-guilt has no objective basis in reality. In other words, *God* is not saying that you are guilty, and that's all that matters. As long as you know that God is happy with you, that's all that *should* matter.

You may know that after General Douglas MacArthur signed the statement on the battleship *Missouri* in 1945, officially signifying that the war was over, there was an island in the remotest part of the South Pacific where they hadn't heard; there, the Japanese and the Americans con - tinued fighting each other. God is saying that he forgives you, but if you can't forgive yourself, then, rather like that incident, you are dealing with a problem that doesn't exist. God has forgiven you.

4. The fourth irony of pseudo-guilt is that the devil uses it to his advantage, and he gets in after all. We betray pseudo-guilt by how we react to bad news. The Psalmist said that the man who fears the Lord will have no fear of bad news (see Ps. 112:7). Jacob received bad news and he panicked; he went to pieces and nobody could deal with him. Pseudo-guilt causes people to blame themselves because they haven't forgiven themselves.

Finally, I quote Proverbs 28:13: *'He who conceals his sins does not prosper, but whoever confesses and renounces them finds mercy.'* True guilt will even - tually be exposed, but I want you to know how completely God will forgive you. In Genesis 45, when Joseph disclosed his identity to his brothers, he totally forgave them. *'It was not you who sent me here, but God'* (v. 8). That was Joseph's way of saying that everything they had done was fulfilling God's purpose. If Joseph could forgive his brothers, how much more can God forgive you?

38

Completely Convinced –
Completely Wrong!

Genesis 37:31–36

In the summer of 1993, I had a most traumatic experience. We were on our way back to the Keys after meeting our son T.R. in Miami. Louise decided to return to Key Largo with him, while I had to make another stop elsewhere. From Homestead to Key Largo the road is absolutely straight with two lanes of traffic, but it is a very narrow 20-mile stretch of road. There are more fatalities on that stretch of road than on any road in America. It's very dangerous because people get impatient and want to overtake.

After a few minutes the traffic came to a standstill, and when that happens, almost always, it's because of an accident ahead. I waited for about 30 minutes. T.R. and Louise were about a mile ahead, and I just had this feeling of horror. Then I saw someone with a mobile phone and I said, 'Look, I'd be glad to pay you if I could just make a call.' He let me use his phone, but when I called home there was no answer. That confirmed my worst suspicions. After about 45 minutes the traffic still wasn't moving, but every so often a car would come from the other direction. When one stopped alongside me, I asked the driver what had happened. 'Oh,' he said, 'it's a fatality – a young man has been killed.'

'Do you know anything about the car?' I asked.

'Yes. It's a silver-grey colour.'

That was the colour of T.R.'s car. I cannot describe my feeling of dread. Finally, after about an hour, the traffic began to move. When we arrived at the scene of the accident, we saw the tangled wreck of a silver-grey car. There was no way anybody in it could have survived. It looked exactly like T.R.'s car. My heart began to pound. I pulled over and I almost staggered up to the policeman and asked, 'Could you tell me who was killed?'

'No, I am sorry, I can't,' he replied.

I said, 'I'm afraid it's my son.' I told him T.R.'s name.

He said, 'It's not your son.'

But I still didn't believe it until I saw T.R. and Louise were safe at home, because all the evidence – an identical silver-grey car, driven by a young man – pointed to the victims being them.

I wonder if you have ever been in a similar situation where you accepted the evidence because it seemed airtight. Fortunately, I didn't have to wait very long. One cannot but sympathize with Jacob. Ten brothers wanted him to believe that his son, their half-brother, was dead. It was an act of deceit and it worked. For 22 years, Jacob believed his son Joseph was dead.

I want us to see three things from this passage:

1. The Danger of Relying on Circumstantial Evidence

The ten brothers handed the bloodstained coat to their father. '*He recognised it and said, "It is my son's robe!"* ' (Gen. 37:33). The evidence was inconclusive; nevertheless, Jacob came to the wrong conclusion. The evidence was circumstantial, strongly suggesting Joseph was dead, but not providing direct proof. You wonder how many innocent people are in prison at this moment, wrongly convicted by circumstantial evidence. Worst than that, you wonder how many people have been wrongly executed over the centuries, solely on grounds of circumstantial evidence.

Maybe, to some degree, you and I are in a similar situation. Like me, you may know what it is like to be misunderstood. Perhaps you have been lied about, and you know that sincere people believe what they have heard about you, and it hurts a lot. Have you ever distanced yourself from somebody because you believed what others had said about them? It terrifies me to think that I would form a conclusion about a particular person in this way; yet I know I have done this, only to discover years later that I had been misled and consequently I had treated someone unfairly.

There are many examples pointing to the dangers of jumping to conclusions based solely on circumstantial evidence, but I want to give only a few.

One example is unanswered prayer. Suppose you have prayed fer-vently for something for a long time, but God hasn't answered. You may have thought, 'I don't think I will pray for that any longer', so you gave up. Let me tell you something: any prayer prayed in the will of God will be answered, but God may not answer it immediately. One instance of this is in Luke 1 where Zechariah had a visitation by the angel who said, 'Zechariah, your prayer has been heard.'

He said, 'Prayer? What prayer?'

'You and your wife have prayed for a son.'

'Oh, that prayer! That was twenty-five years ago.'

Gabriel said, 'God has heard your prayer. Your wife Elizabeth is going to bear a son.'

Zechariah wanted to argue with the angel. He didn't believe him, for he had become convinced that his prayer would not be answered. It is amazing how, when we get entrenched in a particular view, we will not change it. Jacob tore his clothes and all his sons came to comfort him, but he said, 'No! No! Leave me alone. I will go to my grave in mourning!' (see Gen. 37:35).

Let me give you another example of the danger of judging a situation using circumstantial evidence alone. You may have a fixed and biased idea about how God will work. For example, you may be praying for revival and you say, 'If revival comes, I'll know it. If the Lord shows up, I'll recognize him.' The danger of such inflexibility is that if we are not careful we will miss something entirely.

Another example is the foolishness of using circumstantial evidence to question the authority of Scripture. I know what I am talking about through personal experience. I was trained in a seminary where, at that time, the teaching differed little to the liberal theology being taught in Germany. Young men, who had been gloriously converted, who had come from their home churches to study for the ministry, would sit under professors who didn't believe in the infallibility of the Bible. These teachers would use circumstantial evidence to show why the Bible should be approached critically, just like Shakespeare. Those young men would then say, 'Oh, I see. I can't believe in the Bible any longer.' They were never the same again. I remember talking to a man who almost wept. He said, 'I came to this seminary believing in the Bible. But now I know that it is a faulty document. I intended to go into the ministry. Now, I don't know what I am going to do.'

I wonder how many of you have accepted the critical approach to the Bible uncritically, with the result that your faith has never been the same since. You are just like Jacob who said, 'Ah, that is my son's robe! Joseph has been killed by a ferocious animal.' Completely convinced – completely wrong!

I'll give you another example. Here's a person who, by relying on circumstantial evidence, has given up a particular conviction. A few years ago, I was invited by the University of Aberdeen to examine a thesis written by a Korean student on Thomas Goodwin's doctrine of the sealing of the Spirit. They invited me to be the examiner because I am fairly well known to be one who has studied the Puritans and I was familiar with Thomas Goodwin. The thesis was really quite pitiful – if I had wanted to be really strict I could have failed him. But reading between the lines, I could see what had happened. Before he was able to enter Aberdeen, the Korean had studied for a year in Edinburgh, but at a Reformed college where they didn't believe in the sealing of the Spirit. They completely convinced him the doctrine was false. This boy had been converted in Korea and previously had believed it. I looked at him and said, 'You believed what Thomas Goodwin believed before you came over here, didn't you?'

He replied, 'Yes, I did. But they changed me.'

I said, 'Do you know something? I am going to pass you. So don't worry; you have got your degree. But when you go back to Korea, you must preach this doctrine because it is true.'

He was so thrilled because he wanted to believe that, but circumstantial evidence showed there was no possibility of a direct witness of the Holy Spirit. He had thought, 'Oh, I thought I had experienced the sealing of the Holy Spirit, but I see now how it didn't happen to me.' It's amazing how someone can have a conviction until somebody comes alongside and says, 'You can't believe that any longer.'

2. The Danger of a Careless Examination of the Evidence

Notice this: ' *"We found this. Examine it to see whether it is your son's robe." He recognised it and said, "It is my son's robe! Some ferocious animal has devoured him"* ' (Gen. 37:32–33).

Now why would Jacob listen to them – these hot-blooded, jealous sons who had already let him down once before? It shows the importance of a trustworthy witness. Jacob accepted their deceit uncritically. Perhaps you thought you had all the evidence and that you had examined it properly. However, maybe you were too hasty in your judgement and were wrong. Here's what Jacob *ought* to have done. He should have said, 'Wait a minute. If some ferocious animal has devoured Joseph, why wasn't that coat of many colours reduced to shreds? And another thing – where are his remains? We'll go back. Show me where you found the robe and we'll start looking.' No. Jacob immediately leapt to the conclusion that Joseph was dead. Yet there must have been signs that his sons were uneasy and nervous. The truth is that it was a careless examination of the evidence presented to him.

There are further examples of this in the Bible and perhaps you can identify with them. Take the account of Elijah when he gave in to self-pity and said, '*I am the only one left*' (1 Kgs. 19:10). After a while, God said to him, 'Oh, by the way, there are seven thousand who haven't bowed the knee to Baal' (v. 18). Completely convinced – completely wrong!

Or take the example of Mary Magdalene, who went to the tomb of Jesus to anoint his body and discovered that his body wasn't there. She began to cry, and seeing a man standing there, she was completely convinced he was the gardener, but she was completely wrong! She found out she was talking to Jesus himself (see Jn. 20:10 –18).

Perhaps, thinking you examined everything, you reached a conclusion without examining the issue carefully. So often people will say to me on the streets, 'I don't believe the Bible.'

'Really,' I reply. 'Well, that's interesting! Tell me the part you don't believe!'

'Oh, I don't know. I don't want to talk about it!'

They haven't examined the passage, if indeed they had a particular one in mind. Completely convinced – completely wrong!

But you do not have to commit intellectual suicide before becoming a Christian. Giving your life to God and affirming his word is the wisest, safest thing you could ever do. God will not let you down. You will not be ashamed, and I challenge you now in the name of Jesus to take your stand. It's God's word. His honour is at stake. I guarantee you will never be ashamed. 'Defend the Bible? I would as soon defend a lion,' said C.H. Spurgeon.

3. It Was a Calculated Excuse

Jacob tore his clothes, put on sackcloth and mourned for his son many days. All his sons and daughters came to comfort him, but he refused to be comforted. "No," he said, "in mourning will I go down to the grave to my son" ' (Gen. 37:35). He had a calculated excuse, so when anybody came to comfort him, he would say, 'No, I'm all right. Just leave me alone!' Why? He had taken a stand. Joseph was dead! He was not going to hear anything else.

Do you know what I used to notice at the seminary? The students listened to *one* professor and they now believed that the Bible was not true. And if you asked them if they had carefully examined the issue, you couldn't get them to admit that they hadn't. They are the ones now who are the most adamant that you cannot believe in the infallibility of the Bible. Why? It's because they have a calculated excuse; they have committed themselves and, therefore, the Bible is a faulty document.

It is very interesting to note that when we become entrenched, nobody can reach us. I have noticed that, when they have examined an issue carelessly and have relied on circumstantial evidence alone, people come up with a calculated excuse which leaves them so inflexible that it's not months but years before they can bring themselves to think again. It's because of their pride. What happens when we are deceived? We become inflexible, we become unapproachable, we become unteachable.

Think for a moment. Is it possible that this could describe you? How many more years will you waste? If you believe the Holy Spirit is speaking, ask God to have mercy on you and to give you the ability to think clearly. Thank him for speaking like this to you and allow God to begin the process of restoring the years which have been wasted.

39

Overcoming Self-pity

Genesis 37:31–36

All his sons and daughters came to comfort him, but he refused to be comforted. 'No,'
he said, 'in mourning will I go down to the grave to my son' (Gen. 37:35).

Jacob refused to be comforted. This particular part of Jacob's life is a
classic study in self-pity. Although it may be painful for us to admit it,
the truth is that we have all given way to self-pity. Now I am the world
expert on this subject, so I hope you will believe me when I say I
understand this problem. I think you may find this chapter can be helpful
for two reasons. We need to understand exactly what self-pity is, for
that can pave the way to overcome it. Second, we need to see that
self-pity is counter-productive: it doesn't produce good results and it
never achieves lofty goals. Furthermore, the whole time we are wallow -
ing in self-pity, striking out at somebody else, we are only hurting
ourselves.

Self-pity Is Sin

Self-pity doesn't receive as much attention as some sins receive, and it
doesn't necessarily cause the scandal that some sins cause. Sexual sin, for
instance, has a high profile. Everyone is interested and it causes scandal
in the church. But you can see that you can be overcome with self-pity
and it won't be scandalous. You may think that the devil only wants you
to fall into sexual sin. Listen. The devil doesn't care how he gets hold of
you, so if he can get hold of you by causing you to wallow in self-pity,
he will do it.

How can we define self-pity? It is feeling sorry for oneself, and it is
a self-justifying condition. It always seems right. The frightening thing
about it is that sometimes we fail to recognize we *are* in this condition.

Maybe God will use me and I will help you to see that this is your problem. Maybe the Lord will come alongside you, and as he said to the man at the Pool of Bethesda, he will say, *'Get up! Pick up your mat and walk'* (Jn. 5:8).

In that story there is an illustration of self-pity. There was a man who went to the Pool of Bethesda, a place famed for healing miracles: when the angel stirred up the waters, the first person entering the water was healed. Now here was a man who had been there for 38 years. Jesus was there one day and heard about him. What do you think Jesus said to him? Jesus *could* have said, 'Oh, I am so sorry for you. Look here: I have got power, so I am going to heal you. This is not right – spending 38 years in this condition!'

Had he done that, the man would have answered, 'That's right, 38 long years!'

Instead, Jesus looked at him and asked, *'Do you want to get well?'* (v. 6).

There is no doubt about it, some people love being sick and they feel threatened by the thought of being cured. If they are healed, they may have to get a job, lose their disability allowance, lose sympathy and no longer have excuse to complain. Some people are naturally negative in their outlook and love to have something to complain about. They are rather like a friend of mine who was a lifelong hypochondriac. If you had an illness, she would say, 'I know exactly how you feel. I've got it too.'

You would go up to her and say, 'I've got a dreadful headache.'

You hoped you would receive some sympathy from her, but she would say, 'Honey, I haven't been able to hold up my head all day!' You couldn't upstage her.

Self-pity is a self-justifying condition: you have an excuse for it, and you blame somebody else. This man blamed people for not pushing him into the water; somebody else got there first every time (see v. 7). Jacob *'refused to be comforted'*.

Why is self-pity a sin? There are a number of reasons:

1. It is giving in to the devil

The devil loves your self-pity, because once you start feeling sorry for yourself you will be no threat to him. He may leave you alone. He won't bring any other temptation into your life. He will say, 'I've won with that person.' He can now play with you as if you were a little toy. If he wanted to upset you, you'd be like a feather – he would blow, and you would simply fly away. If you stay in that condition you are perilously close to self-destruction, and that's not just sin – that is gross, heinous sin. You are letting the arch-enemy of Jesus Christ have you where he wants you.

2. You are cheating yourself by giving God no opportunity to help

You cut yourself off from those who would help you, from those who would pray with you, saying, 'Leave me alone.' All this time you think that somehow you are making a statement, but you are cheating yourself, and God himself can't get through to you. You've cut off all possibility of communication.

3. You are hurting others

Other people may be affected by your self-pity. Perhaps you say, 'Good! I want others to be hurt.' That is sin. Why would you not let them help you?

4. It's getting angry with God

You are making a statement hoping that God hears clearly in heaven that you are upset with him for allowing what happened and that you blame him for the state you are in. There is a verse in James which says, *'The wrath of man worketh not the righteousness of God'* (Jas. 1:20 AV). You may think that in your anger with him somehow you are going to influence God, to move him, to get him to start helping you. It doesn't work.

5. You are failing to overcome sin

Sin is the hardest condition to overcome. Those who lapse into sin tend to remain in that condition. This man had been an invalid for 38 years. Jacob's self-pity lasted for 22 years. I want to ask you this: 'Do you want to get well? Do you want to be healed? Can't anybody help you?'

The Nature of Self-pity

1. It's a convenience

What's that? That's something very accessible. It's what I would call 'negative pleasantness'. It's not good, but you rather like it. You just get used to it and it becomes quite a pleasant thing. I haven't heard lately of any courses on how to achieve self-pity. There are no A- or O-level or university awards to show that you know what self-pity is because you have passed the course. Self-pity is acquired without any training or discipline. No exam is needed. It is as natural to us as a pig wallowing in mire. It becomes quite pleasant. It is a negative condition, but we say, 'Leave me alone.' That's what Jacob said, *'In mourning will I go down to the grave to my son.'*

2. It's acquired by choice

Jacob made a choice: he refused to be comforted. You need to know that self-pity is a voluntary condition. You are in that state because you have chosen to be. In Jacob's case, it was his way of escaping. Why did he do it? It was convenient; it took no effort. It didn't mean becoming mature and responsible; it didn't mean listening to those around him.

3. It's a cul-de-sac

It's a road that leads to nowhere. The only way out is to go back the way you came. It means making a U-turn. Have you ever made a mistake in driving, but you think, 'I am not going to admit that this is a cul-de-sac'? So you just keep going because you can't bear the thought of turning round. Yet finally, you have to admit defeat, and you decide, 'If I am going to get anywhere, I am going to have to turn around and go back.' Self-pity gets us nowhere. It is a self-defeating and pointless emotion. But we like to think we can prove something by it. Let me tell you how Jacob made a non-verbal statement: *'Jacob tore his clothes'* (Gen. 37:34). I would have thought that was rather a costly thing to do. But self-pity is costly. It will cost you financially.

4. It's curable

That's good news. I will tell you where you begin to find the cure. You begin where Jesus ended his life on earth, at the cross. Until his last breath, he was being tempted to succumb to self-pity greater than any you will ever know. Are you angry because of the injustices you have suffered? Have you ever bothered examining the trial that Jesus had before he was crucified? Years ago, a lawyer came up to me in Fort Lauderdale and said, 'I have made a study of the trial of Jesus. It was the most detailed research I have ever undertaken. I discovered that there was nothing about the trial of Jesus that was fair: it was a wicked injustice.'

Do you think that Jesus had a right to say, 'This isn't fair?' If he had done that, as Satan wanted him to do, in that moment he would have destroyed everything that he had come to earth to do. Jesus came to earth to do what you and I cannot do for ourselves, and that was to live without sinning. That not only meant keeping God's law regarding lying, sexual sin and killing, but attaining a perfect level of righteousness. Jesus couldn't even allow himself a single instant of self-pity, because it is sin. The Jews laughed at him on the cross, nudging one another and jeering, 'Hey, Son of God, come down from the cross and we'll believe! He saved others, but he can't save himself.' But Jesus' response was *'Father, forgive them, for they do not know what they are doing'* (see Lk. 23:34, 35).

Jesus never sinned despite being tempted at all points as we are. He knows what you are feeling, and he understands. But you need to recognize what self-pity is and come to terms with the problem. You have to stop blaming others and admit that you have sinned before God and repent of that sin.

The Cure

1. Listen

The first thing to do is to listen to those who want to help you. Jacob's sons and daughters came to help him, but he didn't want them. After all, this family of his had let him down; his sons had disgraced him and now they are the ones who are coming to sympathize – he didn't want help from them. But the chances are that the people God will send to help you will not be the ones you would have chosen. Listen. Accept help from wherever you can get it.

Many years ago, there was a particular person who stopped coming to Westminster Chapel. He was in a backslidden state. Friends said, 'You need to come and hear our new minister.'

His response was, 'Well, I hear he's an American.'

'Yes, but you need to come and hear him.'

He said, 'I have been hurt by Americans.'

He had worked for an American company who had not treated him well, and he was adamant he would not come. But his friends pleaded with him until eventually he said, 'I'll come – just once.' He came, and sat at the back. I preached on the subject of Jonah who was found out. And at the end, the man was sobbing. God had found him out and used me to bring him back to himself. You may say, 'Well, if I ever got right with God, I'd want it to be in a place like Westminster Abbey, or Westminster Cathedral.' Look. If someone is reaching out to help you, take the help they offer, no matter what its source.

2. Remember

You must also remember that God had a purpose in allowing the event that caused your self-pity. What Jacob couldn't come to terms with at the time was that God had not deserted him. Joseph was still alive, but all Jacob could do was to look at the evidence which seemingly pointed to the contrary. What I am saying to you is that whatever has happened that led to your self-pity has been permitted by God. He has a purpose for you, but you are not going to see his plan realized while you wallow in self-pity.

3. Realize

Next you must realize that nothing that has happened warrants the self-pity to which you have succumbed. Put it like this: things are not as bad as they seem. But you couldn't have told Jacob that. He said, 'Look at my son's robe!' You see, the devil gets in: you look at inconclusive evidence and surrender the hope that God himself had given you. Remember that earlier in this chapter of Genesis, it says that when Joseph told his dream about the sun and the moon bowing down to him, his father kept the matter in mind. Jacob thought then there was something in what Joseph said (see Gen. 37:11). And that is something Jacob would have done well to remember later.

When you give in to self-pity, you are unaware of it, and you cannot be reached by common sense. People reason with you, but you refuse to be comforted. You should realize that nothing warrants the damage you are inflicting on yourself. Jesus heard the story of the invalid, who had been by the pool of Bethesda for 38 years. 'Nobody will push me into the water,' he said. Jesus had divine power. He could have simply put his hands on that man and healed him instantly with his touch. Jesus could do that. But what did Jesus himself do when he heard the whole story? You may not like it. Jesus said to him, 'Get up!' That wasn't very nice. Yet that was exactly what he said. *'Pick up your mat and walk'* (Jn. 5:8). The man was hemmed in and he obeyed.

I would like to think that whatever your problem, God will hem you in too. He will say to you, 'Do something about it.' Jesus didn't reach down and yank the invalid up; the man had a choice to make. So have you, and you can make it now.

40

How God Turns Evil into Good

Genesis 38:1–30

Reading Genesis 38 may not seem to tell you, initially, how God turns evil into good. We are studying the life of Jacob, but Jacob's name does not appear once. Yet had it not been for this particular Bible chapter, Jacob would not have had the future he had. The chapter is included in the Bible for a purpose. We are told, *'All Scripture is God-breathed and is useful for teaching, rebuking, correcting and training in righteousness'* (2 Tim. 3:16).

Does evil have a part in your life? Do you know of a sin you've committed of which you are ashamed? Perhaps your problem is an uncorrected weakness or defect. Perhaps you or your children are the victims of evil and you have never recovered – you are scarred. I want you to know that God brings comfort to the most discouraged person. I will show you how God will turn injustice and evil to good.

The Story

Genesis 38 is about Jacob's fourth son Judah, who was also the son of Leah, the wife whom Jacob had never wanted. For some reason, Judah had left home, got married, and now had three sons of his own. The first was Er, who married Tamar. But because of an unnamed wickedness, God had put Er to death, leaving Tamar a childless widow. In ancient Hebrew tradition it was the responsibility of the surviving brother to produce an heir. So Jacob asked Onan, his second son, to lie with Tamar. Onan slept with Tamar but refused to let her become pregnant (see v. 9). That displeased God and he put Onan to death. The third son Shelah was too young to lie with Tamar, so Judah said to his daughter-in-law: ' *"Live as a widow in your father's house until my son Shelah grows up."* For he thought, *"He may die too, just like his brothers."* So Tamar went to live in her father's *house'* (Gen. 38:11). Meanwhile, Judah's own wife died, and that meant he would have no heirs. Furthermore, he failed to keep his promise to Tamar. But she had an idea:

> *When Tamar was told, 'Your father-in-law is on his way to Timnah to shear his sheep,' she took off her widow's clothes, covered herself with a veil to disguise herself, and then sat down at the entrance to Enaim, which is on the road to Timnah. For she saw that, though Shelah had now grown up, she had not been given to him as his wife.*
>
> *When Judah saw her, he thought she was a prostitute, for she had covered her face. Not realising that she was his daughter-in-law, he went over to her by the roadside and said, 'Come now, let me sleep with you.'*
>
> *'And what will you give me to sleep with you?' she asked.*
>
> *'I'll send you a young goat from my flock,' he said.*
>
> *'Will you give me something as a pledge until you send it?' she asked.*
>
> *He said, 'What pledge should I give you?'*
>
> *'Your seal and its cord, and the staff in your hand,' she answered. So he gave them to her and slept with her, and she became pregnant by him. After she left, she took off her veil and put on her widow's clothes again (Gen. 38:13–19).*

When Judah heard his daughter-in-law was pregnant, he decreed she must be burned to death. We read in verse 24: *'About three months later Judah was told, "Your daughter-in-law Tamar is guilty of prostitution, and as a result she is now pregnant." ' Judah said, 'Bring her out and have her burned to death!'*

To those of you who know the story of David, it sounds very much like David's reaction to Nathan the prophet (see 2 Sam. 12:1–7). You know how self-righteous we can be when we hear of a particular sin somebody else has committed. Sometimes you react strongly to some - thing you have heard of or read about, only because it hits a raw nerve and because you feel vulnerable to that very same temptation.

As she was being brought out to be burned, Tamar sent a message to Judah, saying, *'"I am pregnant by the man who owns these . . . See if you recognise whose seal and cord and staff these are."*

'Judah recognised them and said, "She is more righteous than I, since I wouldn't give her to my son Shelah." And he did not sleep with her again' (Gen. 38:25–26).

It turned out that in her womb were twin boys, Perez and Zerah.

The Lion of the Tribe of Judah

In Revelation 5 a mighty angel proclaimed loudly, *'Who is worthy to break the seals and open the scroll?'* (v. 2). John wept because no one was worthy. Then one of the elders said to him, *'Do not weep! See, the Lion of the tribe of Judah, the Root of David, has triumphed'* (v. 5). That is retroactive to this story. Who would have thought that Jesus Christ, the Son of God, had this kind of ancestry? You talk about scandal! To think that, first of all, Tamar played the harlot to have a child – that Judah should go to a prostitute! It turned out that one of those twin boys would be the only link between Jacob (or Israel) and God's promise to him, coming from Jacob, through Judah, and through the little boy, Perez.

If you begin reading from Matthew 1:3, you find a record of the genealogy of Jesus Christ. Look at it:

> *A record of the genealogy of Jesus Christ the son of David, the son of Abraham: Abraham was the father of Isaac, Isaac the father of Jacob, Jacob the father of Judah and his brothers, Judah the father of Perez and Zerah, whose mother was Tamar, Perez the father of Hezron . . .*

You see, when you look at the genealogy of Jesus, unless you know your Old Testament, you wouldn't know the scandal of the birth of Perez. This was more scandalous than anything we have read recently in *The Times*, or even in the *Sun*. I'll tell you why this is important. In the New Testament we read:

> *In those days Caesar Augustus issued a decree that a census should be taken of the entire Roman world . . . And everyone went to his own town to register.*
>
> *So Joseph also went up from the town of Nazareth in Galilee to Judea, to Bethlehem the town of David, because he belonged to the house and line of David. He went there to register with Mary, who was pledged to be married to him and was expecting a child. While they were there, the time came for the baby to be born, and she gave birth to her firstborn, a son. She wrapped him in cloths and placed him in a manger, because there was no room for them in the inn* (Lk. 2:1–7).

Yet behind all this was a story so scandalous, so awful, but you read in 1 Chronicles 28:4, '*He* [The Lord] *chose Judah.*' He was a man who went to a prostitute who turned out to be his own daughter-in-law. Why should you listen? If you think God cannot turn evil into good, think again.

Planning for the Kingdom

How does this fit in with the life of Jacob? All this was happening while Jacob was feeling sorry for himself. But life goes on and it doesn't stop God working. God remained at work while Jacob was still paralyzed with grief because God works with the future in mind. Jacob had planned to pass everything to Joseph. His firstborn son Reuben had let him down, so he poured out all his affections on Joseph. But then God snatched Joseph away, and Jacob felt he had nothing to live for. Plan B was to be Benjamin, the son of his beloved Rachel. As we have seen, Jacob never loved Leah, who gave birth to Judah. Jacob had no plans for him, but God did. God took over completely and turned evil into good. God said, 'Now I can get to work.' He singled out Judah, the most unlikely of all the sons of Jacob who were to found the 12 tribes of Israel. Judah: no one would have predicted a future for him.

Have you been overlooked or underestimated by your parents in any way? Maybe you weren't your father's favourite or your mother's favourite, and consequently you have been emotionally crippled all your life. Perhaps you were overlooked by a teacher or by a relative. They have put you down, resulting in your having an inferiority complex over the years. God knows that hurt. When God looks high and low over the world, he looks for those nobody else wants anything to do with. He looks for the hurting person for whom no one predicts a future.

In Jacob's case, God was now doing two things at once. He was planning for his kingdom and he was going to preserve Jacob's name. However, he was going to do that when Jacob was out of the picture. Have you ever thought that you would like to have a great name? Wouldn't it be wonderful if someone remembered you? Perhaps you have a plan to bring it about. You are going to do this and that. It's like Absalom, the son of David, who built a monument to himself. He thought he would never be remembered unless he did that (see 2 Sam. 18:18). There are those who plan carefully so they will never be forgotten. Here were two names that would become the two best-known names in all of Israel. One name was Israel, the other Judah. In fact, sometimes the names Israel and Judah are used interchangeably.

I have mentioned before that I used to sell vacuum cleaners and that through certain connections I was able to sell them to the 'movers' and 'shakers' of the United States. I am not joking. I have sold to the president of the Ford Motor Company; I sold to Henry Ford's widow; I sold to the chairman of Coca Cola, and to the founder of Pepsi Cola. I could go down the line of famous and wealthy people I have met. I would sometimes say to them, 'You've been a success. Tell me how you made it.'

Without exception, they all said, 'Well, I've worked for it.'

'Jacob, you have a great name. Tell us, Jacob, how you did it.'

But there was no way Jacob could take any glory for the name God gave him. No way.

'Jacob, tell me about it. You worked hard for your great name, didn't you?'

'No,' he would say. 'I was full of self-pity. I wasn't a very good parent. I did everything wrong, but look what God did!'

I've got news for you: heaven will be populated with Jacobs, with Davids, with failures, because everybody in heaven will have one thing in common – they don't deserve to be there. There will be only one person in heaven who deserves to be there – Jesus. If you compete with what God has done by sending Jesus to die on the cross, God will pass you by. But when you recognize your unworthiness, you will get God's attention.

Jacob's greatest contribution to Israel happened without him knowing it. Joseph was taken out of his hands to be Prime Minister of Egypt. Judah, whose name endures to this day, was a hypocrite, but he was found out, and he realized he was without excuse. He was going to have his daughter-in-law burnt to death until he realized she was the 'prostitute' with whom he had slept. He had been stripped of any claim to goodness. (Later Judah gained respectability, and at the end of Jacob's life it was he who received the patriarchal blessing.)

God turns evil into good. He uses us when we are not even aware of it. He uses us despite our unworthiness and folly. He uses those for whom we have never predicted any kind of future.

When I was the pastor of a church in Fort Lauderdale, I will never forget one evening when I knocked on the door of this simple home. A man let me in and I witnessed to him, his wife and 12-year-old son. The following Sunday they all came forward to the front in an evangelistic service, but I didn't know for certain if the boy had been converted. Some time ago, I was asked to lecture at the Southwestern Baptist Theological Seminary in America and I met him again, then a grown man and studying for the ministry. He said, 'I was converted that night you came to our house.'

You never know who God will use. You may think you are the most unqualified person. If only you knew! God wants you more than anybody. If God could use Jacob, he can use you. If God could use Judah, he can use you. So next time you hear of the tribe of Judah, just remember the link – Perez, the little boy born when Judah slept with his daughter-in-law, thinking she was a prostitute. The facts about Judah were brought out into the open, and people knew about his hypocrisy. You too can confess your sins and they will be washed away. Nobody will know about them, and they will never be held against you. Judah came to terms with his hypocrisy and so must you with yours. Don't think, 'It doesn't matter what I do now because I will get God's attention.' If you take that attitude, you will delay indefinitely what God will do. God doesn't start to work until you own your guilt. Judah did that, and God began to use him.

41

When God Takes Our Hands Off
(Part One)

Genesis 39:1–23

When God brings us to the place where we can no longer manipulate, our hands are taken off the situation. Jacob was the world's greatest manipulator. Reuben, his firstborn, disappointed him, so when Joseph came along he determined to make *him* his firstborn, as Joseph was his firstborn to his beloved Rachel. He wanted to ensure, therefore, that Joseph was a successful man. As the proverb says, *'A wise son maketh a glad father'* (Prov. 10:1 AV). And Jacob was determined that Joseph would make him glad. He probably said, 'I have great plans for Joseph.'

God said, 'Really? I have greater plans for Joseph that you haven't even thought about.'

There was only way that this could happen: God had to remove Joseph from Jacob, so that, whatever happened to Joseph, Jacob could never take any credit for it. We have seen how God took Jacob's hands off the whole situation. As far as the brothers were concerned, Joseph would never be seen again, and, as far as Jacob was concerned, Joseph was dead. Thus, God was now set free to do something with Joseph without Jacob interfering.

Learning without a Father's Help

Why is this chapter relevant to you? First, if you are a parent, you may be concerned that your son or daughter will not grow up in the way you would like unless you have your hand in everything they are doing. You are convinced that the only way your children will turn out well is if you are there to advise and to pull strings for them. But God looks down and says, 'I don't like the way you are manipulating your children.' Perhaps God has had to intervene to bring them to the place where you are no longer in control. It hurts because you know what's right; you know what's best. No one questions the sincerity of your motives, but God says, 'Watch what happens when, without your help, I get into the picture.' The second reason why you should read this is you may know what it is to have a very powerful parent. You can never reach their standard, and they are always telling you what to do. This is to encourage you to see what God will do with you directly.

The truth was that God had greater plans for Joseph than Jacob could ever have imagined. *'No eye has seen, no ear has heard, no mind has conceived what God has prepared for those who love him'* (1 Cor. 2:9).

The Ishmaelites handed Joseph over to Egyptians, and Potiphar, who was a captain of the guard, an officer in Pharaoh's army, bought Joseph as a slave. What do we know from then on? Genesis 39:2 says, *'The LORD was with Joseph.'* Those words are so powerful that, in the book of Acts, when Stephen was telling the story of Joseph before the Sanhedrin, he quoted this very verse: *'But God was with him'* (Acts 7:9). This is all parents need to know when it comes to their children – God is with them. This is all you need to know when it comes to living your life – God is with you.

What God had in mind for Joseph never entered Joseph's head; it never entered Jacob's head. But God was determined that Joseph was going to be the Prime Minister of Egypt. What do we find then? Joseph was a slave in Potiphar's house. Yet, because the Lord was with him, everything he did turned out well. Potiphar was so pleased with Joseph that he put him in charge of his whole household and entrusted everything he owned to his care.

Learning to withstand Temptation

However, along the way, Joseph was going to meet a particular tempta-tion. Sooner or later, you and I will know sexual temptation. It is only a matter of time. You see, God tests us along the way to see if we can be trusted with a greater responsibility.

Potiphar's wife was physically attracted to Joseph, and we are told that every day she would come to him and say, 'Come to bed with me.' But he refused, not only to sleep with her, he even refused to be with her. Now this shows Joseph was trustworthy. Potiphar didn't know how good this man really was. Joseph was discreet. He did not tell Potiphar about his wife's advances to him, and he continued to resist her.

Joseph probably had an opportunity to have the kind of affair that could have continued without anybody knowing about it. Certainly, Potiphar's wife was not going to want to tell. Suppose it did get out? Those who mattered to Joseph wouldn't know, because Joseph was a nobody in Egypt, and no one in Canaan would ever find out, for they didn't even know that he was alive. So if Joseph ever needed an excuse to sleep with this married woman, he had it, humanly speaking. He could have said, 'I didn't ask to be here. If God really cared for me, he wouldn't have allowed my brothers to do what they did. Back in Canaan nobody will ever know if I sleep with her.'

If the truth were known, how many have resisted sexual temptation for one reason – they were afraid they would get caught? But do you know why Joseph resisted? Read what he said to Potiphar's wife: *'How then could I do such a wicked thing and sin against God?'* (Gen. 39:9). What motivated him was his relationship with God. Do you have this kind of relationship with God, where your sole concern is his opinion? Or do you think, 'Will I get caught? No. No one is going to find out!' If that's the case, it is only a matter of time before you fall, because you will tell yourself that, at long last, you have found the opportunity for the perfect affair, and no one will ever know. But the Bible says, *'You may be sure that your sin will find you out'* (Num. 32:23). On the other hand, if your motivation is 'What does God think?' you will be kept from this sin.

So, we are told, Joseph not only refused to go to bed with her, but he refused to be in her company. The reason Christians fall into sin is because of the way they react to temptation and the way they make provision for the flesh. You can avoid sin by avoiding the temptation.

Now, what do you think God did to reward Joseph for resisting Potiphar's wife? 'Hell hath no fury like a woman scorned,' said Victor Hugo, and Potiphar's wife was no exception. She accused Joseph of trying to rape her, and the next thing we know is that Joseph was in prison. How do you suppose he felt then? I wonder how you would feel if you had done the right thing and things got worse instead of better? In 1 Peter 3:13 we read: *'Who is going to harm you if you are eager to do good? But even if you should suffer for what is right, you are blessed.'* When you suffer for what is right, God is honoured.

Joseph was now in prison because he did the right thing. It could be that God has you in an equivalent situation. It's as though you are in prison. You are in a position where you have been hemmed in, and you think, 'God, is this your way of thanking me when I have tried to honour you?' Yet do you know what the Bible says after Joseph was put in prison? *'The LORD was with him'* (Gen. 39:21). It is the same phrase used earlier in verse 2. So when Joseph was prospering, the Lord was with him, and now he was in prison, the Lord was with him.

Some people think that when the Lord is with you, you are going to prosper, but, according to this, it is not necessarily the case. What *is* certain is that you can be accused, you can be in prison, and the Lord will be with you. I want you to know that the Lord was with Joseph as much in prison as he had been when he was prospering in Potiphar's house. You may feel, because you have been hemmed in and because nothing has gone right, that the Lord is no longer with you. Wrong! He is with you. God has promised, *'Never will I leave you; never will I forsake you'* (Heb. 13:5).

Learning not to Manipulate

The next thing we learn is that a hidden temptation came to Joseph. There are two kinds of temptation. There's the temptation that is overt and obvious, like sexual temptation. Then there is the hidden temptation, where you don't know you are being tested, and which God sends to check out where you really are.

One day, Joseph had company in the prison – Pharaoh's baker and his cupbearer. It turned out that they too had dreams. Joseph said, 'You've had dreams? Tell me about them' (see Gen. 40:8). For the first time in many years Joseph felt qualified to speak at the level of his own gifting, which had not really been tapped until this time. All those years he was operating at a level beneath his competence; he was doing things for which he was overqualified. Perhaps you are like that. You have a gift but it's not being used. Probably, the reason for that is your time hasn't come. How do you know whether your time has come? You will be secretly tested.

How was this going to happen in Joseph's case? 'Let me hear your dreams,' he said. So the cupbearer told Joseph his dream. *'In my dream I saw a vine in front of me, and on the vine were three branches. As soon as it budded, it blossomed, and its clusters ripened into grapes. Pharaoh's cup was in my hand, and I took the grapes, squeezed them into Pharaoh's cup and put the cup in his hand'* (Gen. 40:9–11). Then Joseph told him the meaning of his dream. He said, *'The three branches are three days. Within three days Pharaoh will lift up your head and restore you to your position, and you will put Pharaoh's cup in his hand, just as you used to do when you were his cupbearer'* (vv. 12–13).

So far so good. But now, unknown to Joseph, came the subtle test. He said, *'When all goes well with you, remember me and show me kindness; mention me to Pharaoh and get me out of this prison. For I was forcibly carried off from the land of the Hebrews, and even here I have done nothing to deserve being put in a dungeon'* (vv. 14–15).

You may ask, 'What's wrong with that?'

All I can tell you is God said, 'Oh, no! Joseph, you're not ready yet. You're going to need a couple more years in the dungeon.'

Joseph was feeling sorry for himself; he was being defensive and trying to vindicate himself. So God said, 'No, you're not ready yet.' When it came to resisting sexual temptation, Joseph passed the test with flying colours, but, when it came to allowing God to exalt him unaided, Joseph failed miserably. 'Like father like son,' the saying goes, and Joseph had acted as his father once did. Jacob had been the arch-manipulator. Now Joseph was trying to pull strings, and God had to bring him to the place where he would see what God would do alone. God is serious about this matter of receiving all the credit. God is determined not to share his glory with anybody. One day, God would exalt Joseph in such a way that Joseph would be able to say, 'I don't deserve any of this.'

God is going to take you to heaven one day, but only if you are prepared to say, 'I don't deserve this, but Jesus paid my debt on the cross.'

42

When God Takes Our Hands Off
(Part Two)

Genesis 39:1–23

God wanted to show Jacob what he could do with his beloved Joseph once Jacob was out of the picture and unable to be a manipulator. But that's not all. God wanted to show Joseph himself the same thing, and Joseph had to be taken from his father's control before God could use him.

Some time ago, an American lady visited Westminster Chapel and heard me preach on Joseph's gift of interpreting dreams. After the service she came to talk to me. She said that she felt the message was for her, and what struck her was this: she had a particular gift, but she had been rather hurt because God had not yet used this. I pointed out that Joseph had a particular gift and, while there was nothing wrong with his gift, there was a lot wrong with Joseph. So God could not yet use Joseph, and his gift had to wait.

Longing for Vindication

Joseph longed for vindication; he longed to see his name cleared, but now he was in prison, not for doing the wrong thing, but for doing the right thing. Could it be that I am describing someone reading this? You are at rock bottom. You are very low. It's like being in prison. You say, 'Yes, I have been trying to follow the Lord, but now things are worse than before.' This is a common experience for every person who puts God first. They think that God is going to start blessing them simply because they are obedient. Don't ask me why, because I don't have the answer, but often the closer you get to God the more he hides his face from you and allows bad things to happen.

While Joseph was in prison, he saw a chance to be released; he saw the way forward as to how he might clear his name. For the first time in years, Joseph's gift was needed. Joseph, interpreting Pharaoh's butler's dream, prophesied the man would be released in three days and return to his former job. Then Joseph added, 'Show me kindness: mention me to the Pharaoh, and get me out of this place' (see Gen. 40:14).

It's often the case that a person in a responsible position will use that position for personal advancement. I think that some preachers have done this. For instance, I think certain faith-healing evangelists have done it in America. They have a gift, but they take advantage of it. God doesn't like that. He will not let anyone whom he has entrusted with an anointing exploit it. This was what Joseph was doing when he said, 'I can tell you that you are going to get your job back. Take me with you.' That grieved the heart of God, and God said, 'Oh, no!'

And so, I have to ask you this: Have you decided that some well-connected acquaintance is your free ticket, your way out? Do you think you have to do everything in your power to solidify that relationship and not offend them because they are going to help you? That shows you have such little faith in God that God needs to use that relationship in order to move you ahead. What God wanted to show Joseph, what he wants to show his church, and what he wants to show you and me afresh is what *he* is able to do once we take our hands off a situation. However, what happens usually is God has to do that for us. So he humbles us. He puts us out of the picture. He protects us from ourselves because he knows our weakness and sees we are going to exploit a relationship or use our gift in order to get ahead. God says, 'Will you please be quiet! Will you let me see what I can do, without you pulling the strings?'

What happened was Joseph's prophecy was fulfilled. Three days later, Pharaoh's cupbearer got his job back. But we are told that he didn't remember Joseph. This is because God didn't want Joseph to exalt himself; God wanted to do it unaided. And if you had asked Joseph, 'What in your wildest dreams would you like to see God do for you?' he wouldn't have even come close to what God had in mind for him.

What about Jacob – the arch-manipulator? He thought nothing of any worth could happen in this world unless he was involved in bringing it about. He had planned Joseph's life, and God had taken his son from him. But if you had asked Jacob, 'What is the most that you would like to see accomplished in your son?' I guarantee that even Jacob wouldn't have come close to what God himself had planned.

Many years ago, when I was a student at Trevecca College in Nashville, Tennessee, I had a friend who was probably the most brilliant person I have ever met. His first name was Paul. I don't know what IQ he had, but I would guess it was around 170. He excelled at everything, no matter what the subject, be it physics, algebra, theology, or foreign languages. I never saw anything like it. Anything he read, he remembered. But one day, when we were driving down US 41 on our way to my old church, he started to cry. He said, 'I am afraid that nobody is going to know the gift I've got.' Those were his very words. Later, in his impatience, he fell into sin. Louise and I ran into him a few years ago; he was teaching the tenth grade in a High School in Albany, Georgia. That's as far as he went. He was not living for the Lord. It was so sad.

Perhaps you think that God is letting you down, and your way of getting even with him is that you don't intend to serve him. Don't be so foolish. God is telling you that he has a plan for you, and what he will do for you is far greater than anything you can do by pulling strings or by fretting and trying to make things happen. I try to be guided by the Holy Spirit in everything, and I think of the hymn written by John Henry Newman:

> I loved to choose and see my path; but now
> Lead thou me on.
> I loved the garish day, and, spite of fears,
> Pride ruled my will: remember not past years.

Perhaps you know what it is like to be ruled by pride, but God has brought you back. He wants you to see what *he* can do when you don't have your hands on the situation. Jeremiah knew what God could do. Having received a spectacular answer to prayer, he said, 'Nothing is too hard for you' (Jer. 32:17). Joseph could not have dreamed what God would do for him.

See what God Can Do

Where did God turn in order to bring about the next development in Joseph's life? Who would have thought it? He gave the Pharaoh a dream that so baffled him that he called in his magicians, he called in his soothsayers, he called in all those who had interpreted his dreams in the past. Pharaoh's mind was troubled. He described his dreams, but no one could interpret them. Do you know why? It was because God gave this dream and Satan couldn't interfere with it.

The result was that the Pharaoh became desperate. And at last, God caused the cupbearer, who overheard all of this, to remember Joseph. He addressed his royal master like this: 'Today, I am reminded of my shortcomings. Do you remember, Your Majesty, when you were angry with me and put me in prison? While I was there, I had a dream, and a young Hebrew who was in prison with me interpreted it. Everything he said came true. I believe he could interpret your dreams too' (see Gen. 41:9). Pharaoh was now so despondent that he was willing to turn to anybody for help.

God brings such situations about sometimes. I have commented once or twice of late that I myself have been willing to listen to people who ordinarily I wouldn't pay heed to. At Westminster Chapel, we have often been humbled: we take ourselves so seriously; we are so afraid of not being sufficiently sophisticated, articulate and theological, but God has a way of getting our attention. In 1995 my wife became very ill. But God used somebody to whom I would never have turned for help in normal circumstances and miraculously healed her. Perhaps you too need to be humbled. We have to be willing to be open to the way God wants to lead us. Normally, Pharaoh would have turned to those with credentials and a high position in his court. Perhaps you have thought that in order to get ahead you need to know the right people because you believe that in yourself you are nothing. But do you really think you need credentials, recommendations, culture or polish to be of value? God has given you an ability that is unique: nobody is just like you.

Can you imagine Joseph going to an employment agency to hear them say, 'OK, Joseph, fill out this form and tell us your qualifications. Can you type? Have you been to university?'

He would reply, 'Well, the only thing I am good at is interpreting dreams.'

You can see this guy taking down all this information. 'Dreams . . . Um! Thank you very much. We'll get back to you.'

But Pharaoh had a dream which nobody could interpret until the cupbearer remembered Joseph. God has a way of finding you, and he will do it when he takes your hands off the situation.

So one morning before breakfast, a knock came on Joseph's cell door. There stood an official, who demanded, 'Are you Joseph? Are you the Hebrew? Then get shaved and dressed.' And so he was ushered into the presence of the king. Joseph didn't know what was happening. He didn't know what to think.

God does things like this overnight. *'See, I will send my messenger, who will prepare the way before me. Then suddenly the L ORD you are seeking will come to his temple'* (Mal. 3:1). Perhaps you have been praying continually, and you have walked in the light, yet nothing is happening. Maybe you have sought God to no avail and ask, 'Is there a God out there?' And suddenly God turns up. Now Joseph's time had come.

The king came straight to the point. 'We understand that if you are told a dream, you can interpret it.'

Do you know how Joseph answered? *'I cannot do it . . . but God will give Pharaoh the answer he desires'* (Gen. 41:16). This was the new Joseph. Much had happened in the last two years: Joseph had got right with God and had come to the place where he knew, in himself, he was nothing.

Joseph interpreted Pharaoh's dream like this: *'God has shown Pharaoh what he is about to do. Seven years of great abundance are coming throughout the land of Egypt, but seven years of famine will follow them'* (Gen. 41:28). But here's the interesting thing: we discover Joseph has another gift. He begins to make an application. You see, there is an interpretation and application of that interpretation. Something every preacher has to learn to do is not only to interpret the Scriptures, but also to apply them. Joseph interpreted the dream but that was not enough. He said, 'Here is what you have to do.' This wasn't required of him, but the Spirit of God was upon him, so after the interpretation came the application.

Joseph said, *'Let Pharaoh look for a discerning and wise man and put him in charge of the land of Egypt'* (Gen. 41:33). He told him what to do. It would make Egypt wealthy, and all the world would come begging Egypt for food. This new gift emerged and enabled Joseph to speak to Pharaoh like that. And if you wait on God's time, he will not only use that gift you have – however insignificant you thought it was – but he will anoint that gift by giving you more authority, more power, and the ability to do things that you never thought possible. Jesus said, *'Whoever can be trusted with very little can also be trusted with much'* (Lk. 16:10).

But who do you suppose the unsung hero of this story was? It was Pharaoh himself. Let me tell you why. Pharaoh agreed with Joseph and asked, *'Can we find anyone like this man, one in whom is the spirit of God?'* (Gen. 41:37). So there and then, Pharaoh affirmed Joseph and put him in charge, effectively making him Prime Minister of Egypt. One day, he was in prison, the next day he was Prime Minister of Egypt! But Pharaoh deserved the praise. Let me tell you why. What evidence did Pharaoh have that Joseph was right? He just felt it in his heart. That's the way you become a Christian; it happens in your heart. Paul said, *'If you confess with your mouth, "Jesus is Lord," and believe in your heart that God raised him from the dead, you will be saved'* (Rom. 10:9–10). Joseph's time had come and so has yours. Wherever you are, whatever your past, whatever skeleton you have in your cupboard, whatever your sense of failure, you can begin trusting the Lord from this moment on.

43

When God Hides His Face

Genesis 42:1–38

When God is showing his face, you can cope: you can endure things that you could not ordinarily endure. But should he hide his face, then any problem can overwhelm you: you become easily upset; you are prickly and perhaps prone to depression and anxiety. There is a biblical expression in the book of Isaiah that says, *'Truly you are a God who hides himself'* (Isa. 45:15). Sometimes God does this, and it is the essence of what the Bible means by 'chastening' or 'disciplining'. The Bible says, *'The Lord disciplines ('chastens' AV) those whom he loves'* (Heb. 12:6). The Greek word means 'enforced learning'.

Chastening

In this chapter of Genesis, someone was being chastened. Who was it? It was not Joseph but Jacob. Joseph also had endured many years of being chastened because God had a work for him to do. Whenever God lets you suffer as a Christian, it's not without purpose; it's not without meaning; it's because you are special.

Jacob was the one who was further to experience God's disciplining. It had been 22 years since God spoke to him directly. How long has it been since you first heard the Lord? How long has it been since you were walking with him in obedience and you knew his smile? You say, 'He has been hiding his face from me.' I'll tell you why: It's because he loves you. If you know exactly what I mean by this phrase 'when God hides his face', then you are not reading this by accident. John Newton wrote:

> How tedious, how tasteless the hour
> When Jesus no longer I see,
> Sweet prospects, sweet birds, sweet flowers
> Have all lost their sweetness to me.

God hides his face because he wants to get your attention. When you consider the suffering of Joseph, who do you suppose suffered the most? It was Jacob. Whose name appears in the Bible most next to the name of God? It's Jacob's name: Israel. When God honours a person, it's tempered with suffering. The reason for Jacob's suffering at this late stage of his life, when he had already gone through so much, was that he was still under preparation, and he was going to be highly honoured. So if God has hidden his face from you it's because you are special. The greater the suffering, the greater the anointing.

Now let's consider the ten brothers. They were now having to suffer. You see, after 22 years, they thought they had got away with their sin. However, God's hand was on Joseph, whom they had sold; he was now Prime Minister of Egypt, and the prophecy he had given to the Pharaoh regarding the seven years of plenty and seven years of famine had come true. On his advice, during the seven years of plenty, the Egyptians had stored up food, so that when the seven years of famine came Egypt had food to sell. Canaan, where Jacob and his sons lived, was badly affected along with the rest of the world. So the day came when Jacob had to send the brothers to Egypt to buy food. They were not worried about this for they had no idea that they were going to meet their brother. But, before they recognized Joseph, they were to experience a trauma so great that they were able to connect what they had done to him and what was happening to them at that moment. Not that God was getting even, but, sooner or later, if we are going to enjoy blessing we have to put things right.

Now let me ask you this: Have you got away with something until now? Have you hurt somebody? Have you lied about someone? You may say, 'But they have hurt me.' Don't worry about what they have done to you. Have *you* hurt somebody? Is it possible that you have done something you regret and you need to confess it to God? But perhaps you have decided that your sin has gone unpunished and undetected for so long that it was not so bad after all. These brothers weren't at all bothered by what they had done until strange things began happening.

Let's return to Jacob for a moment. What about Jacob's chastening or disciplining? Why did he need it? The truth is that he still had a bad spirit. It showed what a poor relationship he continued to have with his sons. Notice what it says in verse 1: *'When Jacob learned that there was corn in Egypt, he said to his sons, "Why do you just keep looking at each other?"'* We have seen in past studies that Jacob didn't have a very good relationship with his family. You would think that after a few years Jacob would have learnt from his past mistakes. You may have had a bad relationship with your parents or with your son or with your daughter, but do you believe that eventually it's just going to correct itself?

Now, how's this for a strong and loving relationship! Jacob said, *'Why do you just keep looking at each other?'* It shows that Jacob was still no better: he had a bad spirit; he was critical and judgemental. But, worst of all, he was still discriminating with regard to his sons. This is why I have been referring to *ten* brothers, for the Bible says that when the ten brothers went down to buy grain from Egypt, Jacob did not send Benjamin, the other son of his beloved Rachel, with the others, because he was afraid harm might come to him (see Gen. 42:4). After all he had suffered, you would think that Jacob would have learned not be selective. When parents are selective, showing favouritism with their children, they do them no favours. They are not helping the one they are preferring, and they are certainly not helping the others who feel their parents don't care about them.

So, at the end of the chapter, we find that Jacob was full of self-pity. He said, *'Everything is against me'* (v. 36). Thus, God continued to deal with him. Maybe that is happening to you, and you don't understand why God hides his face. It's not because he wants to get even; it's simply that, to make you the kind of vessel that he wants you to be, he has to refine you, and it's painful.

Vindication

What about Joseph? As I said, his time had come. You can be sure that what he wanted more than anything was his dream that his brothers would bow down to him to be fulfilled. Joseph lived for vindication. By vindication, I don't mean by being Prime Minister of Egypt. He never aspired to be that. In fact, that was one of the reasons why God put him in that position. God often exalts a person to a position they never wanted so they don't become conceited. Joseph was an effective Prime Minister, but that wasn't where his heart was. Yet what he longed for most was withheld from him until, one day, God said, 'Now you can even be trusted with this.' That day had come.

Here came ten of his brothers. Speaking through an interpreter, Joseph accused them of being spies. Some have misunderstood this, thinking it was Joseph's way of getting even. But that was not the case. He had so brilliant and so loving a strategy. He wanted to get them all to the land of Goshen. Joseph knew what they didn't know: there were many more years of famine to come and they were not going to be able to cope in the land of Canaan. He wanted them to move to Egypt where they could eat and live well, but he knew it would not be easy to get them there. There was one other thing: he didn't want their father to know what they had done to him. You say, 'He must have wanted that.' But it was not the case. Similarly, the Bible says, God *'does not treat us as our sins deserve or repay us according to our iniquities'* (Ps. 103:10). The thing those ten brothers feared the most was that their father Jacob would find out. God knows how much pain we can bear.

Restoration

I want to end this chapter by talking about the ten brothers because, at long last, God dealt with them. What interests me most is that the chastening that they received was so minimal and so brief by comparison. Think about it: they had only a short time when they were to think about what they had done. We read in Genesis 42:22 that Reuben spoke up and said, *'Didn't I tell you not to sin against the boy? But you wouldn't listen! Now we must give an accounting for his blood.'* They were certainly aware that something was happening, for verse 28 says, *'Their hearts sank and they turned to each other trembling and said, "What is this that God has done to us?"'* For a brief period, those ten brothers were experiencing a nightmare. God was dealing with them.

And if you have done great wrong, it is only a matter of time before God will begin dealing with you. Did you think you could get away with it.? Let me tell you what it means if you do. This is awful – but you need to know. It means that God does not love you; he is passing you by. God will just wait and deal with your sins in hell. Any coming to terms with sin in *this* life, however, is by the gracious mercy of God. Maybe, he is using this message to get your attention.

Now, I want to show you something else. Consider what these ten brothers did: selling their brother to the Ishmaelites and letting their father believe that a wild beast killed him. If you were Joseph, perhaps you would think, 'Those ten brothers of mine – I hope they get their comeuppance one day.' The interesting thing is they are made to come to terms with their sin, but in comparison to what Joseph went through, and in comparison to what Jacob continued to suffer, the ten brothers had the easiest deal. This is why. They were not sovereign vessels; they were not chosen for a special work. God dealt with them because they were in his family. You may ask, 'Surely they should have suffered more?' Ah, God may allow *you* to suffer because he has a great work for you to do, while perhaps the one who has hurt you the most doesn't suffer at all.

Let me give you an illustration of this. Corrie ten Boom was a woman who suffered greatly in World War II because her family wanted to hide Jews in Amsterdam. When Corrie was in prison, she got a good look at the guard who was so cruel to her sister who died in prison. Later, after Corrie was released, she visited various places, spreading the gospel and giving her testimony. In one of the services, she saw that prison guard who, in the meantime, had been converted. When she saw him in the audience, she felt a terrible anger. 'Who does he think he is? Why is he here – that man, who did what he did to my sister?' She had to pray fervently, and the love of Jesus filled her heart. After the service, he came up to her and said, 'Isn't God good? He is so gracious. He forgives us.' With that, he walked away. He wasn't a sovereign vessel.

You may wonder why God doesn't deal with this person for what they have done to you. Never mind, God's hand is on you and he has a work for you to do. Remember, the greater the anointing, the greater the suffering. But Jacob's sons, Joseph's brothers, did have to come to terms with their sin, and you have to do this too. I don't know whether you are a sovereign vessel and God has chosen you for a special work. I don't know what God has up his sleeve for you. But if God is dealing with your sin, come to terms with it.

44

Living Between the Times

Genesis 42:24–38

As we look at the life of Jacob, Richard Bewes' lovely phrase 'between the times' seems to fit the story in Genesis 42 well. Joseph was living between the times, the ten brothers were living between the times, Jacob was living between the times. Joseph was living between the time of the vindication he never wanted and the vindication he was seeking so earnestly. The ten brothers were living between the threat of starvation and God finding them out.

What do we mean by this phrase? To begin with, that is what life is – a series of events linking the past and the future. Most are mundane happenings, but others are so special in their nature. Oswald Chambers put it like this, 'Routine is God's way of saving us between our times of inspiration.' We all like those moments of inspiration, and we are reluctant for them to pass into history. For example, when Jesus took Peter, James and John up into a mountain where they saw Jesus transfigured before them, Peter said, 'This is good. I like this.' And he just wanted to remain there (see Mt. 17:4). There are times when the Lord blesses you so powerfully, and you think, 'If only this could last for ever!' These are special times, like the Day of Pentecost, when the Spirit of God came down in power (see Acts 2:1–4). Or take the moment of answered prayer – isn't it good when you see God is doing something – when something is actually happening? Between the times is when you are waiting for it to actually happen.

Could it be that is where you are? Perhaps you feel that you are living between the times. You may not realize that God has brought you to this place, but you will discover that God is up to something. Something may be happening to you, and you are not yet aware of it. Why is it that God makes us wait, and often the era between the times is so long? There are three things I want us to see:

1. Some Things Take Time – Even for God

Do you know God took six days to create the world? Mind you, he could have done it quicker than you could bat an eyelash. But God took time. God could have sent his Son into the world sooner than he did, but he waited until two thousand years ago. The Bible says, *'When the time had fully come, God sent his Son, born of a woman, born under law, to redeem those under law'* (Gal. 4:4–5). The point that I am making is that all that took time, and even God must wait. How many of you have ever said in your prayers, 'O Lord, how much longer?' But what about God? He has to wait too. He has the power to end everything, but, for reasons that we will not understand until we get to heaven, God subjected himself to the conditions he created whereby he too must wait. I happen to believe that the one being in the whole universe who has suffered the most is God himself. There is a side of theology that many are afraid to study: it is too painful. It is easy for us to dismiss the suffering of God, and we ease our own pain by saying that God doesn't feel anything wrong.

We see Joseph in a situation where he waited, and yet he was in a position of not having to wait. He could have done something that he once wanted to do more than anything in the world and that was to vindicate his name with his brothers. Now that he was Prime Minister, he had power to send chariots back to Canaan to fetch his father. Accompanied by bodyguards, he could have taken a chariot himself and returned to Canaan. He could have walked right up to his father and said, 'It's me, Joseph.' In the same way, God could do this or that, but he waits. So remember, some things take time.

2. Between the Times There's Something for Us to Learn

Joseph needed to learn restraining grace. He himself was being tested to the hilt. The fact that he was Prime Minister of Egypt did very little for his ego. Never in his wildest dreams had he aspired to that position, and yet it was in this country he was doing such a useful work. Sometimes God will make a success of a person in a particular part of the world that means nothing to them. I have often thought that if I were to preach to a million people in Africa it wouldn't do anything for my ego at all. Yet fill my church with two thousand souls, and I could say to my friends back in America, or to my dad, if he didn't have Alzheimer's disease, 'Look what God is doing.' God knows what we can bear; he knows our problem – our pride.

Joseph could be trusted with being Prime Minister because he never wanted this task. What he wanted was vindication in the eyes of his family and now that was within his grasp. He could clear his name instantly, but he had to wait. The proof that you are pliable in God's hands is that the day comes when you could clear your name and vindicate yourself, but you still wait for God to do it his way. Joseph proved he had learnt this lesson.

In Genesis 42 we see the evidence of what his brothers meant to him emotionally. It says, *'They did not realise that Joseph could understand them, since he was using an interpreter. He turned away from them and began to weep'* (vv. 23–24). The same Jesus who could weep with Mary and Martha when their brother died is at the right hand of God, and he weeps. So if you are hurting at this moment, if you are grief-stricken, if you are troubled, even though the Lord knows that your grief will pass, he doesn't say, 'Cheer up. Shame on you for crying! Don't you know it's going to work out all right?' No. He weeps.

So Joseph wept because the time had not come to reveal himself to his brothers. What about the ten brothers? They were between the times: the threat of starvation behind them, and before them the time when God would begin to deal with them. They had swept under the carpet, as it were, the dirt, the filth for which they were responsible. Twenty-two years before, they had done this awful thing to their brother. It seemed they were getting away with it. After a few years when nothing happens, one begins to breathe more easily and thinks, 'That's good! It happened so long ago. I'm not going to have to worry about that now.'

I wonder if you have done wrong, maybe a long time ago, and it seems you have escaped the consequences. So you think, 'Well, that's it.' But you have to accept the fact that unconfessed sin will be dealt with sooner or later. It will be dealt with either at the judgement seat of Christ or be dealt with in this life. I want you to know that *now* is the time to deal with it, because after your life is over it will be too late. You may feel this is very painful and say, 'I don't think I like hearing this.'

Yet neither did the ten brothers like what was happening to them. But God was beginning to deal with them. In verse 21 they said, *'Surely we are being punished because of our brother. We saw how distressed he was when he pleaded with us for his life.'* Their consciences were now troubling them, and they had to face the enormity of what they had done. If something similar is happening to you, know that God is doing you the greatest favour. If you can come to terms with your sin now – it won't be dealt with later. While there is yet time, confess it to God and say, 'I am sorry.'

Maybe you need to put something right with somebody. You will know if you should. Sometimes the hardest thing in the world is to own up to something you have done, but doing this will give the greatest peace. There is a place for making restitution, and until you put a matter right you will feel troubled.

The wonderful thing is that God forgives everything totally. This is what happened when Jesus Christ went to the cross and our sins were put on him. So you are not going to get things right by going to the person you have wronged and bypassing the cross. No. You have to come to the cross and admit your sin, but unless you truly repent in your heart then you are not yet ready.

What about Jacob? He was living between the times. He had the same old problem – self-pity. He had completely lost sight of God's promises, and he was still blaming everybody else. So he said to his sons: *'You have deprived me of my children. Joseph is no more and Simeon is no more, and now you want to take Benjamin. Everything is against me!'* (Gen. 42:36). I wonder if you can identify with this. Perhaps you are a mature person, yet you still wallow in self-pity. If that is the case, you need to seek a fresh and wonderful outpouring of the Holy Spirit.

3. Between the Times, God Still Looks After Us

We read in verse 35, *'As they were emptying their sacks, there in each man's sack was his pouch of silver!'* Think of that: they needed food; they took money to pay for it, and when they returned they discovered that Egypt didn't need their money. This shows that God was looking after them. But the effect it had on them frightened them silly.

Some people misunderstand the fact that God takes care of their needs and they think, 'I have been blessed. I have made more money in recent times than ever before. This shows that God is with me.' Now, it *may* show that God's with you, but it doesn't mean that everything is right with you. It was God's plan the money be returned to the brothers and they should find it in their sacks because God wanted to get their attention. People sometimes confuse prosperity with the fact that God is blessing them because they are so good. There was nothing that these men had done to deserve that. You need to see that the fact that you are blessed is not because you are worthy of it but because God loves you. God loved these ten brothers.

Why do we have to wait? Notice two things:

- Some things take time. From our viewpoint it is sometimes difficult to understand why God doesn't act sooner. But when, eventually, he acts, we come to see that it couldn't have happened sooner, and it is a mercy that it didn't. I don't know what God is doing, but I am prepared to trust him, and I know that everything is on schedule. So with you, remember that God is on your case. Why do we have to wait? Some things take time.
- It takes time to see our sin. Do you know why that takes so long? It is because we cannot come to terms with our own sense of shame. If you were to ask these ten brothers why they treated Joseph so badly, they would reply, 'Look at the way our father treated us by making Joseph his favourite son. Look at the way Joseph lorded it over us,

strutting around in that coat of many colours, telling us we are going to bow down to him.' And I have no doubt that the reason they were able to sweep the dirt under the carpet for 22 years was that they still blamed their father and brother.

In verse 28, it says, *'Their hearts sank.'* Could it be that the Holy Spirit has driven something into your heart like a laser beam, and you are hurting because you have this deep-seated fear? God is saying, 'Time is up. This matter has to be sorted out.' The brothers blamed their father long enough, and now they were beginning to feel God was closing in on them. Why didn't he deal with them before? I don't know the answer to that. But when God deals with us, he has a way of boxing us in. The second thing is they came trembling; they were scared (see v. 28). It was like the time when King Belshazzar saw the handwriting on the wall; he was trembling; his knees knocked (see Dan. 5:6).

One Christmas, some years ago, I had a Christmas card from Mrs Jean Watson, a lady I haven't seen since 1963. She reminded me that she was converted when I was the pastor at the church she attended. She told me that when the Holy Spirit began to deal with her she thought she was losing her mind. You see, you may have been able to throw off your belief in God, in hell, and in the Bible. But you know when the Holy Spirit is dealing with you and you are being hemmed in.

Joseph's brothers would have been able to identify with the way Jean Watson felt. They began to fear God and said, *'What is this that God has done to us?'* (Gen. 42:28). I will tell you why God acted in the way he did. He wanted them to put things right so that they could experience joy. God doesn't want us to be sad and live with the burden of our guilt. If we confess our sins, God forgives us (see 1 Jn. 1:9). You will know if God has you in mind.

45

Coping with Stubbornness

Genesis 42:35 – 43:14

Jacob was the prime example of stubbornness. In Genesis 42:38 he said, *'My son will not go down there.'* He intended sticking to his guns, for he wasn't going to risk losing Benjamin, the only other son born to his beloved Rachel.

Joseph had nothing but love for his family. His plan was that they should all come to live in Egypt because he knew that the famine would last several more years. But he had to set about it in very delicate way, and it seemed as though he was just giving them a hard time. He accused his brothers of being spies – a charge they strenuously denied.

'Then prove you are not spies,' said Joseph. 'Where's your other brother?'

'He's with our father and he won't be coming.'

'Ah,' said the Prime Minister. 'I want to see your brother. If you don't bring him, then you get no food. In fact, to prove that you are not spies, you are going to leave one of your number here.'

Stubbornness

So Simeon was left there, as collateral as it were, and the brothers knew they *had* to bring back Benjamin. They went home to Canaan and explained how roughly the Prime Minister had treated them. They told Jacob that there was no point in going back for more food without Benjamin. Jacob's response was, 'My son will not go down there. End of story.' But when they ran out of food, Jacob said, *'Go back and buy us a little more food'* (Gen. 43:2). It was as if he hadn't been listening. That's an example of a stubborn person, not giving in, not even admitting that they know there is a problem.

Stubbornness means being unteachable, inflexible, holding firmly to your own opinion and not giving in. Maybe you admit you are stubborn. If so, you are a rare person because this is the kind of fault we don't admit to very often, and if we do we justify it or laugh about it. But it could be that you have to deal with another person who is obstinate. What we know is that a stubborn person is incorrigible, they never improve; they don't seem to learn. They will not admit to a fault and nothing seems to change their mind. Have I described you? Do people who know you best think this about you? The chances are, if two or more people have thought it, there may well be something to it.

However there are two kinds of stubbornness: there's the stubborn - ness that can flow from the Holy Spirit, and there's is the stubbornness that flows from the flesh. The word 'flesh' is a Bible word that describes the way we are by nature without any help from God. In other words, there's the good kind of stubbornness and the bad kind. The good kind is where you have been persuaded of something by the Holy Spirit, therefore you stick to your guns. You have made a commitment to the Lord, and you can say with the Apostle Paul, *'I know whom I have believed, and am convinced that he is able to guard what I have entrusted to him'* (2 Tim. 1:12).

I am talking now however about stubbornness in the flesh. What *are* we like when left to ourselves? We find we are proud; we have big egos that don't want to admit to a wrong. But pride has another side – insecurity. The person who has the biggest ego is equally the most insecure person there is.

I spent three years at Oxford, which is a rather respectable university, and I learnt something about the typical Oxford don. When you speak of Oxford dons you are talking about the brightest minds there are. Do you know what I discovered about them? They love flattery if it has anything to do with their intellect. You would think that brilliant people like that wouldn't need any encouragement, and yet that is the case. Do you know why? It's because those who have the biggest egos are the most insecure.

By nature, we are motivated by fear, and the fear of losing face if we change our mind. You know this is a delicate problem for me as minister of Westminster Chapel. I don't like to climb down. I think that if I do it too often the church members won't respect me. It is easier not to admit that I have changed my opinion about something. But I have learned one thing: I have to make a choice whether I keep their approval or whether I seek to honour God.

It is not easy to admit that you might have got it wrong about this or that, but over the years I have watched people who became inflexible simply because they made a public statement or put their viewpoint in print: no matter what, they would never alter it because that would dent their pride, and they feared they would lose face. I have watched those who want to blame others, their parents perhaps, or blame the conditions in which they live; in defending their positions, they have become so entrenched that they have gone too far. It is so sad. For example, many marriages have broken up simply because one partner would not give in and admit, 'I was wrong.'

The Signs of Stubbornness

1. The first thing to see is that you blame others rather than yourself. Notice how Jacob did this in verse 36. Looking at his ten sons, he said, *'You have deprived me of my children . . . and now you want to take Benjamin'* (Gen. 42:36). Jacob admitted no responsibility for anything that had happened – he simply blamed others. Sometimes parents don't realize how much guilt they transfer to their children. We all tend to believe what our parents say. And if you say to your son or daughter, 'You are never going to amount to anything', they grow up believing that. Blaming others is the easiest thing in the world to do.

2. There are also feelings of self-pity. Look again at verse 36. Jacob said, *'Now you want to take Benjamin. Everything is against me!'* He was in bondage to his own self-pity. However, one tries to justify one's feelings. In verse 38 Jacob said, *'My son will not go down there with you; his brother is dead and he is the only one left. If harm comes to him on the journey you are taking, you will bring my grey head down to the grave in sorrow.'* That was his rationale. That was his reason for sticking to his guns. We all have a way of justifying our position. It's a way of protecting ourselves. Jacob was trying to avoid further pain. You need to know that people have a problem with stubbornness partly because they are protecting themselves. They don't want any more pain. It's the easy way out.

Feelings of self-pity can deepen to the extent that you feel there is nothing to live for. In verse 36, Jacob says, *'Everything is against me!'* In verse 38 he says, *'You will bring my grey head down to the grave in sorrow.'* Have you come to that position where you feel that there is little to live for? If it is not dealt with, stubbornness leads one to a borderline clinical depression.

3. You avoid reality. And so we read in verse 2 that Jacob said to his sons, *'Go back and buy us a little more food'* (Gen. 43:2). What did he expect them to say? They had already told him there was no point in returning unless they took Benjamin. After a while, he began to live in a fantasy world. But a person who has this problem of stubbornness, tends to avoid reality.

4. Sadly, it all leads to insensitivity in the way in which you speak. I want to show you something that I regard as most extraordinary, cruel and heartless. I wonder if you have ever noticed it? Jacob said, *'My son will not go down there with you; his brother is dead and he is the only one left'*

(Gen. 42:38). Imagine that! Talking to your other sons and saying, *'He is the only one left.'* How do you suppose that made those sons feel? It made them want to shout, 'Hey, Dad! We're here. We're your sons too.' Jacob was so insensitive.

How to Cope

What do you do if you have to cope with a person who is stubborn? First, you have to remember this verse: *'If someone is caught in a sin, you who are spiritual should restore him gently. But watch yourself, or you also may be tempted.'* That means that you recognize that you also are vulnerable (Gal. 6:1). Next, you have to get the person to face facts. Judah said to his father, *'The man warned us solemnly, "You will not see my face again unless your brother is with you"'* (Gen. 43:3). Then you must answer their questions honestly. You see Jacob had asked, *'Why did you bring this trouble on me by telling the man you had another brother?'* They replied honestly that the man had questioned them closely about themselves (see Gen. 43:6, 7).

Yet, at the end of the day, only God can change a person. But in Jacob's case, we discover that he gave in. Why? First, he had no other choice. Sometimes the only way a stubborn person is dealt with is where God himself brings them to the place where they are hemmed in and there is only one way forward. That is God's gracious way of dealing with them. I know what it is to have God box me into a corner, leaving me with no choice. It is painful at the time, and yet I know it is God's way of getting my attention.

There is one other thing we must note. Judah, who had been trying to reason with his father the whole time, added this: *'Send the boy along with me . . . I myself will guarantee his safety; you can hold me personally responsible for him'* (Gen. 43:8, 9). That's what ended up working.

Look at these words: *'I myself will guarantee his safety; you can hold me personally responsible for him . . . I will bear the blame before you all my life.'* In taking the blame for all our sins on the cross, that is exactly what Jesus did for us.

46

The Guarantee We Will Go to Heaven

Genesis 43:8–23

In the last chapter, we saw how Judah stepped into a situation where Jacob, full of self-pity and so stubborn, refused to send Benjamin with his brothers to get food. Judah said, *'Send the boy along with me and we will go at once, so that we and you and our children may live and not die'* (Gen. 43:8). Now here's the verse I want to focus on: *'I myself will guarantee his safety; you can hold me personally responsible for him. If I do not bring him back to you and set him here before you, I will bear the blame before you all my life'* (v. 9).

The guarantee that we will go to heaven is Jesus, who was born of the tribe of Judah. Judah now stepped forward to intervene, to intercede and to plead with a stubborn man. 'Guarantee' is the word that is used in the New International Version here. It is used again in Genesis 44:32, when Judah again intercedes, but this time before Joseph. Some of you who know the Authorized Version well will already know the word 'surety'. This is why so many hymns, when referring to the intercessory work of Jesus at the right hand of God, refer to him as our 'surety'. It's an archaic word, probably; the word 'guarantee' brings it into the twentieth century. In the Hebrew, the word means to 'offer security', for instance, when you exchange something, a gift or money which is forfeited if your promise is not kept.

Now, I need to tell you that this word in its equivalent Greek form is found in Hebrews 7:22 which says: *'Because of this oath, Jesus has become the guarantee of a better covenant'* (NIV) or *'a surety of a better testament'* (AV). It means a 'pledge' – where one agrees to undertake for another who is unable to discharge his own obligations. And that is what Jesus does for us.

His Guarantee Is Needed

The requirement for you getting into heaven is that you fulfil the law of God perfectly in thought, word and deed, 60 seconds a minute, 60 minutes an hour, 24 hours a day, every day of your life. You may not have murdered anybody, but if you have a grudge against anybody, according to Jesus, that is breaking the sixth commandment. You may never have committed adultery, but if you have lusted after a woman in your heart, according to Jesus, that is committing adultery. By the time you get to the tenth commandment which says, *'You shall not covet'* (Exod. 20:17), if there had been any doubt up to now, it becomes obvious that nobody can keep the law, for we all covet; we all want something we don't have. The point is that the law is perfect, and the law demands perfection. To get to heaven, you have to keep the law in thought, word and deed all your life. On that basis, none of us can believe that we qualify to go there.

Yet if I asked another question: How many of us believe that we *are* going to go to heaven? Many of us would say, 'Yes, I *know* I will go to heaven.' We do not say this because of our good works or because we do our best. We say it because we know we have a guarantee, a surety – Jesus – who came down to earth for that purpose. *'For God so loved the world that he gave his one and only Son, that whoever believes in him shall not perish but have eternal life'* (Jn. 3:16).

His Guarantee Is Certain

Hebrews 7:22 says that one reason Jesus has guaranteed our eternal life is that the guarantee was preceded by an oath. The Bible makes a distinction between a promise and an oath. You may promise something, but if you ever break your oath that is doubly serious. In fact, Jesus said, 'Keep your *promise.*' We are not supposed to swear an oath (see Mt. 5:33). But in the Old Testament, if there was a doubt whether a person could be trusted, you would ask them to swear an oath, because if one swore an oath and didn't keep it, it was a very serious matter.

But this is an amazing thing: God himself, on occasion, swears an oath to us. Why? Isn't his promise enough? His promise is, indeed, secure, but some promises from the Bible are given upon condition. As a matter of fact, I just quoted John 3:16. *'For God so loved the world that he gave his one and only Son, that whoever believes in him shall not perish.'* This is a condition: if you don't believe, you will be lost. So even though Jesus is the guarantee that you go to heaven, you won't if you don't believe on him. But once in a while God swears an oath. What's the difference? If he swears an oath, there are no conditions. The outcome is certain: it is going to happen. In Psalm 110:4 we read: *'The*

LORD *has sworn and will not change his mind. You are a priest for ever, in the order of Melchizedek.*' Hebrews 7 says that Jesus was the one whom the Psalmist referred to in Psalm 110, the priest after the order of Melchizedek, the one to whom God swore the oath, and he, being our intercessor, would guarantee that anybody he prayed for would go to heaven.

Here's what happened. When Jesus died on a cross, he did what Judah said *he* would do, and that was to take all the blame. On the cross, Jesus took the blame for all your sins. The wonderful thing is that when God sent his Son into the world to die, Jesus, as it were, said to the Father, 'Blame me.' And God did blame him. So I want you to know, your guarantee is that somebody has already fulfilled your obligation to keep the law. You couldn't do it, but Jesus stepped in and took the blame for your failure.

Jesus was raised from the dead on Easter morning. Forty days later, he went to heaven and anybody he prays for will go to heaven too. Hebrews 7:25 goes on to say: *'He is able to save completely those who come to God through him, because he always lives to intercede for them.'* Jesus is now praying for everybody who comes to God, but does so in his name. This is why it's not good enough to say, 'Try your best.' Listen to me. If you want a guarantee that you will go to heaven, then you must come to God through Jesus. He is the *only* guarantee. In fact, the only way anybody is saved is through him. Jesus said, *'I am the way and the truth and the life. No-one comes to the Father except through me'* (Jn. 14:6).

His Guarantee Is Sufficient

Let us return now to the story of Jacob. Jacob felt defeated: he had lost Joseph, and now he was afraid he was going to lose Benjamin. Then Judah spoke up. It was so wonderful. This same Judah, the son of Leah, the wife Jacob never loved, was the one who was to give a guarantee. We can never predict the one God will use. The person we didn't appreciate sometimes turns out to be the link. This man Judah was now trying to make Jacob see sense.

But there's another thing I need to show you about Judah. He went so far as to say to Jacob, 'Not only must you let us go and take Benjamin with us, but we must do it *now*' (see Gen. 43:10). If you come to Christ, and I pray that you do, one of your regrets will be that you didn't do it sooner. Time is wasting. There is always an urgency when it comes to the gospel, because if you miss going to heaven, you've lost everything. You can gain the whole world but lose your soul (see Mt. 16:26). You can become popular, you can become rich, you can have an obituary in *The Times*, and be lost. This is why the Bible says, *'Now is the time of God's favour, now is the day of salvation'* (2 Cor. 6:2).

In that same epistle to the Hebrews, we have God swearing another oath: he swears in his wrath that some will not enter into his rest (see Heb. 3:11). You see, when God swears an oath, it means nothing can change. The worst thing that can happen after you have heard this gospel is that you say to yourself, 'Well, if I don't respond now, I will one day. Perhaps next week.' But that may be too late.

Jacob's reaction was typical of unbelief. But finally he agreed to go. He said, *'Put some of the best products of the land in your bags and take them down to the man as a gift – a little balm and a little honey, some spices and myrrh, some pistachio nuts and almonds'* (Gen. 43:11). But the Prime Minister didn't want pistachio nuts and almonds, he just wanted Benjamin.

You may say, 'All right, I'll become a Christian. Look, God, I am going to do this for you.' That might be good, but it's not what God wants. He wants you to affirm that his Son paid all your debt on the cross. If you think Jesus did *almost* enough but you need to add to what Jesus did for you, then I have to tell you that you will remain as lost as ever. If you come to the place where you're not going to add *'pistachio nuts and almonds'*, and you're not going to bring extra baggage, God will ensure you will go to heaven. But you have to come to terms with the fact that God wants only the blood of Jesus to be your guarantee, your surety.

> Nothing in my hand I bring,
> Simply to thy cross I cling.
> A.M. Toplady

You know this seems almost too good to be true, but that is God's message for you.

47

The Tenderness of Jesus

Genesis 43:24–34

Deeply moved at the sight of his brother, Joseph hurried out and looked for a place to weep. He went into his private room and wept there (Gen. 43:30).

The brothers had returned with Benjamin. Seeing his youngest brother, Joseph was moved and hurried out, looking for a place to weep. 'Was that like Jesus?' you ask. That was exactly like Jesus. John 11:35, says, *'Jesus wept.'* Indeed, the words used in reference to Jesus in John 11 are the same as those in Genesis 43 referring to Joseph. Notice again, in Genesis 43:30 are the words, *'deeply moved'*. In John 11:33 we read: *'When Jesus saw her weeping, and the Jews who had come along with her also weeping, he was deeply moved in spirit.'* The same words are in verse 38: *'Jesus, once more deeply moved, came to the tomb.'* This is the way Jesus is. An aspect of him you should know about is his tenderness – his love, the way he felt about people.

What was Jesus like? He was full of compassion. In Matthew 8:1 we read how, when he came down from the mountain after giving the Sermon on the Mount, large crowds followed him, but only one person went up to him with a request, and that was, of all people, a leper. In those days a leper was regarded as somebody you avoided like the plague. People thought that if you touched a leper you would develop the disease too. In fact, lepers were regarded as the scum of the earth. They were isolated and no one would go near; if they walked into a crowd, people scattered in every direction. So lepers knew their place.

Being Accepted

All of us can tell whether another person is going to accept us. We can almost feel it. You must have some inkling if you came to see me whether or not I would listen, whether I would care. What I wish is that I could radiate the love of Jesus, that you would feel that I want to be like him.

The leper knew that if he went to Jesus he would be accepted. We are told that he fell before him and said, ' *"Lord, if you are willing, you can make me clean."*

Jesus reached out his hand and touched the man. "I am willing," he said. *"Be clean!" Immediately he was cured of his leprosy'* (Mt. 8:2).

In Matthew 9:36 we are told: *'When he saw the crowds, he had compassion on them, because they were harassed and helpless, like sheep without a shepherd.'* He accepted people just as they are.

In Luke 19 we read about a man by the name of Zacchaeus who was a tax collector and therefore hated by everybody because tax collectors kept a lot of money for themselves, and so nobody trusted them. He was curious about Jesus, so he climbed up a sycamore tree to have a good view, and when Jesus saw him he said, 'Zacchaeus, come down; I want to spend some time with you' (see v. 5). People were astonished and appalled. Jesus knew everything about Zaccheus, yet he simply accepted him. Zacchaeus was so amazed. He said, *'Here and now I give half of my possessions to the poor, and if I have cheated anybody out of anything, I will pay back four times the amount'* (v. 8). Some people teach that a precondition to becoming a Christian is that you have to do this or that, and only then will Jesus accept you. What we see here is that Jesus just accepted Zacchaeus as he was, and lo and behold, Zacchaeus wanted to do the right thing. Jesus is still the same today. He accepts you as you are.

In fact, we are told in John 8:3–11 that Pharisees, who were a legalistic, self-righteous people, brought in a woman caught in adultery and said to Jesus, 'According to the law of Moses, this woman should be stoned. What do you say?' Jesus bent down and starting to write in the ground with his finger. Then he said to these people, *'If any one of you is without sin, let him be the first to throw a stone at her.'* Hearing that, they all left. Then Jesus said to the woman, *'Where are they? Has no-one condemned you?'*

The woman said, *'No-one sir.'*

And then Jesus declared, *'Then neither do I condemn you. Go now and leave your life of sin.'*

What did he do? He accepted her. That is his way. Jesus displays such tenderness. I could give one example after another to assure you that whatever may be in your past, whatever it is that you've done, this Jesus will accept you.

You may think, 'If I went to church and people knew what I am really like, they would have nothing to do with me.' Sadly, there are a lot of Christians who are like that. But I am not speaking about church or Christians, I am talking about Jesus who was so tender that if he saw people in distress he stopped what he was doing to comfort them. The most stunning truth that I can get over to you is that he hasn't changed.

Jesus Accepts Us

Isn't it wonderful that the God-man we are talking about, the Creator, the God who made you, who came to this earth, was not the kind who went around telling people that they had reach a certain standard before he would accept them. He didn't make people feel small because they weren't from a certain class or because they didn't have a certain status; he accepted people as they were. For the first time, the poor people had a hero. The tenderness of Jesus. If you don't need this kind of message now, maybe one day you will see you need the One who will take you as you are.

Jesus hasn't changed. When he went to heaven, he didn't have to change to get there. That's not true of you and me. I am going to go to heaven one day, but something has to happen to me before I get there. The Bible says I am going to be changed. This body will change: there will be no decay; we won't die in heaven. My spirit will change, my soul, everything that is not right about me will be corrected, because no unclean thing shall enter therein (see 1 Cor. 15:51–54). So to get to heaven, I will have had a change. When Jesus went to heaven, he didn't have to change at all, he simply entered straight in. He's the same Jesus. As it says in Hebrews 4:15: *'We do not have a high priest who is unable to sympathise with our weaknesses.'*

Joseph – A Picture of Jesus

I want to talk about Joseph now, because we have a picture here of how Jesus, who is at God's right hand, sees us. We can't see him, but he can see us clearly. He has the advantage: he is in the position of seeing the whole picture. It is just like Joseph who, when he saw his brothers, saw everything clearly. They were having to speak through an interpreter. But he understood them as soon as they spoke. When we pray, we sometimes struggle, trying to make ourselves heard. Yet the Bible says that all things are naked and open before his eyes. Jesus listens to us even though he knows everything before we speak. This is the way Jesus sees us. He sees us clearly. Joseph saw his brothers clearly, but his brothers didn't see him like that.

Another interesting point is that they bowed down. Joseph's dream was fulfilled. The Bible says: *' "As surely as I live," says the Lord, "Every knee will bow before me, every tongue will confess to God" '* (Rom. 14:11). What the brothers were doing was the picture of the way it will be when all that was promised of Jesus has been fulfilled and we stand before God.

Joseph was interested. He began to ask questions (see Gen. 43:27–29). He asked, *'How is your aged father?'* He saw Benjamin and asked, *'Is this your youngest brother, the one you told me about? . . . God be gracious to you, my son.'* These weren't perfunctory questions – Joseph cared. He wanted to know about them because they were his family. I want you to know that *he* loves you, this Jesus, as much as Joseph loved his family. Jesus cares about you and about every detail of your life. Joseph was deeply moved. As soon as Joseph had spoken to Benjamin, we read: *'Deeply moved . . . Joseph hurried out and looked for a place to weep. He went into his private room and wept there'* (Gen. 43:30). The word 'tenderness' means 'easily moved to pity'. This tenderness was not apparent to the brothers. The Bible tells us that the Jesus in heaven, where we cannot see him, is the same Jesus as he was on earth and that he is touched with the feeling of our weaknesses. When you have a difficult time, perhaps you wish for someone with whom you can share your problem, somebody who would understand what you are going through. You may think of somebody and say, 'I wonder if I could tell this person? No, they wouldn't understand. They will just pat me on the back and say, "God bless you." They wouldn't appreciate how I feel.'

We are not able to see Jesus, but we know he is touched by our pain. The brothers couldn't know that Joseph was in the next room, weeping. But Joseph was touched, deeply moved. Jesus has not changed. Are you hurting? Are you looking for somebody to weep with you? Jesus will. The Lord knows how things will turn out for you, but he weeps for you now because he loves you and he knows how you feel.

Maybe, you have been involved in something for which people have condemned you; they have judged you. Do you know what Jesus would say? 'I don't condemn you. Go, sin no more!' He will accept you, so that from this day forward you may live the kind of life that will give you a sense of dignity and honour. Jesus will take you just as you are. To think that Jesus would see you and pick you out just as he did Zacchaeus! Sometimes I will look over a crowd and wave at somebody; it's nice to feel affirmed.

Many years ago, when he was running for office, John F. Kennedy came to Fort Lauderdale, and a friend of ours who had been completely opposed to him went to see him. She came back flustered and excited. She said, 'He looked right at me!' I think she would have voted for him there and then. To think that Jesus would look at us so tenderly! Are you used to someone pointing the finger at you? Do you know what it is to be harassed, constantly reminded of everything that's wrong? Is there anyone who can take *me* as I am? Yes. Jesus tenderly looked at me.

Joseph prepared a banquet. What do you think his brothers had done to deserve that? They were the ones who had been so mean to him. They were the ones who had sold him into slavery. But now they are being given a feast by the Prime Minister of Egypt! There were hundreds and thousands of people coming from all over the world to Egypt to buy food. Yet how many of those had a meal with the Prime Minister? This didn't happen to everybody; in fact, it didn't happen to anybody, but it happened to them. He was according them a great honour. Not only that, they were being treated with dignity. Did they deserve it? Absolutely not.

What God promises you is dignity and honour and a place in heaven. Most people aren't going to heaven. I have to tell you the Bible says, *'Small is the gate and narrow the road that leads to life, and only a few find it'* (Mt. 7:14). Don't ask me why; I don't understand it, but if you are reading this, God has been singularly good to you. You may have felt that nothing good has ever happened to you. Listen. You're reading about the gospel; you're hearing about a God who loves you. That is more precious than an invitation to see the Queen. That is more precious than a job paying £100,000 a year. Do you know, he does this for you despite knowing all about you?

Joseph knew what his brothers had done to him. He knew them so well that we are told that when the men were seated, they found themselves sitting in the order of their ages, from the firstborn to the youngest, and they looked at each other in astonishment. They realized that something strange was happening.

God has given me a message just for you: You matter to him. Joseph laid on this banquet knowing everything about his family. And knowing everything about you, Jesus went to the cross of Calvary and took your sins upon himself. If you recognize that you've sinned and you are sorry, then his tenderness is apparent: he forgives you. Jesus looks at you tenderly. You don't need to be lost. You will never find another person who loves you more.

48

The Toughness of Jesus

Genesis 44:1–34

Dr James Dobson has a phrase: 'Love must be tough.' Tenderness is central to Jesus' nature, but so is toughness. Jesus himself said in Revelation 3:19, *'Those whom I love I rebuke and discipline.'* Now, to complicate matters, I am going to use the word 'antimony'. It means two principles, irreconcilable, yet both true. Jesus is God, yet Jesus is man. You can't reconcile the two, but they are both true. Jesus is tender, yet Jesus can be tough.

In the previous chapter, we saw how Joseph wept when he saw his brothers, especially Benjamin. They would not have known what was going on, any more than we can see that, behind the scenes, Jesus is touched with the feeling of our weaknesses. But in this passage, we also see the toughness of Jesus when we see how tough Joseph (a picture of Christ) was with his brothers. And yet it was for one reason: he loved them. Perhaps you feel God is being tough with you. You can feel a certain kind of hostility, a strangeness, and you wonder, 'Is this God?' I am prepared to tell you that God does that because he loves you.

What is happening here? Joseph was being tough with his brothers to test them. He wanted to know two things. First, he wanted to know their attitude towards his brother Benjamin, because Benjamin was Joseph's full brother (the others were half-brothers), and Joseph, unfor - tunately, was preferred by his father. It was not right that Jacob should have been partial to Joseph, but he was. Joseph knew this, and he knew that his father would feel the same way about Benjamin. Joseph wanted to know what his brothers felt about Benjamin. The second thing he wanted to know was how they felt about his father, their father. And so, they were tested.

The Toughness of Jesus

Jesus tests us to this very day because he wants to know how you feel about *his* Father. Let me tell you something: There is a lot of talk from people who say, 'Jesus, I can accept, but I don't like the God of the Bible.' Or some people say, 'I like the God of the New Testament but not the God of the Old Testament.' However, they need to understand that the God of the Old Testament is also the God of the New Testament. Not only that, the God of the Bible is the Father of Jesus. You may think that you are endearing yourself to Jesus by saying 'Jesus, I can take you, but I don't like your Father.' But that will incur his anger. You could not have said anything worse.

Before you are saved, you have to be reconciled with God, the Father of Jesus. There is no way you can avoid the God of the Bible if you are going to go to heaven. Jesus makes it clear that his Father is the God with whom you must come to terms. He wants to test you. He wants to see how you are going to react, how you feel about his Father. Perhaps, years ago, you became disillusioned with God; you felt he had let you down, that he hurt you in some way. You believed then that your feelings were justified. Jesus wants to know how you feel about God now.

How do we know about the toughness of Jesus? In the New Testament, Jesus showed his toughness in a number of ways. For example, on Palm Sunday he went into the Temple, overturned the tables and drove out the money-changers (see Mt. 21:12, 13). Artists have often portrayed Jesus holding a lamb, or with children around him, and sometimes with a halo over his head. However, I haven't seen many pictures of Jesus throwing the money-changers out of the Temple!

Take, for example, when Jesus saw his disciples on the sea of Galilee in a storm; they were rowing, but making no headway as the winds were so strong. Jesus saw them. He could have gone to their rescue immedi - ately. He didn't. He waited. That meant he had to be tough, even though what he wanted to do was to go at once.

Again, take the account in Mark 7:25–30, when a Greek lady asked Jesus to cast out a demon possessing her daughter. Jesus refused, at first, to have anything to do with her. He said, *'First let the children eat all they want, for it is not right to take the children's bread and toss it to their dogs.'* Then the woman began to sob and said, *'Even the dogs under the table eat the children's crumbs.'* We see the toughness of Jesus. He appeared so rude, but then he gave in. He said, 'It's all right. Your daughter is healed.' Jesus was testing her to see if she really wanted help. So love is tough. And he will test you too.

The God of the Bible is the architect and author of the most offensive doctrine I know, and that is the teaching of eternal punishment. There is no way I can reconcile this doctrine in my mind. There is nothing about that teaching that I like. I don't understand it. But Jesus endorsed it and never apologized for it. That was toughness. He described a place which the devil would have you believe does not exist. Sometimes it is called hell. Sometimes it is called the place where there is weeping, and gnashing of teeth. It is sometimes called 'outer darkness where the worm doesn't die, where the fire is not quenched' (see Mk. 9:48). Never mind that some churchmen today seldom talk about this doctrine, never mind that theologians water it down, never mind that you have not been confronted with it, search the Scriptures for yourself. Jesus taught it.

There was a time when Jesus had to say to Peter, one of the disciples to whom he was very close, one of his inner circle, *'Out of my sight, Satan!'* (Mt. 16:23). This shows that no relationship must so sentimental that you cannot rebuke someone who is closest to you. Love must be tough.

Maybe we don't realize what is going on at the moment, and the Lord withholds certain things that we want. Maybe, like the disciples, we are out at sea, rowing and waiting for the Lord to get into the boat. But we must wait on his timing. The Lord is tough. When you are a compas - sionate person, it's hard to be tough. Jesus is tender at heart, but he loves us so much that there are times when he has to be tough.

Joseph and Benjamin

Let us look now at the way Joseph dealt with his brothers with reference to Benjamin. The first thing we discover is that Genesis 43:34 says, *'When portions were served to them from Joseph's table, Benjamin's portion was five times as much as anyone else's.'* Joseph did that, partly because he loved Benjamin, but mostly to see what the ten brothers would do. He did not need the interpreter he was using; he understood every word they were saying and he was watching their every expression. They didn't know it, but they were being tested.

This is the way it is in life. We aren't aware that we are being tested. It may be that God has earmarked you for a certain promotion. He may have a certain inheritance he wants to give you, but he tests you to see if you are ready, and he is watching you. Joseph not only gave them food, but verse 34 also says, *'They feasted and drank freely with him.'* The wine flowed. Do you know the phrase, 'in wine, the truth'? Joseph let them have all the wine they wanted because he wanted to find out what they thought of Benjamin.

And so, you too are being tested. The test is, 'What do you think of this gospel?' The word 'gospel' means good news. The good news is that Jesus himself died on a cross, shed his precious blood that you might have forgiveness of all your sins. You are being tested, and it may be that, like these ten brothers, you are getting a second chance, but you don't realize it.

Showing that You've Changed

That brings us to the next event in the story (see Gen. 44:1–2). Joseph now said to his servants, *'Fill the men's sacks with as much food as they can carry, and put each man's silver in the mouth of his sack. Then put my cup, the silver one, in the mouth of the youngest one's sack, along with the silver for his corn.'* This was an opportunity for Joseph's brothers to show that they had changed. If they were going to treat Benjamin the way they had treated him, they would react to Benjamin now in the same way they had once reacted to him, because they knew that their father had now transferred all his affection to Benjamin. The way Jacob once felt about Joseph, he then felt about Benjamin. These ten brothers had hated Joseph, and now, possibly, they would hate Benjamin. So unknown to them, they were given a test to see how they would react when they discovered that the silver cup was in Benjamin's bag.

When they reached the edge of town, one of Joseph's officials caught them up and demanded, 'Who has stolen my master's cup?' They were horrified and protested, 'None of us would do that.' The brothers agreed that whoever had it would surely die. That was fine because they were so sure that none of them would do that (see Gen. 44:9). However, the official softened the penalty the brothers proposed, saying the guilty person would become his slave.

Of course, what happened was a 'set up'. Joseph had put the silver cup in Benjamin's bag. Do you see what was going on? Joseph was giving the ten brothers a perfect opportunity to do with Benjamin as they once did with him, because they could just say, 'Well, sorry, Benjamin, we didn't know you had done that. Good riddance – you get what you deserve!' If they had done so, it would have shown that they were still the same as they used to be. But they had changed. They had the perfect excuse to let Benjamin go, but they didn't.

Have you ever wondered if you really have changed? Are you ashamed of something you did in your past and you cannot live with the guilt? Your guilt can disappear when you confess your sins to God and repent of them. The truth is that sometimes this doesn't help, and the only way we can live with ourselves then is when we know that we really have changed. So what God does, in many cases, is to give an equivalent temptation – a secret test – to see if you have changed. When you realize that you had an opportunity to be as you once were, but you didn't give in, you can begin to live with yourself.

Joseph wanted to know that they thought of their father. They had been jealous and one can understand that, but they had also shown scant respect for their father. Yet there was a way to find out if this was still the case. The truth about this emerged when Judah intervened.

Once it was agreed that whoever had Joseph's cup would be enslaved, it looked certain that Benjamin would be left in Egypt. But when the brothers were taken before Joseph, Judah stepped in. Talk about having an advocate, talk about pleading, you have never heard such a powerful intercession in all your life. Judah began to make the case and his final words are in verse 34: *'How can I go back to my father if the boy is not with me? No! Do not let me see the misery that would come upon my father'* Note, he didn't say, 'his father', he said *'my father'*. Joseph could see this man was different. By being tough, Joseph found out what his brothers were like.

What then were the reasons for his toughness?

- To show his love at the proper time. More than anything, Joseph wanted to disclose his identity to his brothers. He could hardly wait to tell them. He wanted them to know and to love them. But, by being tough, by waiting, he found out what they were like. When Jesus saw the disciples rowing at sea, the time came when Jesus said, 'I've got to go now.' And he stepped in.

- To see if they had changed and to give them a second chance. John Newton, the composer of 'Amazing Grace', refers to God as 'giving us the second look', and he comes to you a second time. The Bible says of Hezekiah that God left him to test him and see what was in his heart (see 2 Chr. 32:31). God has given you an opportunity. And he has set it up to test you.

49

Total Forgiveness

Genesis 45:1–15

Joseph had to come to terms with the bitterness he felt, but the question is, had he totally forgiven his brothers? 'Total forgiveness' is a phrase I borrow from another Joseph, Joseph Tson, an old friend, who happened to be passing through London a few years ago. I was going through what was, at that time, the deepest trial I had ever known. I can't tell you how desperate, how bitter, how angry and how hurt I was. I told nobody about it, but I was seething inside. When Joseph came, I said to myself, 'This is one man with whom I can share this.'

Yet I have to be honest and tell you that the only reason I decided to tell Joseph was so that he would pat me on the back and say, 'R.T., you are right to be angry. Go ahead. Get it out of your system.' If I told you the story, I don't know what your reaction would be. Perhaps you would say, 'Oh, that's awful! It was unfair. It was unjust. No one should be treated like that!' That's how I would have wanted you to respond if I had told you years ago. And that's what I wanted Joseph Tson to say to me. So I shared my problem with him, and he then asked me, 'Is there anything more?'

I said, 'No, I think you've heard it all.'

'Look, I'd like to take a nap,' he replied. 'Give me 15 minutes.'

He kept his word and came back 15 minutes later. Then he looked at me and said, 'R.T., you must totally forgive them, because until you do you will be in chains. Release them, and you will be released.'

Nobody had ever talked to me like that. Yet, as the proverb says, 'Faithful are the wounds of a friend.' It was the greatest word anyone had ever given me privately or, for that matter, that I have ever heard publicly. 'Release them.' Such simple words, such a biblical principle. I said, 'Joseph, I can't.'

'You must,' he answered.

It was the hardest thing I ever did.

Some years later, when preaching on the life of Joseph, I saw in this passage from Genesis how we may know that we have totally forgiven someone. People sometimes say to me, 'I wish I could be sure. I *think* I have forgiven, but how could I know for certain?' Maybe you're like that. I don't write this to give you a guilt trip; I write it to set you free, because when you forgive that person totally, you are the winner. You see, we somehow delude ourselves into believing that by not forgiving others we are hurting them. Nothing could be more foolish! When I don't forgive totally I am the impoverished one. I am hurting myself. As Joseph put it, I am in chains.

In the previous chapter we saw how Judah interceded so powerfully on Benjamin's behalf. Judah was prepared to sacrifice himself for his brother. It's a perfect picture of how Jesus took our place and intercedes for us.

'How can I go back to my father if the boy is not with me?' pleaded Judah. *'No! Do not let me see the misery that would come upon my father'* (Gen. 44:34).

But the Prime Minister could take no more. *'He cried out, "Make everyone leave my presence!"'* Now there were only Joseph and the 11 brothers. And without an interpreter, speaking now in Hebrew, he said, *'I am Joseph!'* (Gen. 45:3). Those men were terrified.

Knowing We Have Totally Forgiven

Now the question is, how do we know that we have totally forgiven another person?

1. You keep their identity secret and conceal what they did

Joseph's intention in all this was to get all the family to move to Egypt. However, he didn't want anybody in Egypt to know what his brothers had done. So he sent everybody out, including his interpreter, and their reunion took place in private. Joseph wanted his brothers to come to Egypt and be loved and admired by the Egyptians. He wanted them to be treated as heroes, so no one was to know what they had done 22 years ago. He wanted to protect them.

Has someone hurt you? Maybe you don't want people to admire them, you want others to despise them, you want them to see what they are really like. But Joseph concealed what his brothers had done. The proof that you have totally forgiven is that you protect the identity of that person who hurt you, so that no one will ever know.

What is the promise in the gospel? Jesus died on the cross for our sins, and when we come to the Father, trusting in the blood of Jesus, we are promised total forgiveness. Let us suppose for a moment, though, that you had confessed all of your sins to God. Then this big screen comes down, and God flashes on the screen all that is known about you, everything that was in your past. You would cry, 'It's all true! But I thought I was forgiven. I thought these things would never be held against me. How could God reveal that?' You would know that God hadn't kept his word. But the promise in the gospel is that all of our sins are covered by the blood of Christ. I want you to know that if there is anything in your past of which you are ashamed nobody will ever know. God will protect you from their knowing. And, when you stand before God at the judgement, nobody will ever know. *'As far as the east is from the west, so far has he removed our transgressions from us'* (Ps. 103:12).

2. You set them free from fear

Joseph said, *'I am Joseph! Is my father still living?'* (v. 3). But his brothers were not able to answer him because they were terrified at his presence. Then Joseph said to his brothers, *'Come close to me.'* What he wanted to do was to make them feel it was all right. He wanted to weep on their shoulders; he wanted to feel close to them. But they couldn't believe it. You see, the proof that we haven't forgiven is that we want another person to be afraid of us. This way we can control them. For example, if I know that you have spoken against me, I will go to you and act in such a way that it makes you a little edgy. You think, 'Oh, he knows!' Why am I doing it? To make you nervous, to intimidate you, to make you fearful and ashamed. It's because I am bitter; I have not forgiven you. In 1 John 4:18 we read, *'Perfect love drives out fear.'* Then it makes the interesting point: *'because fear has to do with punishment.'* It means that if you want another person to be afraid of you it's because you haven't forgiven them, so you punish them, holding their misdeeds over them to keep them fearful.

Let me ask you this. Husband, has your wife treated you badly in some way and you constantly remind her of this? Wife, has your husband let you down in some way and you won't let him forget it? Remember, *'Love keeps no record of wrongs'* (1 Cor. 13:5). Why do we keep a record of wrongs? It's because we plan to use it. But, when we have totally forgiven, we will tear up that record, burn it, and never look back. The proof that you have totally forgiven is you set a person free from fear.

3. You want people who have hurt you to forgive themselves

Look at verse 5: *'Now, do not be distressed and do not be angry with yourselves for selling me here.'* Think about that. Yet that is the way God forgives. He forgives, and he wants you to forgive yourself. Perhaps you have said, 'I believe that God forgives me, but I can't forgive myself.' Let me tell you something: that does not make God happy. If you don't forgive yourself, you don't really believe that God has forgiven you. If he has decreed that it is just and right for him to forgive you, and then you go around saying, 'I can't forgive myself,' that makes God angry. That's a sign of self-righteousness. When God forgives he wants us to enjoy his forgiveness, and he wants us to forgive ourselves. Joseph could say, 'Don't be angry with yourselves.' Have you ever seen a person who is sorry, and you still won't forgive them? They would do anything if they hadn't done what they did. When you have totally forgiven them, you set them free and enable them to forgive themselves.

4. You let them save face

Look at verses 7 and 8: *'But God sent me ahead of you to preserve for you a remnant on earth and to save your lives by a great deliverance. So then, it was not you who sent me here, but God,'* What does 'to save face' mean? It means that you keep a certain dignity. I don't know how many of you have read Dale Carnegie's book, *How to Win Friends and Influence People* (Chancellor Press). It's not a Christian book, but every Christian should read it. One of the points he makes about winning friends is to let the other person save face. To an oriental this is particularly important: if the Japanese lose face, they may commit suicide. And, you see, when we forgive the other person, we do not want them to feel humiliated, we let them have a sense of dignity.

How do we do this? Let's see how Joseph did it. When I consider what they did to him and how bitter he had been, what he said was amazing. He was saying, 'Look, it's all right. God sent me here first. It wasn't you who sent me here. God knew a long time ago that there would be famine in the world, and he wanted to save our family. Somebody had to get here first, and I am the one chosen.' It was a way of saying, 'I am no different to you. I would have done what you did.'

You have to come to terms with this: when you begin pointing a finger at another person, and when you shame them for what they did, you don't realize that you are capable of doing the same thing. Joseph knew what he himself was really like now. The best way to find out what *you* are really like is to enter into the presence of God and allow his Spirit to focus on your heart. You will discover that you will be like Isaiah, who said, *'Woe is me!'* (Isa. 6:5 AV). Joseph had reached the place where he knew what was in his heart, and he knew he was the sovereign vessel, chosen to be the first one to reach Egypt. Joseph could let them save face and say, 'Look, it was God who did it. God sent me here.'

It is one of the sweetest truths of the Bible that God doesn't want us to feel guilty, and the reason I can say that is true is that he tells us in Romans 8:28: *'We know that in all things God works for the good of those who love him.'* Why does he do that? So that we can look at our past and not feel so bad.

5. You protect them from their greatest fear

Those ten brothers had one fear. They could live with almost anything except their father Jacob finding out what they did. Joseph could have said, 'I forgive you, but you have to go back and tell our father what you did.' They would have been horrified. All the forgiveness that Joseph had manifested would have meant nothing if they had to do that. But Joseph knew that. I find it very interesting because it was the first thing on their mind: 'Oh, no! This is Joseph and our father is going to find out.'

Yet do you know what he said to them? *'Hurry back to my father and say to him, "This is what your son Joseph says: God has made me lord of all Egypt!"'* (Gen. 45:9). He repeats it in verse 13: *'Tell my father about all the honour accorded me in Egypt and about everything you have seen. And bring my father down here quickly.'* The one thing he wouldn't let them do was tell their father. In fact, his instructions were, *'Don't quarrel on the way!'* (v. 24).

Many years ago, Senator Edward Kennedy of Massachusetts had the most brilliant political future of any person on the face of the earth. All he had to do was throw his hat into the ring and he would have been elected President. He was his father's last hope. His brother John Kennedy had been assassinated; Robert Kennedy was assassinated; there was only Ted Kennedy left. Then came Chappaquiddick. The only fear that Teddy Kennedy had was not that he would not get to run for President. It was not that people would find out the truth about Chappaquiddick; he could live with that. He had one fear – that his ailing father would hear about it. They kept the old man from seeing TV, but he eventually found out, and Teddy Kennedy was crushed. For him, it was the worst scenario.

Joseph knew that these brothers could live with anything except Jacob finding out. Look at the way Judah was. He couldn't bear the thought of returning without Benjamin. The brothers wouldn't do that to their father. They couldn't live with their father finding out about their terrible crime. But Joseph protected them. Perhaps you have held that threat over somebody. It is your way of blackmailing. You haven't forgiven.

6. You maintain your forgiveness

We turn now to the end of the book of Genesis. Seventeen years later, having moved to Egypt, Jacob died. Joseph's brothers were now con - vinced that he had simply waited for the day of his father's death to take vengeance on them. So they went to him and made up the story that their father had sent word to Joseph saying, 'Forgive the boys for what they did.' In Genesis 50:18, it says: *'His brothers then came and threw themselves down before him. "We are your slaves," they said.'*

Joseph couldn't believe it. He said, 'I forgave you!' He couldn't believe they would do this. However, they couldn't believe they were really forgiven. But Joseph said, *' "Don't be afraid . . . I will provide for you and your children.*" *And he reassured them and spoke kindly to them'* (Gen. 50:21). It showed that 17 years later he had not retracted his forgiveness.

Maybe you think you have done something great because you have forgiven once. But showing forgiveness is an ongoing process. It's a life sentence. How would you like it if God forgave you for a year of two, and then, after seventeen years, he said, 'I have been thinking about what you did. It's just too much!' No. The blood of Jesus washes away sin; it will never be held against you.

I end this chapter on a very practical point. You will say, 'But Joseph's brothers knew what they had done and they were sorry. The people I am worried about don't think they have done anything wrong. Do I have to forgive them?' My answer is that in 90 per cent of the cases where total forgiveness is required, the people you have to forgive sincerely don't know they have done anything wrong. Did you know the bitterness I had? I guarantee you, those I had to forgive would say, 'Why do you need to forgive me? What have I done?' I say this for this reason: Don't make the mistake of going out and saying, 'Paul, I forgive you for what you said.'

'Oh, what did I do?'

'You don't *know* what you did to me?'

Now I have upset him.

Almost without exception, the people I have had to forgive are sincerely unaware of what they have done. The problem is with *me*. I have had to deal with it. Those who have hurt me haven't known for sure what has been going on in my mind. It doesn't matter. What matters is that in my heart there's no bitterness. What is the biblical basis for forgiving others who are unaware of what they have done? Jesus on the cross said, *'Father, forgive them, for they do not know what they are doing.'* (Lk. 23:34).

50

Shaken by Good News

Genesis 45:16–28

They told him, 'Joseph is still alive! In fact, he is ruler of all Egypt.' Jacob was stunned; he did not believe them (Gen. 45:26).

We have now reached the point in the story where Jacob is the focal point once again. Have you ever been shaken by good news? Normally, we think of being shaken by bad news. The Psalmist says that the one who trusts in the Lord, the righteous man, will have no fear of bad news (see Ps. 112:7). But Jacob was shaken by *good* news. In fact, it was the greatest news he ever heard in his life and he was stunned. His 11 sons reported a scenario that exceeded his wildest imagination. Joseph was alive and Prime Minister of all Egypt!

God Loves to Surprise Us

The news to Jacob was unexpected. God loves to do things like that. Sometimes he plans and prepares for a long time. He waited thousands of years before he finally sent his Son into the world. Yet sometimes God likes to do something so suddenly that no one is quite prepared for it. For instance, in the days of the early church, I doubt it entered the minds of the Christians to pray that Saul of Tarsus, who hated the name of Jesus and was doing everything he could to wipe out Christianity, would get saved. But, while Saul was on his way to Damascus to arrest more Christians, a light suddenly beamed down from heaven blinding him, and he fell to the ground. Saul of Tarsus was saved (see Acts 9:1–6). It happened suddenly, and overnight the whole situation for the Christian church changed.

For Jacob, the news that Joseph was alive was stunning. He fainted (according to the AV). As for Saul, when he was converted, he fell to the ground.

Later, after Saul became the Apostle Paul, there was an occasion when Paul and his new friend Silas were put in prison (see Acts 16:16–40). At midnight, we are told that they began to sing praises to God, but suddenly there was a violent earthquake and the foundations of the prison were shaken. The prison doors flew open and everybody's chains fell off. The jailer woke up. When he saw the prison doors open, he drew his sword and was about to kill himself because he thought the prisoners had escaped. But Paul shouted, 'Don't harm yourself! We are all here.' The wonderful news that they hadn't run left this jailer shaken. He was stunned and fell trembling before Paul and Silas crying, 'What must I do to be saved?' Sometimes the best news in the world comes suddenly, and it leaves us stunned, trembling. Maybe that is happening to you.

The news about Joseph surpassed anything Jacob had ever expected. If you were to ask Jacob what was his wildest dream, he would not have named what his sons told him. He had already concluded that Joseph was dead – that he was out of the picture. I wonder if you have already reached conclusions about which you are so certain that you are unable to conceive any alternative situation.

The wonderful thing was the news that Joseph was alive, but then to learn that he was the lord of all Egypt was almost inconceivable. God loves to do that. He loves to do that which surpasses anything that we ever thought of. When the Queen of Sheba came to Solomon, she said, 'I had heard of your fame, I had heard of your wisdom, I had heard of your riches. Having seen it, even the half had not been told to me' (see 1 Kgs. 10:7).

The Apostle Paul said that when we pray God does that which goes beyond what we ask for or even think about. *'No eye has seen, no ear has heard, no mind has conceived what God has prepared for those who love him'* (1 Cor. 2:9). God has a plan for every single one of us. When we see what he has in mind, it will surpass anything we thought possible. As St Augustine said, God loves every single person as though there were no one else to love. He wants to give us the desires of our hearts beyond anything you thought possible.

Reacting to Good News

Jacob reacted with scepticism. Notice how it was put to him: ' *"Joseph is still alive! In fact, he is ruler of all Egypt." Jacob was stunned; he did not believe them'* (Gen. 45:26). That is often the first reaction to the greatest news that ever was. We go out from Westminster Chapel every Saturday, and we try to present the gospel on the streets. God blesses the Pilot Light ministry; it is the sweetest time. Yet we find the hardest thing to put over when we present the gospel is that it is really true. People say, 'Now, just a minute, are you saying that I will go to heaven because Jesus died for

me on the cross? Surely, there's more that we have to do to get to heaven!'
They find it difficult to accept the idea that getting to heaven rests on
something someone else has already done. The first reaction is often
scepticism.

Jacob received the news with silence. How do we know that? It's
because his sons kept on talking, but he said nothing. Silence. But, you
see, what often happens is that we don't want to talk to anybody
immediately. I recall a young nurse who had been brought by friends to
hear me preach. That particular evening, I spoke about eternal punish -
ment, about hell. This sophisticated young lady was so upset, and so angry,
that after the benediction the people who had brought her were afraid to
speak. She sat there seething until they said gently, 'Well, would you like
to come back for a cup of coffee?'

She refused saying, 'I didn't think anybody believed in that. I want to
go home.'

All the way home there was silence. So the people who brought her
tried to apologize a little, saying, 'Perhaps Dr Kendall wasn't at his best
tonight.'

Still trying to smooth things over, they let her out of the car and
thought they would never see her again. But on the Friday of that week,
the nurse phoned and asked to join them at church on the following
Sunday. They couldn't believe it. That Sunday evening she was con -
verted.

Jacob reacted slowly to the good news. First, he needed clarification.
Jacob asked, 'Have I heard you correctly?' And so they told him
everything Joseph had said to them and what Joseph told them to tell
him. But he needed more: he needed corroboration. Genesis 45:27 says:
'When they told him everything Joseph had said to them, and when he saw the
carts Joseph had sent to carry him back, the spirit of their father Jacob revived. And
Israel said, "I'm convinced! My son Joseph is still alive. I will go and see him
before I die." '

Perhaps you have heard the gospel many times, and now, for the
first time, the penny has dropped. But you need corroboration. God
knows what you know. He knows how honest you are, and he also
knows the tokens he has given you whereby you know in your heart
that this is the truth. He knows that you realize that if you were to go
against what you already know to be true, when you stand before the
judgement you will have no excuse. You won't be able to say, 'God,
you didn't tell me this.' He will be able to say, 'I *know* what you know.'
This gospel has been corroborated. That means you have known the
truth and God has made himself real across the years.

I was talking to my friend Paul Cain about Genesis 45:27, where it
says that Jacob saw the carts that Joseph had sent to carry him back. Paul
said, 'One day, some years ago, I was thinking about that verse and I had
an open vision. I was allowed to see the very carts, the wagons that

Pharaoh sent to pick up Joseph's father. You have never seen anything in the twentieth century quite so ornate, so beautiful in their colours of red and gold.' I can see why Jacob had never seen anything like them. They *had* to have come from Pharaoh. That's the way God works today. He will show you what you have never seen before, in such a manner that you *know*.

Jacob then knew. What had convinced him otherwise, 22 years before, had been circumstantial evidence only. He had taken one look at the bloodstained coat his sons brought him and assumed Joseph was dead. He looked for no further corroboration. Have you accepted evidence given you that, maybe, destroyed your faith in the Bible as the final authority? How will it make you feel when you find out that this book is true, that God is alive and God is on your case? It will leave you stunned.

I want to say three things before I end this chapter: (i) God forgives you for everything in the past. (ii) He hasn't finished with you yet. (iii) Make a start in the right direction now.

After Jacob said, *'I'm convinced!'* we are told that *'Israel set out with all that was his'* (Gen. 46:1). If God has dealt with you, set out on your Christian journey. Tell others what Jesus has done for you. Then that all that God has in mind for you can begin to be fulfilled.

51

Surprised by a Brilliant Future

Genesis 45:25–46:7

Now Jacob was a very old man; he had reached that time in life when he lived almost entirely in the past. Jacob had known great visitations of God. He had had direct encounters with God. But all that had changed. For the last 22 years there was no evidence that he had any real communion or intimacy with the Lord. Rachel, the love of his life, had died years ago, and he had probably never recovered from that. What he had tried to do was to pour out his affection on the son Rachel gave him, his beloved Joseph. And he had wanted to relive his life through Joseph – parents often do that sort of thing – but God took Joseph from him, and he felt he had nothing to live for. You are talking about a bitter old man, filled with self-pity, filled with a critical spirit. No one enjoyed being around him: whenever anyone tried to come close to him, there was the pointing of the finger. And it took every effort on the part of his sons to show respect for their father.

I feel sorry for people like Jacob who develop a critical spirit and become filled with self-pity. Yet I have to confess that I wouldn't be any different. I think of these words from 1 Corinthians 4:7, where Paul said, *'Who makes you different from anyone else?'* That's a question that ought to be addressed to anyone who wants to point the finger. The truth is that we are all like Jacob.

Yet, if you feel you have nothing to live for, God understands. At the right hand of God is Jesus, who is touched with the feeling of our weaknesses (see Heb. 4:15). And even though there may be a Christian or two around you who may point the finger and make you feel miserable, I am telling you that Jesus will understand, and he will accept you as you are. Moreover, he will surprise you with the kind of future you never thought possible.

There are a number of things to consider:

1. In a Matter of Seconds Jacob Was Given a Brilliant Future

One moment Jacob had nothing to live for, and the next moment he had *everything* to live for. In fact, all that happened exceeded his wildest dreams. In Ephesians 3:20 we have these words: *'To him who is able to do immeasurably more than all we ask or imagine . . .'* This is an example of how God does that which surpasses all you have expected. The Bible says that with God all things are possible (see Mt. 19:26). There is a verse in 2 Chronicles 29 which says: *'The service of the temple of the LORD was re-established. Hezekiah and all the people rejoiced at what God had brought about for his people, because it was done so quickly'* (vv. 35–36). Every time I come across that verse it grips me how, in an instant, God can change everything.

In a matter of seconds, God changed everything for Jacob, and that's what he wants to do for you. He wants to give you a future. It comes in two stages:

- Stage One: He wants you to know for sure that you will go to heaven when you die.
- Stage Two: He will give you a life to live until that time.

You may say, 'I am interested in Stage Two first.' No. That's not the way it will be. If you want the future that God has in mind for you, you are not ready to live until you are ready to die. The first thing you have to do is to get right with him and ensure that if you were to die today you would to heaven. You need to affirm that Jesus died on the cross to pay your debt. For those who do this, there are fringe benefits: he does care about your life, about your job, about your income, and he does care about your health. But don't put the cart before the horse; the first thing is to do it God's way.

2. Jacob Had to Leave Familiar Surroundings

Notice how it is put in Genesis 1:46: *'So Israel set out with all that was his.'* That means Jacob had to turn his back on surroundings he had known that had given him so much pain.

There are two points to understand here:

- His surroundings were familiar. We are talking about the home that Jacob was used to. Perhaps you are 'at home' with a certain lifestyle, you are 'at home' walking over people; you are 'at home' abusing your body, or just living for pleasure.
- His surroundings had given him so much pain. But I ask you: those

familiar surroundings, haven't they given you so much anguish? Isn't it true that the reason for the distress you are suffering is that you have been 'at home' doing those things that have robbed you of your peace and your joy?

Thus, to enjoy the brilliant future that lay ahead, Jacob had to turn his back on familiar surroundings in which he had experienced such great suffering. He was really hemmed in. If he wanted to see Joseph again, Jacob had no choice but to leave. God doesn't give you a choice, unless you chose to reject what he offers. Jacob could have said, 'I am going to stay here. Let Joseph come to me!' But I am telling you the truth: if you are going to be like those who say, 'Let God come to me,' the chances are you will die and go to hell. But God has been so good to you, hemming you in, pointing the way and showing you exactly what to do. You would be a fool to reject this message.

3. He Had to Be Willing to Go Where He Had Never Been

We are told:

> *Israel set out with all that was his, and when he reached Beersheba, he offered sacrifices to the God of his father Isaac.*
> *And God spoke to Israel in a vision at night and said, 'Jacob! Jacob!'*
> *'Here I am,' he replied.*
> *'I am God, the God of your father,' he said. 'Do not be afraid to go down to Egypt'* (Gen. 46:2–3).

God knew Jacob was afraid. He was going to have to go where he had never been. There is something frightening about venturing out into unfamiliar territory. Becoming a Christian may be something you have never done. Coming to Jesus means that you are putting your whole future in his hands. But he says, 'Don't be afraid, because I will be with you.' Among Jesus' last words were, *'I will be with you always, to the very end of the age'* (Mt. 28:20).

4. Jacob Heard God Speaking to Him Once Again

He received confirmation that he had done the right thing. Do you know what it was? The old communion, the intimacy with God was restored. I find this one of the most moving phases in Jacob's life. It had been 22 years since he had heard God speak in an intimate manner. Now he was on his way, and God had spoken to him in a vision. God's voice was the sweetest sound he had heard in years.

If you will do that which honours his Son, and leave those surround -
ings which have caused you so much pain, and head out into an unknown
future, God will be with you, and you will feel his presence and his power.
If you are a backslider, but you would love to hear God speak to you
powerfully and intimately again, it will happen when you turn from those
surroundings which have given you so much pain. If you are prepared to
return to him, you will hear him speak. How long has it been since the
Lord spoke to you?

What was the future that was given to Jacob?

- He had a renewed communion with God. That means intimacy with
  him. Do you know intimacy with God? I honestly believe this means
  more to me than anything else in the world. And God wants you to
  see for yourself how intimately you can know him. That means you
  can know your Creator: you can know the God who made the
  universe, and he will deal with you as though you were the only one
  out there.
- Jacob experienced God's presence. Jesus said, *'I will be with you always'*
  (Mt. 28:20). That means you will have protection and you will feel he
  is with you. Sometimes God hides his face, but when you feel his
  presence it is wonderful. God said to Jacob, 'Don't be afraid. I will be
  with you' (see Gen. 46:4). That's what he is saying to you.
- Jacob was given security. God will supply your need. I'm not saying
  that you are going to drive a Mercedes Benz; I am not saying you are
  going to shop at Harrods every day. But I promise you this: God will
  supply your need, to the penny. Sometimes his provision comes at the
  last minute, when you think you can't survive another day, but God
  is never too early, never too late, he is always on time. Jacob was given
  the security of knowing he was going to live in the land of Goshen
  and would be taken care of for the rest of his life. God will do that
  with you.
- Jacob's future was glorious. Not because he himself had done anything
  to earn it, but because of Joseph. Jacob could now live in another
  country in light of Joseph's glory. God will do that for you. We are
  called to glory. It is not conditional on anything we have done, but on
  what someone has done for us.

God offers you an identical future to that of Jacob. He offers you intimacy
with him. He offers his presence, security and glory. However, Jacob
wasn't able to enjoy it until he set out and said goodbye to familiar
surroundings.

52

When It's Time to Move On

Genesis 46:1–7, 26–30

> Broken wings take time to mend
> Before they learn to fly again.
> On the breath of God they'll soar,
> They'll be stronger than before.
> Don't look back into the past,
> What was fire now is ash.
> Let it all be dead and gone,
> The time is now for moving on.
>
> Janny Grein

With his direct descendants (66 persons in all, not counting his sons' wives), Jacob, at the age of 130, prepared to leave Canaan, the land God promised to Abraham, never to see it again. But for Jacob that was in the past; the time had come for moving on.

Perhaps you are in a dilemma. Is it time to move, perhaps to a new house in another area or even in another country? Perhaps you are considering changing your job or the church you attend. But the greatest decision that you ever make is when you change your point of view. The time has come to move on, to abandon the ideas, opinions and the lifestyle that you have lived. You must say goodbye to that past. The Apostle Paul said, *'If anyone is in Christ, he is a new creation; the old has gone, the new has come!'* (2 Cor. 5:17).

How do we know it is time to move on? I can give you three indications:

1. You Have Little or No Choice

You will know it is time to move on when circumstances have coalesced in such a manner that you have been hemmed in, and you just say, 'I can

see there is only one thing to do.' It is when God takes things out of your
hands. Do you know what Christian conversion is? It is when God has
caused things to happen in such a way that you really had no choice. God
has sent one signal after another, and you know the only way forward is
to move on. That's what I am challenging you to do now – to make the
step.

In Jacob's case, there were economical issues; there were the bare
essentials to think about. How would they survive if they remained where
they were? There was famine in Canaan, but there was food in Egypt.
When it comes to the issue of when it is time to move on, one does have
to consider things like income.

Then there is another matter about which you have little or no
choice, and that is when you realize what is drawing you forward. In
Jacob's case, it was the thought of seeing Joseph. God said to Jacob, *'I
will go down to Egypt with you, and I will surely bring you back again. And
Joseph's own hand will close your eyes'* (Gen. 46:4). Think about this.
Jacob's chief problem was that he loved Joseph too much. He favoured
Joseph, and he neglected the rest of the sons. All the bad things that
had recently happened could be traced to this. Then we find God telling
him that Joseph's own hand would close his eyes. God said that to him
because he knew that would please him. One could argue, Jacob didn't
deserve kindness like that. Yet this is just an aspect of God's tenderness.
That's the way God is. When you think he's going to discipline you,
you find out that he knows what you are thinking. He knows what's
dear to you. How tender God was, affirming Jacob in this manner.

What was drawing Jacob forward was the fact that he was going to see
Joseph again. Never seeing Canaan again meant nothing to Jacob. There
was the famine there; while ahead, in Egypt, was Joseph. He didn't really
have a choice. Do you have any choice? Look at where you are and all
that is there – famine – that which gives you no hope. Now look at what
lies ahead: God promises you life and he will take care of you. Consider
the possibility that one day you will go to heaven and you will see Jesus
face to face. You will discover exactly what he looks like, what his voice
sounds like, how tall he is. You will see him. You will enjoy complete
security: there will be no worries about employment, about where your
next meal is coming from, about having to take exams, or having to prove
yourself in some way. In heaven there will be eternal security, peace and
joy, no tears, no pain, no sorrow.

So I ask which would you prefer? Do you choose to go to heaven or
live on this earth for another year or two of pleasure? How much time
do have you left? Do you really want to cling to that habit, that lifestyle,
that viewpoint, which have brought you near to ruin when the alternative
is going to heaven?

2. The Thought of Moving On Makes You Feel Thankful

Notice how verse 1 puts it: *'So Israel set out with all that was his, and when he reached Beersheba, he offered sacrifices to the God of his father Isaac.'* Why did he offer sacrifices? It was because he was thankful. The New Testament uses the phrase, *'sacrifice of praise'* (Heb. 13:15). I would challenge any Christian reading this, sometimes, to spend your time in prayer without asking for a thing. Instead spend the whole time thanking the Lord. Sacrifice what you would like to ask him. Sacrifice the time: just give it to him, and be thankful. You have so much cause to be thankful.

Why did Jacob have reason to be thankful? First, was the sudden brilliance of a new future. Joseph was alive and he was Prime Minister of Egypt. Jacob was going to see him, and God himself had said Joseph was going to close his eyes. How do you suppose that made Jacob feel? God had affirmed him despite Jacob's past failure. Don't ask me how he does it, but God has a way of causing everything that is in your past to work together for good: the sore spot, the hurt, your folly, the skeleton in the cupboard. Name it. God will do it.

This is what God was telling Jacob, and so he was thankful for an unexpected future. He was thankful for the utter faithfulness of God. There were times when Jacob was so discouraged that he had given up. He thought somebody had got it wrong. It seemed as though nothing that had been prophesied regarding him could possibly be true. Take, for example, the patriarchal blessing his own father Isaac had given:

> *May God give you of heaven's dew and of earth's richness – an abundance of grain and new wine.*
> *May nations serve you and peoples bow down to you.*
> *Be lord over your brothers, and may the sons of your mother bow down to you.*
> *May those who curse you be cursed and those who bless you be blessed* (Gen. 27:28–29).

That's quite a promise; Jacob had believed it once. Then everything had turned out in such a way that he said, 'I can no longer believe that.'

Think of the word God gave him in Bethel in Genesis 28:

> *Your descendants will be like the dust of the earth, and you will spread out to the west and to the east, to the north and to the south. All peoples on earth will be blessed through you and your offspring. I am with you and will watch over you wherever you go, and I will bring you back to this land. I will not leave you until I have done what I have promised you* (vv. 14–15).

Before he heard that Joseph was alive, Jacob had said, 'I used to believe that, but I don't now.' Twenty-two years. That's how long Jacob's life had been in a state of collapse. Note the words: *'All peoples on earth will be blessed through you and your offspring.'* You see, what Jacob hadn't known was that it was his son Joseph, being in Egypt, who turned a potentially disastrous situation around. If it weren't for Joseph being there, Egypt would have had no corn; it was Joseph who had prophesied that they should prepare for famine lasting seven years. Egypt had the wealth; Egypt had the corn. It was a nation who would be grateful to Jacob. But Jacob was unaware what was happening.

I want you to know that God was at work in your time of unbelief, when you felt nothing was happening, and you thought, 'I can't believe any longer.' When the day comes that you realize that God had been so faithful, you will look at him and think, 'I am so ashamed that I could have doubted him.'

Now everything was coming together, and Jacob had the renewal of the promise and knew the utter faithfulness of God. Not only that, he had a united family. Sadly, Jacob had never found any great degree of happiness in his family life. There had always been a strained atmosphere. There had been so much sorrow, so much sadness and tension. Then, lo and behold, something happened and overnight his family was united, and we read that *'Those who went to Egypt . . . who were his direct descendants . . . numbered sixty-six persons'* (Gen. 46:26). He had his children and his grandchildren together. How glad that must have made Jacob feel. 'All's well that ends well.'

3. God Confirms that the Change Is Right

Call it communion, call it fellowship, but God affirms the change in such an intimate manner that you know that it is right. You see, there is no value in change in itself. What's the point of change if it doesn't do something good? But the proof that you are right to make a change is that you have a great sense that God is with you. As we have seen, Jacob had not heard God speak for 22 years. Then he was told to do something that seemed to go totally against what God himself had made clear. God gave to Abraham, Jacob's grandfather, a promise that *Canaan* was the land that they were going to live in. Canaan was the land of promise. Yet now, Jacob must go to Egypt, although he would never return to Canaan because he was 130 years old. How could Jacob let Abraham down? How could Jacob do that which went so completely against the promise? Canaan was regarded as the wave of the future, and Jacob was leaving. He was having to say, 'The immediate future, the wave of the future, is Egypt.'

Indeed, sometimes changes do seem to go against what you sincerely thought God himself had previously made plain. You say, 'This can't be God because he said, "Canaan is your home", but now he is saying, "Go

to Egypt." ' Figure that out. Isn't this a dilemma? Perhaps you are in that
very situation where the way God is leading you goes against what you
thought he had made clear. So Jacob needed confirmation from God, and
after he offered sacrifices to God that intimate relationship was restored.

> *God spoke to Israel in a vision at night and said, 'Jacob! Jacob!'*
> *'Here I am,' he replied.*
> *'I am God, the God of your father,' he said. 'Do not be afraid to go down to Egypt,*
> *for I will make you into a great nation there. I will go down to Egypt with you, and*
> *I will surely bring you back again'* (Gen. 46:2–4).

I do not know whether Jacob knew it, but when the Lord spoke to
Abraham, he said: *'Know for certain that your descendants will be strangers in
a country not their own, and they will be enslaved and ill-treated four hundred
years'* (Gen. 15:13). So what Jacob was doing, though it could be argued
that he was going against what God had said to Abraham, was actually
fulfilling what God said to Abraham.

God doesn't lead us directly from A–Z, but as long as you know it is
his voice, as long as you know that it is he speaking, you can continue.
People may misunderstand you, they may not know how you can justify
what you are doing, they may think you are crazy, but the same God
who led Jacob is leading you. Notice how it is put, *'I am the God of your
father.'* It was a break with the past but, at the same time, continuity with
the past.

Nothing in life is permanent and one day life itself will end. Nothing
stays the same. The greatest trauma of all is not moving house, but when
you are coming down to the end and you think, 'This is it.' We read in
Hebrews 9: *'Just as man is destined to die once, and after that to face judgment,
so Christ was sacrificed once to take away the sins of many people; and he will
appear a second time, not to bear sin, but to bring salvation to those who are waiting
for him'* (vv. 27–28).

When Jesus died on the cross for you, he took your place; you were
in the heart of God from the foundation of the world. All that God
had in mind for Jacob, he has in mind for you; all that was carefully
planned for Jacob, has been carefully planned for you. You don't want
to miss it. And if you trust that blood, God will say, 'That man, that
woman, is going to heaven.' So, unless Jesus comes first, when it comes
to your time to die, you will be moving on, saying goodbye to this
world. Are you ready for that moment?

53

Knowing God Hasn't Finished with Us Yet

Genesis 46:26–34

Although he had long since given up any such hope, Jacob suddenly discovered he had a future. Is it possible for us to discover that God hasn't finished with us? Perhaps you feel you have no real future. Perhaps you can look back on that time when everybody said, 'Oh, what a future!' But that's all over now; you feel there is nothing to live for, you've made real mistakes, and there is no way that God could use you now.

In 1 Corinthians 9:27, Paul said: *'I keep under my body . . . lest that by any means, when I have preached to others, I myself should be a castaway'* (AV). By 'castaway' he meant being rejected or disqualified. Paul had the fear that somehow he could preach to others and be a blessing to them, but then, somehow, he might so grieve the Lord that he would be put to one side. He expressed what is also my own worst fear. It is a fear shared by others. I am not making this up or exaggerating in the slightest, but Billy Graham once told a friend of mine that his greatest fear is that God would take his hand off Billy Graham.

Do you feel that your greatest days are behind you? That is what Jonah feared. Do you know about Jonah – the man who ran from God because God said, *'Go to Nineveh'* (Jonah 1:2)? Jonah had been intimidated by the thought, so he said, 'Don't ask me. I can't do it.' So he ran from the Lord, and God sent a fish to swallow him up. We are told that in the belly of the fish, Jonah began to pray, saying, *'I have been banished from your sight; yet I will look again towards your holy temple . . . When my life was ebbing away, I remembered you, L ORD'* (Jonah 2:4, 7). Then we read in Jonah 2: *'Those who cling to worthless idols forfeit the grace that could be theirs'* (v. 8). That simply means running from God wasn't worth it. Jonah's fear then was that he would never have another opportunity. I'll tell you the interesting thing about Jonah: the worst words he ever heard were *'Go to Nineveh!'* Yet the time came when he felt that if God would only repeat those words, they would be the sweetest words he would ever hear. God caused that fish to eject Jonah on to dry land, and the happiest words in the book of Jonah are these. *'The word of the LORD came to Jonah a second time: "Go to Nineveh!"'* (Jonah 3:1). Jonah couldn't believe that God was giving him that same call, and what once horrified him, now thrilled him.

Jacob was now an old man. He had made many mistakes, almost every mistake possible, and he had come to the place where he anticipated nothing but sorrow. He felt there was nothing to live for and anticipated the worst. Are you like that? You feel you are finished. You know the greatest feeling in the world is to feel needed, to feel useful, and the greatest honour in the world is to be used by God. I can think of nothing more wonderful than knowing that God is using me. Perhaps you have known better days when God *did* use you in a particular situation, and you would give anything in the world just to know that it could happen again.

However, something did happen to Jacob. Out of the blue, he discovered what he never dreamed possible, and Jacob and his family had now come to Egypt. Joseph had heard Jacob had arrived in the land of Goshen. I wonder what must have been in their minds as they hadn't seen each other for 22 years.

Do you know what it's like not to have seen somebody for such a long time? Mickey Hemlepp was a boy who lived across the street from me back in Ashland, Kentucky. He was the nearest thing I had to a brother, and we were constantly in each other's houses. Until I was 17 we did everything together. Then, in 1953, he moved to another part of Kentucky and I went away to Trevecca to study for the ministry.

One day in 1990, I had a phone call. My secretary said, 'A Mickey Hemlepp is at Heathrow Airport. He has six hours in London and wonders if he could see you.' I was so excited, even though we only had a couple of hours together. I remember waiting for him. It had been 37 years since we last met and I wondered, 'What will he look like? Will I recognize him?' But as soon as I saw him I knew it was Mickey and we embraced each other. I don't say that I wept, but I almost did.

That emotion was just a drop in the ocean compared to what was happening in Egypt. There was Jacob, frail, leaning on his staff, and in the distance he saw dust from the wheels of what could only be the royal chariot with his son in it. Adrenaline ran high, and his heart beat faster. The moment came, and we read: *'As soon as Joseph appeared before him, he threw his arms around his father and wept for a long time'* (Gen. 46:29). Then Jacob said this: *'Now I am ready to die, since I have seen for myself that you are still alive.'* The irony was that now he was ready to die, he was ready to live.

The Best Is Yet to Come

The irony was that Jacob's best days were yet to come: his happiest days, his greatest glory, his greatest usefulness, his greatest legacy, were in the future, because he had yet to do what God had raised him up to do: to give the patriarchal blessing to those twelve sons. I can promise you on the authority of God's word that if you come to the cross and get right with God, your happiest days, your greatest days, lie ahead. I guarantee it.

The irony is that you are not ready to live until you are ready to die. I have to tell you something else about the gospel of Jesus Christ: it is designed with particular reference to your death. Speaking generally, I think that for some reason, when it comes to reaching the world with the gospel, we have reached the place where the church has done everything wrong. The idea today is that the reason you should become a Christian is that you are going to be so much better off in your lifetime. Listen. The Apostle Paul said, *'If only for this life we have hope in Christ, we are to be pitied more than all men'* (1 Cor. 15:19). You will not become a Christian simply because you see there is some advantage in it for you. You will never be converted until you realize God is a God of justice and hates sin.

The reason Jacob was ready to die was because of whom he saw, and he said to Joseph, *'Now I am ready to die, since I have seen for myself you are still alive'* (Gen. 46:30). The whole of Jacob's life had now come together. I have referred to Joseph unwisely telling his dream, and you will remember that when he told his father as well as his brothers his father rebuked him; nevertheless Jacob kept the matter in mind. Somehow Jacob believed it; so all those years he couldn't understand how Joseph could *not* be alive. And when he saw his son standing there before him he said, *'I have seen for myself'*, and the whole of his life had meaning.

That's not all. We come to the point where our life isn't so dear to us after all. Sometimes God has to put us through something whereby we realize that we are not as important as we thought and life can go on very well without any of us. I suppose that if I died tomorrow there would be a few weeks when those who knew me would be sorry. But realistically, in about three months they would have put it behind them. You see, it is so easy for each of us to think we are all-important. But God has a way of bringing us to the place where we do not love our own lives; we just want to honour him.

You will remember reading earlier about Corrie ten Boom, the Dutch lady who was part of a family that sheltered Jews from the Nazis. She was put in prison and sentenced to death. But because of a clerical error she was told, 'You are free!' She found out later that the clerk made a mistake and had selected the wrong person. Corrie ten Boom was set free. Her situation had seemed hopeless, but God had not yet finished with her.

She realized that she didn't deserve to be alive and was so thankful that she gave the rest of her life to serving the Lord.

The Way Ahead

How do we know then that God is not finished with us, and what is our responsibility?

1. We must be willing to accept a stigma. What is a stigma? It denotes that which is offensive. The church today is so afraid of offending people by preaching about hell and about the cross. These brothers of Joseph had a new stigma. They were going to live with the stigma in an alien land. They were going to be made separate from Egyptians. Joseph said to them, *'When Pharaoh calls you in and asks, "What is your occupation?" you should answer, "Your servants have tended livestock from our boyhood on, just as our fathers did." Then you will be allowed to settle in the region of Goshen, for all shepherds are detestable to the Egyptians'* (Gen. 46:33–34). So what we find is that they would be separate from Egyptians because of the stigma of their occupation.

Christians too have a stigma. The Bible says that we are in the world, but not of the world (see Jn. 15:19). A part of being a Christian is, though we are indebted to everybody around us, we are different. Jacob would be indebted to Pharaoh, but he was different. These brothers and their wives would be indebted to the Egyptians, but they were different. You may be indebted to someone who has done something for you and you are grateful, but you are still different. Perhaps they are relatives and you are grateful to them. Maybe you have been in an awkward position where someone has done a lot for you, perhaps where you work, at university, or at home, and you are grateful to them, but you still had to take a stand. Jacob's family had a stigma in an alien land. Are you willing to live with that offence and bear that stigma?

2. We must be willing to be indebted to another. The family had to be willing to accept the help of the one who had given them the prophecy that one day they would all bow down to him. That was humiliating for them. Jacob himself had to be willing to accept the help of the one he had once tried to control. Remember, Jacob was the world's greatest manipulator.

Maybe you have tried to control God and to dictate to him. How many of you have said, 'Well, God, if you will do this for me, then I will do this for you'? In trying to make a deal with God, you are dictating the conditions on which you will serve him. Before God will use you again, you must be willing to accept the help of the One you once tried to control. This is the very essence of this gospel. It means that you need a Saviour. You need someone who will do it all for you. You will have to be indebted for the rest of your life because of what he did for you.

Jacob and his family were going to have security; for this, they were indebted to Joseph and they could never repay him. How could we ever repay God for choosing us from the foundation of the world, for sending his Son to die on the cross for us, for sending the Holy Spirit to convict us of our sin, then giving us faith? It is all simply handed to us. Suddenly, we realize that we have been given eternal life, we have been forgiven, we have been saved – it is what God did.

Some people find that so distasteful, they can't accept it They can't handle being so indebted to God. Yet that is the God of the Bible. We owe him everything and can never repay him.

3. One has to be willing to live in grateful dependence from now on. It was so humbling, particularly for Jacob. Not only had he been such a manipulator but he was a hard worker and he had always earned his keep. He was wealthy, but now he just had to let someone else give him everything. It was humbling. The whole family had to accept the situation as it was; it was no use trying to pretend. They were living in a foreign land where, as shepherds, they were detestable to the Egyptians. They had to accept that they would never return to Canaan. The Bible says *'They have brought along their flocks and herds and everything they own'* (Gen. 46:32). Everything came with them. They didn't say, 'Let's leave a little security back in Canaan in case we want to return.' No. They brought everything with them. If God is going to use you again, you have to make the break. You have no chance of going back. No way! You are going forward. Jacob's greatest days were now ahead. He had something to live for. God hadn't finished with him, and he hasn't finished with you.

54

All's Well that Ends Well

Genesis 47:28–49:33

By faith Jacob, when he was dying, blessed each of Joseph's sons, and worshipped as he leaned on the top of his staff (Heb. 11:21).

This verse in Hebrews 11 refers to the events in Genesis 47:28 – 49:33. Consider how important Jacob was – his name, Jacob, or Israel, is used more than any other in the Old Testament. Yet when you consider that in Hebrews 11, the writer is going from Abel to Enoch, to Noah, to Abraham, and when you consider that Abraham had more than a dozen verses written about him (even Sarah was mentioned), and Moses had five verses – isn't it surprising that Jacob gets only *one*? Have you ever wondered about that?

As I said in the preface, Hebrews 11:21 is a verse I understand. Some years ago that verse suddenly gripped me. Bold, as if written in letters of gold, the words leapt out at me and, like a laser beam, showed me the whole life of Jacob at a stroke. In fact, it was this that made me want to preach on the life of Jacob in the first place, which I did, initially at Keswick.

Jacob's life had so much in it that had been chaotic; it had looked so bleak, and nothing seemed to add up at the time. There was so much injustice, and Jacob was often so foolish, and yet, at the end, everything came together for him. You can picture the old man looking back – and imagine his staff, that maybe was as high as his chest or up to his shoulders, and he's hanging on to that staff and worshipping. He's reflecting upon his life. It had all come together; not one promise of God had failed after all. He had his family with him, and before he died everything ended so well.

Now the passage in Genesis 47:28 – 49:33 refers to two events brought together in Hebrews 11:21. I return to this question, therefore: Why did the writer of Hebrews give Jacob only one verse when he was so important?

For one thing, Jacob hadn't been exactly a man of faith. He had been a man of great complaining, of considerable doubting. He was the man who manipulated things. You talk about one who wanted to *make* the promises happen – that was Jacob. Here was a man who had run from Esau for much of his life – no faith there. I don't want to repeat all that I've written already, but if you look for faith in the life of Jacob, I'll tell you there wasn't much! He had so much promised to him, so much handed to him, yet he had so little faith. He doubted all the time. And even after he was reunited with Joseph, whom he had thought was dead, when Joseph presented him to Pharaoh, the King of Egypt, Jacob immediately started complaining! He said, 'Well, I've lived a hundred and thirty years, but it's nowhere near as long as my father and grandfather lived' (see Gen. 47:9). He was still filled with self-pity; he was so negative, a man who had so little faith.

But the writer of Hebrews, who apparently said to himself, 'I have to mention Jacob. How shall I refer to him?' And having thought about it, he wrote, 'By faith he worshipped, leaning on the top of his staff.' But that was about the *end* of Jacob's life.

And yet, there's something so sweet about it. Here was a man who suffered most of his life. Here was the man who was the controller, but at the end he believed and could see that every promise had been fulfilled. Jacob finally got it right.

By the way, there's a warning here if you're one of those who say, 'Well, I'll get it right before I die. Eventually, I will get right with God.' Charles Spurgeon used to talk about the thief on the cross who was saved just before he died – perhaps only an hour or two before he died. Spurgeon put it like this: 'There's only one example of this, only one, so that none need despair, but only one, lest there would be those who would presume.' Indeed, you may not have the opportunity at the end of your life; you never know how it will be. You may not even be alert. In 2 Corinthians 6:2 we read, *'Now is the day of salvation.'* As to waiting, the Bible says, *'Seek the LORD while he may be found* (Isa. 55:6). You can't always find him. He said, *'My spirit will not contend with man for ever'* (Gen. 6:3). And so you may be so sorry if you think you can wait till the last minute. Nothing could be more foolish. What is more, those who become Christians so often say, 'Why didn't I do it sooner?'

Now, at the end of his life, Jacob was so happy; everything came together for him. I want us to note four things about this time.

1. Jacob's Family Was Restored

His family had been divided for so long. We recall the trouble with Dinah and the Shechemites (see Gen. 34). We remember the problem with Judah and Tamar (see Gen. 38), and then, of course, how Jacob was separated from Joseph and thought his son was dead. So much of Jacob's life was wrapped up in Joseph. Now we read in Genesis 46:30, *'Israel said to Joseph, "Now I am ready to die, since I have seen for myself that you are still alive." '*

And so his family was restored, and every single one of them went to Egypt; not one was left behind. Alec Motyer put it like this: 'The greatest antidote to parental depression is the gathering of the family.' All's well that ends well.

2. Jacob Reflected on God's Faithfulness

In Genesis 48:3 Jacob said to Joseph, *'God Almighty appeared to me at Luz in the land of Canaan, and there he blessed me and said to me, "I am going to make you fruitful and will increase your numbers. I will make you a community of peoples, and I will give this land as an everlasting possession to your descendants after you." '*

Jacob now recalled that word and must have felt rather embarrassed that he hadn't really believed it as he should have done. God gave the promise to him, but Jacob was afraid that Esau would kill him. Wrong. Nevertheless, Jacob was so worried and tried to protect himself.

A few years ago, Carl F.H. Henry and I were driving around Buckingham Palace on our way to Westminster Chapel, and I said quite casually and spontaneously, 'Carl, do you have any regrets about life? What would you do if you could relive your life?'

He paused, and then he said, 'I would remember that only God can turn water into wine.'

So often we all try to make things happen, and consequently we lose the joy from seeing what God alone would actually do.

But now, life was nearly over, and Jacob had to admit that God had kept every promise. It is as though he was thinking, 'I have no complaints.' But in the meantime, there hadn't been much faith.

Do you know what makes faith, faith? It's when you don't have the evidence but you still believe! Hebrews 11:1 says, *'Now faith is being sure of what we hope for and certain of what we do not see.'* You don't have the evidence, but you still believe. Faith is believing God because God said it. If you are one of those who say, 'If I have evidence, *then* I'll believe,' you don't realize that it's not faith then. You see they said at the cross of Jesus, 'Come down from the cross, then we will believe' (see Mk. 15:32). But that's not faith. Faith, to be faith, is where you don't have the evidence, yet you *still* believe.

And now, at the end of his life, as he worshipped on his staff, Jacob thought, 'Oh, God has been so good. God has been so good.'

3. Jacob Had a Revelation of the Future

This is where, perhaps for the first time, Jacob showed that he believed God completely. Hebrews 11:21 says, *'Jacob, when he was dying, blessed each of Joseph's sons.'* At the end of his life, Jacob was given the opportunity to show that he really had faith, and we see it in the account of him blessing the sons of Joseph.

What happened was this. Joseph brought his two sons, Ephraim and Manasseh, for he wanted the patriarchal blessing, the blessing of Jacob on his sons. And Genesis 48 says: *'When Israel saw the sons of Joseph, he asked, "Who are these?"*

'"They are the sons God has given me here," Joseph said to his father.

Then Israel said, "Bring them to me so that I may bless them" ' (vv. 8–9).

Now, since the greater blessing came from the right hand of the patriarch and the lesser from the left hand, Joseph positioned his firstborn Manasseh, so that Jacob's *right* hand would be on Manasseh, and his left hand on Ephraim.

And Jacob, who was almost blind, prepared to bless them. But he switched hands! Then he began to pray.

Displeased, Joseph stopped him saying, 'Oh, Father, you don't realize, this one is Ephraim, *this* one is Manasseh. You're putting your right hand on Ephraim, and Ephraim's going to receive the greater blessing. You must switch hands.'

But his father refused and said, 'I know, my son, I know. He too will become a people, and he too will become great. Nevertheless, his younger brother will be greater than he, and his descendants will become a group of nations.' He blessed them that day and said, 'In your name will Israel pronounce this blessing: May God make you like Ephraim and Manasseh.' So he put Ephraim ahead of Manasseh.' (Gen. 48:19–20).

Why did Jacob do this? Why should the younger brother be the greater? It is partly because this showed Jacob was doing something that wasn't really trying to please Joseph. His big problem had been that he was so partial to Joseph; he had just wanted to please Joseph. He had made him that coat of many colours, and had done everything possible for him. His whole life had been wrapped up in Joseph. But now he showed he would only listen to God. At the end of his day, he put that right. All's well that ends well. It was Jacob's finest hour.

4. Jacob Rectified a Mistake

In Genesis 49 Jacob said:

> *I am about to be gathered to my people. Bury me with my fathers in the cave in the field of Ephron the Hittite, the cave in the field of Machpelah, near Mamre in Canaan, which Abraham bought as a burial place from Ephron the Hittite, along with the field. There Abraham and his wife Sarah were buried, there Isaac and his wife Rebekah were buried, and there I buried Leah* (vv. 29–31).

He put that right too. Leah was the wife he never wanted. Leah was the wife he never loved. You would have thought that he would have wanted to be buried with Rachel. Leah, however, was the one who bore him the sons who ultimately mattered most to the future of the kingdom of God: Leah was the one who gave him Levi and Judah. The Messiah would come from Judah's line, not from Joseph's. And Jacob, in his final moments, looked back upon his life and realized that he hadn't been very nice to Leah. And so he said, 'I'm about to die. Here's where I want to be buried. There Abraham and his wife Sarah were buried. There Isaac and his wife Rebekah were buried. And there I buried Leah. I will be buried with Leah.'

> Depth of mercy! can there be
> Mercy still reserved for me?
> Can my God His wrath forbear?
> Me, the chief of sinners, spare?
> Charles Wesley

And so here is a life where everything about it had been so wrong. And yet God loved Jacob. *'Jacob I loved'* (Rom. 9:13). *'And we know that all things work together for good to them that love God, to them who are called according to his purpose'* (Rom. 8:28 AV). All's well that ends well.

Scripture Index